THE STRUGGLE OF THE MODERN

The Struggle of the Modern

by

STEPHEN SPENDER

University of California Press

BERKELEY AND LOS ANGELES

University of California Press
Berkeley and Los Angeles

© *Stephen Spender 1963*

First California Paperback Printing, 1965

TO NATASHA AT BERKELEY

CONTENTS

vii

PART THREE

NON-RECOGNIZERS, RECOGNIZERS, AND OVER-RECOGNIZERS

PART FOUR

THE REVERSAL OF THE MODERN

INTRODUCTION

THIS is a book of personal reflections about those qualities in literature and art in the present century which I consider modern. I say personal, because I discuss, autobiographically really, books I have read and some pictures I have looked at, recollecting and commenting on the characteristics which relate to the problems of inventing a specifically modern kind of art.

In publishing this, I am conscious that it is a book which leads in many directions which might have been followed. For example, there are many manifestos by imagists, expressionists, futurists, surrealists, and so on, together with many articles in 'little' magazines which form part of an immense documentation of modern art. In writing these loosely connected chapters, I have been haunted all the time by another book, an authoritative, extensive survey which could be written. My book contains some of the thoughts one might have when reading such a survey.

This book is in some respects the fulfilment of an obligation to the University of California. In 1959, I gave the series of Beckman lectures at Berkeley, with the understanding that I should publish them. Parts Two, Three and Four are offered as a substitute for publishing these lectures. They have very little resemblance to the lectures given, the last traces of which I have eradicated in proof.

The first section, *The Modern Imagination*, is based on the lectures I gave in 1961 in Washington at the Library of Congress under the auspices of the Gertrude Clarke Whittall Poetry and Literature Fund.

★   ★   ★   ★

Some of the pairs of 'opposites' which run through this discussion of the modern are 'contemporaries' and 'moderns', 'recognizers' and 'non-recognizers'. I see the 'moderns' and the 'recognizers' as deliberately setting out to invent a new literature as the result of their feeling that our age is in many respects unprecedented, and outside all the conventions of past literature and art. I see the 'contemporaries' and the 'non-recognizers' as being at least partly aware of the claim that there is a modern situation. Yet they refuse to regard it as a problem special to art. The 'contemporaries'—of whom H. G. Wells was an early example and C. P. Snow a recent one—see the changes that have taken place in civilization as the result of the developments of scientific technology, and think that, on the whole, the duty of writers is to enlist their art to support the cause of progress. The 'moderns', on the whole, distrust, or even detest, the idea of progress, and view the results of science as a catastrophe to the values of past civilization; nevertheless, opposite to this, there have been some moderns who were sustained by the idea that, instead of progress enlisting art, artists might convert scientists to a modern aesthetic vision which would transform the external appearances of our whole civilization; through architecture, ballet, music, sculpture, painting and poetry, taming the souls of men.

Here I am chiefly concerned with writers and artists who show in their work a consciousness of modern art as an aim, whether they accept or resist it.

There are also a great many writers whose works I do not discuss who as it were 'carry on' and simply ignore the problems involved in being, or refusing to be, modern. It is not that they

have nothing to say about modern life but that they seem unconscious of the need, which has so obsessed some of their colleagues,
of making abrupt changes in form and idiom.

An example of this consciousness of modern life as subject, but
unconsciousness of it as a problem of form, is the autobiographical
hero, the 'I', in Christopher Isherwood's novels. Stuart Hampshire has recently discussed this in a way which suggests how
different Isherwood's treatment of this hero might be, if he were
more conscious of it as a 'modern' artistic problem. Discussing
Mr. Isherwood's most recent novel, Mr. Hampshire writes:
'Literary egoism of this kind is the expression of a fluid personality, of an uncentred 'I.' The memoirs of an egoist help to provide him with a centre. The fluid ego flows into a succession of
situations, modifies each of them a little, and is temporarily shaped
by them; but each time it resumes its way along other channels.
Any shape that can be discerned is discernible only in the succession of incidents; these are the situations in which, to his surprise,
and, as it seems, through no purposes of his own, the unidentified
hero successively found himself.'

If we did not know that Mr. Hampshire was discussing *Down
there on a Visit*, we might suppose him to be writing about the 'I'
in *Molloy*, by Samuel Beckett. So the problem of projecting a
whole succession of autobiographical 'I's as the lenses in which
other characters are focused, which Mr. Isherwood has solved by
the seemingly conventional method of fictitious autobiography,
might be solved by what E. M. Forster calls 'a new system of
lighting'. All through the 'modern' phase there have been
writers who did not choose either to be realist or poetic-image
novelists, 'contemporaries' or 'moderns', in the way in which
Arnold Bennett is an example of the first category, Virginia
Woolf of the second. Graham Greene, Evelyn Waugh, Henry
Green, Angus Wilson, William Plomer are serious novelists of
modern subject matter: but here I do not write about them
because I am only discussing obvious examples of modernism or

anti-modernism; except where I consider those, like the Georgian poets, from whom the moderns—the imagists—reacted.

E. M. Forster observes in his Introductory Lecture to *Aspects of the Novel*: 'All through history writers while writing have felt more or less the same. They have entered a common state which it is convenient to call inspiration, and having regard to that state, we may say that History develops, Art stands still.' He reinforces this by adding that human nature itself scarcely changes: 'Four hundred years is nothing in the life of our race, and does not allow room for any measurable change.'

Unless human nature changes, then the novel need not do so either. Forster, writing in 1927, reverts to this, perhaps with some uneasiness: 'If human nature does alter it will be because individuals manage to look at themselves in a new way and there are people—a very few people, but a few novelists among them—trying to do this.' He goes on to say: 'Every institution and vested interest is against such a search: organized religion, the state, the family in its economic aspect, have nothing to gain . . .', all of which would incline one to think that Mr. Forster himself favours it. But he contemplates it with no equanimity . . . 'Anyway—that way lies movement and even combustion for the novel, for if the novelist sees himself differently he will see his characters differently and'—as I quoted above—'a new system of lighting will result.' It is startling, but revealing, to compare Mr. Forster's remarks with Virginia Woolf, in 1924, asserting, in *Mr. Bennett and Mrs. Brown*: 'On or about December 1910 human character changed.' This sounds a bit abrupt, but later she fills it out in words which definitely put her on the side of the moderns and against both the 'contemporaries' and those who carried on. In about 1910, she emphasizes, 'all human relations have shifted—those between masters and servants, husbands and wives, parents and children. And when human relations change there is at the same time a change in religion, conduct, politics, and literature.'

Enough has been cited here to demonstrate the reason for

the difference between the traditional novels of Forster and the poetic-imagist ones of Virginia Woolf. Forster is recording the kind of changes which take place in manners, behaviour and ideas within the unchanging constant which is human nature. Virginia Woolf is seeking to turn her fiction into an instrument which records changed human nature: a shift not just in the taste that sensibility reveals, but in the quality of sensibility itself. 'A new system of lighting' has to be introduced.

The moderns are therefore those who start off by thinking that human nature has changed: or if not human nature, then the relationship of the individual to the environment, forever being metamorphosized by science, which has altered so completely that there is an effective illusion of change which in fact causes human beings to behave as though they were different. This change, recorded by the seismographic senses of the artist, has also to change all the relations within arrangements of words or marks on canvas which make a poem or novel, or a painting.

*　　*　　*　　*

Apologies and acknowledgements. Apologies are due to the University of California Press, for having kept them waiting so long; worse, or profounder apologies, to my publisher Mr. Hamish Hamilton for my having involved him once again in that crime against printers, of rewriting a book very extensively in proof.

Thanks are due to the editors of *Partisan Review*, *The Saturday Review*, and *The Listener*, for passages of earlier versions which they have published; to Mr. Roy Basler of the Library of Congress; and to Sir Herbert Read for his generosity in allowing me to print his letter in the chapter 'Dialogue with a Recognizer'.

PART ONE

THE MODERN IMAGINATION

I

THE ROMANTIC IMAGINATION

THE Situation of the Poet is certainly a topic much discussed at literary conferences. Often, the discussion takes the form of poets telling a large audience that they cannot communicate with its members. Sometimes, it takes the more practical one of discussing how to give economic aid to poets by making them do other things than write poetry—teaching, for example. Anyway, it offers a picture of poets as being peculiarly helpless in the circumstances of modern life.

The question, 'What can poets do to save civilization from destruction?' is often asked by some member of the public at the very conference where the poet is on show in his role of helpless, hopeless anachronism. This suggests that poets, though neglected, somehow command the secret of the time in which we are living. If the Voice of the Imagination were heeded, enemies would be reconciled and the hungry fed. Two confusions are involved here. Firstly, there is a tendency, in the mind of a public, for the poet to be more a matter of concern than the poetry. The other is the idea that if poetry and the poet were given their true place, this would really have some effect on a world distracted and tormented with fear. The second of these propositions is one that poets—that is, imaginative writers (whether they write poetry, fiction, or drama)—sometimes share.

The belief that poets can alter and have altered the world is

contained in Shelley's famous claim that poets are the unacknowledged legislators of mankind. No modern poet would regard this
as anything but preposterous. Yet underneath the denials, the idea
that the life and works of the imagination somehow provide an
incandescent centre in which human personality and even social
forms can become molten and transformed, certainly persists, in
Lawrence, in Rilke, even in Joyce.

So much preoccupation with the situation of the poet, and with
the function of the poetic imagination, results doubtless from the
feeling that in the past poets fitted better into the community, and
their poetry was better understood. Certainly, we are right in
feeling that there was a difference, but I doubt whether this was it.
There were perhaps merely different expectations on the part of
the poets, different misunderstandings on that of the public. What
may be a modern peculiarity is that poets today expect to be
understood for the qualities that they regard as intrinsic to their
poetry being poetry, just as painters expect their paintings to be
admired not for their subjects, or their beauty, but for qualities
called painterly, perhaps even for the texture of the surface of the
pigment.

No one could say that the poets of the Victorian era—Tennyson,
Browning, and Arnold, were neglected, or even went unappreci-
ated. And yet they seem rather like displaced persons who acted
to their audience the Victorian public's idea of 'the poet', rather
as a refugee may, in his exile, find himself having to act out the
accent and behaviour which his neighbours expect of someone
coming from the country of his origin. 'Vex not thou the poet's
mind, With thy shallow wit,' Tennyson growled at a public
expecting the cloaked and bearded poet to growl. And if one
glances back rapidly from precedent to precedent of English poets
across the centuries, one finds poets who were courtiers, cavaliers,
politicians, customs inspectors, ambassadors, writers of flourishing
dedications to patrons, lunatics, gangsters, but rarely a situation
which could be regarded as favouring them simply because they

wrote their poetry. This is true even of the greatest. We feel that Milton belonged to the conscience of a puritan revolution (though he had friends who were poets and scholars), that Shakespeare belonged to a very fertile period of history and a group of players, that Chaucer was one of his own Canterbury pilgrims, that Wordsworth was the property of the Wordsworthians, that the Romantics belonged to their biographies, that Tennyson belonged to Arthur Hallam and Queen Victoria.

If we are discouraged by the thought that modern poets don't 'communicate' we may find comfort in the reflection that there can have been few periods when their poetry communicated *as poetry*. In the opinion of his contemporaries Shakespeare seems to have been only one among a number of playwrights who were doubtless judged not for the poetry but for the play being the thing. He comes rather low on the list of playwrights supplied by his contemporary, Meres.

Yet I would not care to dispute the truth of the observation of someone who said that a modern poet, launching forth his slim volume of verse today, is like a person dropping a feather over the edge of the Grand Canyon and then waiting for the echo. Nevertheless, certain living poets get back a considerable reverberation. We ought to remember this. What is more important, there never was, as I have suggested, a period in which the arts were more appreciated for the specific qualities which are considered peculiar to each art. In fact, the arts run the risk of being over-purified, and artists of feeling obliged to produce some quintessential extract of the qualities of their art, so great is the pressure of critical connoisseurs on them to produce only the real, right thing.

It is really as though, in an age of specialization, poetry only has to communicate along the pure packed line which Keats, reproaching Shelley, said should be 'loaded with ore'. This means that we do ask ourselves, 'Is this poetry?' where in the past people might have asked, 'Does it tell a story?' 'Does it praise the king?' 'Has it a moral?' 'Does it conform to the standards which we call beautiful?'.

Poetry is an end where previously it was often regarded as a means, a vehicle for carrying flattery, beauty, melodrama, religion, moral, or just the world. And this situation seems acceptable to some poets, notably to Robert Graves who draws the logical conclusion that poets should only write for other poets, and should take in one another's washing. In one of his early letters, Ezra Pound declares that a poet should not expect to find more than thirty readers who appreciate his work for its true qualities.

I do not take it for granted that poets today have a grievance. Nevertheless, we do feel rightly, I think, that whether poetry is admired for the wrong or the right reason, there is, as it were, a reduction of scale in its relation to a world of machines, scientific inventions, world-power-politics. This diminution corresponds perhaps to the ratio of modern man to the almost annihilating scale of the time-space universe; of modern man even to his own inventions. There is perhaps not so much a breakdown of communication as a kind of shrinking of the imagining, feeling, flesh and sense tissues through which the poetic communicates, in relation to the great exaggeration of impersonal, inhuman forces.

Critics have offered many reasons for this state of affairs. Ever since Matthew Arnold, they have been telling us that there is a decay of the institutions which communicate values in society itself, and that therefore poetry cannot today become (using Matthew Arnold's own epithet, in his lecture on *The Function of Criticism at the Present Time*) 'important'.

It is symptomatic perhaps that, in the late nineteenth century, Arnold used the word 'important' with regard to poetry, where we should probably write 'significant'. We avoid 'important' because it sounds too public; 'significant' can be as private as we want it to be. If you say an art is 'important' you imply that there is a confluence of subject matter, interest, values, within the art, with things outside that are important by standards outside it. Our current use of the word 'significant' can have no reference to anything outside the standards set up by the work itself, just as a symbol can with the Symbolistes symbolize only itself. What was important to Matthew Arnold was important to Mr. Gladstone. Nothing that is significant to me is important to Mr. Harold Macmillan. So in using the word 'significant' in modern criticism, we limit ourselves to that which is signified within the terms of the art, to the reader trained to receive what the poem communicates.

So it has come to be accepted that what is significant along the channels of communication between poet and reader is not important in public thought. Poetry—and hence imaginative literature —has become 'significant' when it has ceased to be 'important'. Poet and reader are inmates of the prison cell shared by Lear and Cordelia when Lear has abandoned all power and most claims on life:

> . . . Come, let's away to prison:
> We two alone will sing like birds i'the cage;
> When thou dost ask me blessing, I'll kneel down
> And ask of thee forgiveness. So we'll live,
> And pray, and sing, and tell old tales, and laugh
> At gilded butterflies, and hear poor rogues
> Talk of court news; and we'll talk with them too—
> Who loses and who wins, who's in, who's out. . . .

We accept the idea that there is an almost autonomous outside world of science, inventions, power, evolving and revolving according to laws of economics, etc., which has become unimaginable within the individual consciousness. This was not so for Shakespeare or Milton. Their imaginations roamed over the whole world, and over the forces that controlled the history of their time. Here, surely, there is a real difference between past and present.

The reasons for regretting the separation of the automatism of social forces from the shrunken inner world of individuated experience are not so obvious as might at first appear. The common misunderstanding started by Shelley is to regard the separation as a public catastrophe, as though poets might save civilization and are prevented from doing so by the forces of machinery and politics. It is not a catastrophe and poetry cannot save nations, and could not ever do so, though perhaps we should not overlook the capacity of poets in the past to create what politicians today call an 'image'. Virgil set out to create a pattern for Romans in *The Aeneid*, and Shakespeare (perhaps more successfully because less purposively) certainly created an 'image' of England's country and soldiers, which perhaps helped to win the Battle of Britain. It certainly seemed incarnate in the few who won the cause of the many. Whitman, in *Song of Myself*, became the experiences of all America, in order to provide Americans, in his self-portrayal, with an image of America, personalized, for which they might live.

Everyone would agree, though, that today poetry cannot save civilization. It may be a misunderstanding to infer from this that poetry cannot and should not make inner worlds of elements in the public world which are 'important'. There seems to be a tendency today to think that poets should not reconcile outward things with inner life in their poetry, but they should only deal with such things as are already inner, personal, private, or literary. One can sympathize with this tendency which can become both stoic and playful in poems as excellent as those of Philip Larkin. Nor am I suggesting that there is some obligation on poets to be socially responsible, if I add that the mind which creates from imagination should be able, ideally, to imagine what seems impersonal, or even unimaginable. Robert Graves, answering a questionnaire, in the *London Magazine* of February 1962, has declared that 'personal issues are what interest people, not newspaper issues', a statement which can only be taken to mean that Mr. Graves thinks that nothing of public concern, which is discussed in the newspapers, can be felt by the reader to be his personal concern. Since questions involving the survival of the reader, and of his loved ones, are newspaper issues, this seems an ostrich-like attitude. It also seems characteristic of a habit among modern writers of setting up false dichotomies between 'public' and 'private', 'personal' and 'impersonal'. The contradiction between 'personal issues' and 'newspaper issues' disappears when one reflects that no newspaper issue is a subject for art unless it is felt by the artist as one affecting him personally—as the bombing of Guernica affected Picasso. If contemporary poets are not any of them able to compose inner worlds which include elements of the public world—the world that was felt in *The Waste Land* as in Auden's *Spain*—then contemporary poetry reflects a partial failure to imagine the disturbing modern environment. The reader or aspiring young writer (over-impressed perhaps by C. P. Snow's *The Two Cultures and the Scientific Revolution* or concerned with the Bomb) may find himself apparently confronted by a choice between the limited private, personal, literary-academic world of the imagined, and the abstract, threatening, open world of the unimaginable. There is the suspicion today that poetry is the playground of perpetual students—or perpetual professors—who have achieved their maturity at the price of refusing to have dealings with the world. In the past there was major and minor poetry, but no idea that it was honourable for all poetry to be personal, and poetically disgraceful to attempt the major themes of the whole of life viewed as a whole. There was no idea that the world of art was somehow the opposite of the world of historic action.

When Matthew Arnold set himself up as the advocate of the Function of Criticism, his plea (more influential than the one on another occasion that poetry might replace religion) was that 'creative power works with elements, with materials', and that if these are not present, 'it must surely wait till they are ready'. In the present century critics like T. E. Hulme, I. A. Richards, and T. S. Eliot have explained that the elements which are lacking are values and beliefs, fragmented and decayed in modern scientific and materialist societies. In some quarters, the decline of institutions in society upholding values and beliefs has led not so much to the view that criticism can prepare the ground for 'important' poetry, as that it must take the place of major creative effort, by keeping open the connections with the past organic society of living values, through the selection and analytic study of those works which are truly in the Great Tradition. The Great Tradition and the analysis of the values in these works replace both poetry and religion.

The view is that, poetically, we live in a vicious circle which completely conditions literary creation. There are no effective institutions of faith and values because there are not the faith and values, and there are not the faith and values for poetry to draw on because there are no such institutions. This vicious circle is also held responsible for the 'breakdown of communication' in poetry.

This depressive analysis leaves out one thing. It does not explain why, until recently, there have been poets of the stature of Yeats, Eliot, and Frost writing great poetry. Moreover, it should be pointed out that this very habit of explaining the situation of poetry in terms of the collapse in values, itself shows one of the symptoms of the situation complained about—a desperate dependence on outward circumstances, a materialist tendency to explain the inner state of the individual artist as entirely the result of outward conditioning.

I think criticism has been too preoccupied with conditioning circumstances. It is inevitable that it should be so. Critics deal, after all, with things given, what is already written, what they find going on in the life around them, the already read, not the as yet unwritten. One of the things that creative talents do is change into favouring circumstances the unfavourable conditions out of which they create. Eliot, writing as a critic, easily demonstrates the impossibility of Eliot's writing *The Waste Land*. I cannot accept altogether the view that poetry is the result of analysed circumstances. So what I have set myself to do here is to separate, for the time being, the idea of poetic imagination from the context of conditioning history, consider it as an activity *per se*, take it, as it were, out of the context of conditioning non-values.

*   *   *   *

Shakespeare wrote comparatively little about poetry. When he describes the process of making poetry, he suggests the operation of an independent creative faculty upon things immediately apprehended:

> The poet's eye, in a fine frenzy rolling,
> Doth glance from heaven to earth, from earth to heaven;
> And as imagination bodies forth
> The forms of things unknown, the poet's pen
> Turns them to shapes, and gives to airy nothing
> A local habitation and a name.

The citation is so familiar, and itself so airy, so Mozartian, that it slips by almost unconsidered. But what is said is surely astonishing: that the form of things remains unknown until the poet, standing midway at the centre of his universe, bodies them forth; that the airy imagination is a pure activity, making named forms out of nothings.

It is noteworthy that Keats and the other Romantics returned to this Shakespearean view of the imagination as an independent sovereign activity centred in the poetic genius, and owing allegiance to no superior intellectual authority. In doing this, the Romantics rejected the practice of the Augustan poets who put their great imaginative gifts at the service of theological, aristocratic, and rationalist philosophic views of their times. Eighteenth-century poets like Pope considered the imagination to be the servant of the intellectual rationalizations of that age which seemed to reconcile the reasoning of God with that of scientists. To the Augustans, poetry was an intellectual synthesis which, in its transparent imagery, had the ambition of resolving discords between different spheres of contemporary reasoning.

Keats returned to the view which he derived from certain passages of Shakespeare, that imagination is a primary faculty of the poetic sensibility, whereas fancy, wit, are secondary, illustrating already conceived ideas. Imagination can be thought of as purely inventive, conjuring shapes out of nothing, or as the centre of poetic sensibility acted upon by experiences. It receives these experiences and transforms them so they can be related one to another within the harmonious unity, the world in little, which is the poem. Imagination comes before intellectual concept, whereas wit or fancy or illustration demonstrates idea.

The Romantics rebelled against their predecessors, the Augustans, against the poets of wit, because in them the imagination had become adjectival, imaginative. The imaginative was put to the service of reason. The Romantics returned to the concept of the imagination as verb, the word made flesh, the dream which is Adam's. As Coleridge wrote: 'To contemplate the ANCIENT of days with feelings as fresh, as if all had then sprang forth at the first creative fiat.'

The great revival of interest in Shakespeare which we find in Blake, Wordsworth, Coleridge, and Keats was a return to the Shakespearean as source in English poetry of primary imagination. The Romantics bring us back to the idea of poetic imagination as dreaming yet revealing consciousness in which the circumference of brute facts, experiences, and disparate ideas becomes self-aware, and, in the moment of self-awareness, is transposed into symbols and images harmonious within the complex unity that is the poem.

Ideally, the circumference comprises the whole world of knowledge, experiences, and events, past and present, which are undigested, in the sense that they can only be interpreted into the significance of inner life, through the power of the imagination to relate them within the unity of the poem. The force of Shelley's *Defence of Poetry* which remains impressive—however many holes may be picked in his argument—is his vision that, ideally, the real world is material potentially capable of being transformed by the imagination. He realized, too, that the world—in its most ancient history as in its most recent inventions—is always contemporary consciousness, coming alive within the awareness of people living at a particular moment, people having the attitudes of their generation, their situation in time and place.

Shelley in his view of poetry was, of course, concerned with an ideal, not with a programme that could be laid down for poets. He was writing of a desideratum, not of what was necessarily within the capabilities of his contemporaries when he wrote in 1820:

> The cultivation of poetry is never more to be desired than at periods when, from an excess of the selfish and calculating principle, the accumulation of the materials of external life exceed the quantity of the power of assimilating them to the laws of nature.

Here imagination is regarded as the transforming centre of poetic consciousness, a task, and perhaps a body of contemporary achievement above and beyond any individual poet 'imagining that which we know' for his generation, as task and sum of scientific knowledge stand beyond the individual scientist.

In spite of the reaction today against the Romantics, modern poetry and criticism have taken over the view of the imagination as a centre acted upon by experiences and inventing its own harmonious inner world; and, in spite of talk of revival of classicism, they have not returned to the essentially classical view that imagination is the power of illustrating theology, monarchy, or philosophy, dressing up, as it were, preconceived ideas about the important values of living. Baudelaire was anti-Romantic, theologically minded—yet he regarded the imagination as standing above the experiences on which it operated:

> The whole visible universe is but an array of images and signs to which the imagination gives a place and relative value; it is a sort of fodder which the imagination must digest and transform. All the faculties of man's soul must be subordinated to the imagination, which can call upon them all at once.

Coleridge, in one of the most famous passages of *Biographia*

Literaria, defines imagination as 'the power in which one image or feeling is made to modify many others, and by a sort of fusion to force many into one'.

And, in a still more famous passage:

> The poet, described in ideal perfection, brings the whole soul of man into activity, with the subordination of its faculties to each other according to their relative worth and dignity. He diffuses a tone and spirit of unity, that blends and (as it were) fuses, each into each, by that synthetic and magical power, to which I would exclusively appropriate the name of imagination.

In the present century, at a later stage of modern poetry, imagination begins to be regarded as arbiter in a world of fragmented values, or, in the thought of Rilke, as the molten memory of traditions which have vanished from the world, in Yeats as mouthpiece of the 'Images in the Great Memory stored'. Rilke is perhaps the twentieth-century poet most seized with the idea of the poet having a task of fulfilling the past so that it redeems the present. In doing this, imagination becomes the force in which memory of traditions which once gave living significance is re-invented. In a letter to Witold von Hulewicz explaining the purpose of his *Duineser Elegien*, Rilke writes:

> The Elegies show us engaged on this work, the work of the perpetual transformation of beloved and tangible things into the invisible vibration and excitability of our nature, which introduces new 'frequencies' into the pulsing fields of the universe. . . . And this activity is sustained and accelerated by the increasingly rapid disappearance today of so much of the visible which we cannot replace. Even for our grandfathers, a house, a fountain, a familiar tower, their very clothes, their coat, was infinitely more, infinitely more, intimate. . . . The lived and living things, the things that share our thoughts, these are on the decline and can no more be replaced. *We are perhaps the last to have known such things.* The earth has no alternative but to become invisible in US.

So Rilke regards the task of poetic imagination to be that of setting up a kind of machinery which connects the reinvented past with the present. The angels in the elegies might be compared to vast transformers standing above a human landscape, converting the energy of the divine and the traditional into power which flows over and redeems the banal life of the fair in the valley below whose values are those of money.

Rilke's purpose calls to mind Matthew Arnold's suggestion that 'religion . . . will be replaced by poetry'. This idea has, on the whole, received a bad press from critics, especially those, like Eliot, who think that poetic imagination should at some point fuse with impersonal authority, and who would reinforce authority with irrefutable dogma. However, Rilke could not accept the Roman Catholicism in which he had been brought up. For him it is clear that poetry is not so much a replacing of religion as a path hewn out leading back to that in religion which is not dogma but imagined idea. 'For poetry,' writes Arnold, 'idea is everything,' whereas 'our religion has materialized itself in fact, the supposed fact.' But religion is, at some point, imagination identical with idea, and the attempt of the *Duineser Elegien* might be defined as that of tracing back both poetic symbol and religious belief to the place where the word becomes flesh.

In the letter already quoted Rilke goes on:

> If one makes the mistake of applying Catholic conceptions of death, the Hereafter and Eternity to the Elegies or the Sonnets, one isolates oneself completely from their conclusions and becomes involved in a fundamental misunderstanding. The angel of the elegies is that Being in whom the transmutation of the Visible into the Invisible, which we seek to achieve, is consummated.

For Rilke imagination was, as it were, an acted-upon instrument played through by traditional things and exposed to the modern environment. His sensibility—deliberately weaned from the Catholicism of his childhood—was to him the channel whereby religious symbols could become poetic ones, and his religious attitudes evolve within his poetry.

No two things could be more different than Rilke's view of poetry severed from dogma, and the idea put forward by I. A. Richards in 1929 of modern poetry's being severed from *all* beliefs. Dr. Richards argues that the beliefs which for past generations were held to be objectively valid can be reasserted today in all their force if it is accepted that they do not compete with science in making statements about external reality. They can be accepted, he argues, because they express attitudes justifiable in themselves through being serviceable to the whole personality of the individual poet and reader. In other words, what was once thought to be valuable because it described the truth about the world around us, is now reaffirmed as valuable because it projects on to the outward scene pictured complex structures true of our inner needs and natures.

I. A. Richards' essay was important because it raised the question of what kind of truth is stated in poetry where the poet draws on past beliefs and myths, without the poet himself having the intellectual certainty that he knows them to be true, and with the likelihood that the reader will think them untrue. By raising questions which might have remained dormant (in the same essay Richards attacked Yeats and Lawrence for believing in absurdities) Richards probably hastened the acceptance of Christian dogmas by Eliot (whom Richards had congratulated on writing, in *The Waste Land*, a poem severed from all belief). First Eliot and, much later, Auden supported orthodox Christianity, as converts, and in their stated views. But whereas Eliot's dogmatic faith seems to distinguish him sharply in his life and intellectual attitudes from a poet like Rilke (and still more from a Christian heretic like D. H. Lawrence), in *Four Quartets* and the *Duineser Elegien*, their *poetic* attitudes are not opposed. In the long run, and despite Eliot's earlier attacks on him, even Eliot and Lawrence meet in their having religious imaginations. It would be far truer to say that in the *Four Quartets* the poet uses theology and dogma in order to release his mystical imagination, than to say that he uses his imagination to illustrate his dogma. Perhaps Auden sometimes falls into a kind of Christian classicism—but this is where he is most willed and least convincing. Rilke the non-Catholic, but with his Catholic upbringing, uses his angels, saints, and dead souls, much as Eliot uses sanctified places. The central experience of the *Four Quartets* is the pure imagining of ecstatic and mystical states of awareness—timeless within time, the striving of prayer towards identification of the self with the past of ritual.

★　　★　　★　　★

We can now distinguish three main attitudes towards the role of the poetic imagination in our time. First, the theory of Rilke in the *Duineser Elegien* that it is a machinery for redeeming the past, and relating it to the present. Secondly, the basically utilitarian 'psychological' view of Richards that poetry is a means of arranging the order of our internal lives by making a harmonious pattern of extremely complex attitudes, once thought to refer to an external order of metaphysics but now seen to be a symbolic ordering of our inner selves. Thirdly, there is the rejection by Eliot, and more recently by Auden, of this utilitarian interpretation of metaphysical ideas, and their acceptance of dogma.

What is common to all these views—and I think to all major attempts in modern writing—is the view of imagination. The imagination has been restored in modern literature to its position of Verb. The reinstating of imagination as primary, central, the verb, was perhaps the attitude responsible for the greatest modern achievements: works like the last novels of Henry James (particularly *The Golden Bowl*), *Finnegans Wake*, Yeats' Byzantium poems, the *Duineser Elegien*, put these writers in the God-like position of being isolated within their own creations, of having to reinvent the world and all its values within their art.

★　　★　　★　　★

It is now possible, perhaps, to reconsider the problem of

communication today, in a way that is not the stereotype of sociological and analytical critics. As I remarked earlier, many of the
misunderstandings which poets, and critics for them, complain
about seem to have been always true of their situation, although it
becomes clear that today an ancient problem takes special form.
For example, I suppose, it has always been true that poets and
other artists are isolated. But in the past this has only been so in the
sense that others also are alone. Shakespeare seems able to rely on
the fact that the situation of Hamlet or Lear going to his doom is,
in its essential relation to the human condition, only an extremely
conscious and developed example of what each member of his
audience might feel. The peculiar modern nightmare is that the
artist appears to be working in circumstances where he is not only
solitary in his exceptional awareness to the human condition, but
where he feels, it seems, alone in being alone. He is operating on an
awareness of being alive, in a world where people are encouraged in
every way to identify themselves not with the other people around
them, all trapped in the same human situation, but with a whole
machinery of getting through life which distracts them from the
fact that they are spiritual animals. This produces the special kind
of modern incommunicability. If you are a poet, often you are
talking about things which are real to you, and which have been
real to people in the past, but to which many contemporaries
appear to have deadened themselves, assisted in the deadening
process by all the machinery of advertising and distraction.

At this point there appears to be a failure of nerve, and a demand
on the part of writers that they should return not to their humanity
but to the traditional institutions which have, as it were, knocked
into people's heads the situation of living a shared awareness as it
was in past times; hence, the return to dogmas and establishments
and critical interpretations of past literature, the insistence on the
selected volumes of the Great Tradition and their accompanying
exegeses as Holy Writ. I wonder, though, whether the flight from
creative into critical attitudes, which has been so much a feature of

the past two decades, is itself not an escape from the main reality to be faced—the common fact of the humanity of each of us isolated within his modern situation. The point I am labouring is put far better than I can make it in Joseph Conrad's *Heart of Darkness*, that work which seems to go further than any other into the implications of modern materialism. When Conrad's narrator, Marlow, has gone far into the jungle of the Belgian Congo (the passage has the significance of prophecy realized today)—with his dehumanized fellow-explorers, who, in their search for ivory, are driven to their own deaths and to mass-murdering natives—he hears through the jungle the great roar of the savages, who, concealed from the white traders, have been watching their approach. Suddenly he sees these hordes:

> They howled and leaped, and spun, and made horrid faces; but what thrilled you was just the thought of their humanity—like yours—the thought of your remote kinship with this wild and passionate uproar. Ugly. Yes, it was ugly enough; but if you were man enough you would admit to yourself that there was in you just the faintest trace of a response to the terrible frankness of that noise, a dim suspicion of there being a meaning in it which you—you so remote from the night of first ages—could comprehend. And why not? The mind of man is capable of anything—because everything is in it, all the past as well as all the future. What was there, after all? Joy, fear, sorrow, devotion, valour, rage—who can tell?—but truth—truth stripped of its cloak of time. Let the fool gape and shudder—the man knows, and can look on without a wink. But he must at least be as much of a man as these on the shore. He must meet that truth with his own true stuff—with his own inborn strength. Principles won't do. Acquisitions, clothes, pretty rags—rags that would fly off at the first good shake. No; you want a deliberate belief. An appeal to me in this fiendish row— is there? Very well; I hear; I admit, but I have a voice, too, and for good or evil mine is the speech that cannot be silenced.

It seems to me that we have paid too much attention to the circumstances that condition the creating imagination. We lament the breakdown of beliefs, the decline in traditional values, the havoc wrought on civilization by the mass media—all these things—which add up to what we call the breakdown of communication. In painting ourselves as products of our social conditioning, we have not paid sufficient heed to the common and continuing human condition, the shared existing and experiencing within differing environments which is the real basis of communication.

If it is true that the poet today experiences alienation, it may also be true that there is a humanity of the non-literary which he partly ignores. There is the poet, situated perhaps at the university, with all his loyalties and his special interests those of the literary group, and with his mental picture of the world of modern people whose attitudes he views as the results of the mass culture which is the worst enemy of his poetry. He regards his poetry as conditioned because he regards this public as conditioned. He only regards those who have critical consciousness, who are immersed through their reading and writing in values outside the contemporary ones, as being liberated from conditioning. But it may be the case that this picture of a public wholly conditioned by advertising, television, etc., may be at least partly false, and that the literary intellectual's view of his isolation may be due to his having cut himself off from those equally aware of their human situation, but who are as little able, in the circumstances created by his élite culture, to communicate with him as he is with them.

The difference between the poet with his view of catastrophe which seems to have become isolated in his literary consciousness, and the same view when it is an agonized state of consciousness shared with other lives, is demonstrated by comparing two major works written out of the mood of World War I: these are *The Waste Land* and that little-known masterpiece, *In Parenthesis* by David Jones. It does not make any difference to my argument that *In Parenthesis* is written in a style which owes something to Joyce and Eliot and that it is a book which confronts the 'common reader' with difficulties. The point is that *In Parenthesis* celebrates communication of awareness, as the result of a common suffering, between the consciousness which is that of the poet, and that of the group of soldiers whom it concerns. Both Eliot and David Jones see the same modern scene of the physical collapse of Western civilization. But the characters of the bank clerk, the secretary-typist, the pub-talkers in *The Waste Land* are psychological stereotypes projected by the surrounding moral chaos. The characters of the soldiers in *In Parenthesis* are made aware by that realization which is the result of having to act in the circumstances that were the Western Front: 'the "Bugger! Bugger!" of a man detailed, had often about it the "Fiat! Fiat!" of the Saints'. Thus, the soldiers are redeemed through the awareness revealed in their acceptance of duty and suffering, into the writer's vision of Arthurian legend, Shakespeare's histories, and the offices of the Roman Catholic Church. They become the present which is also the past of Shakespeare and Welsh mythology through the suffering which enables them to transcend themselves and enter into the communion of the lives of the soldiers who died at Agincourt, and who live in Shakespeare's *Henry V*. It is just this redemption which seems impossible for 'the young man carbuncular' and his young lady, and the pub crawlers in *The Waste Land*. The possibility of its being attained through living and suffering is repudiated by those who say that the only way of entering into the life from which the tradition sprang is by studying the works of the tradition. Is there not something at once too depressive and too assured in thinking that consciousness of the past and present can only be attained in literature, where this consciousness is expressed? And if it were true that the literary consciousness was the only consciousness of living values, then would not this mean the isolation of literature, as though it were only capable of experiencing itself? I think one has to believe that suffering and intensity of living and experiencing are themselves forms of expression, and always have been. So that in the deeply felt experience of soldiers and lovers (for example) the consciousness of the poets, who have made language of their experience, is in communion with that intensity of living. The hero is incapable of expressing himself, but if he is really a hero, his deeds are fully lived, and are as it were presented to the epic poet as a form of consciousness which he interprets in his poetry.

It may be important to rail against our education, the conditions of our cultural life, advertising, corruption, etc., but to say that the life of the past can only be reached through literary criticism and the study of chosen books, is a point of view as vulgarly materialist as that complained against. For life, the values of life as it was most intensely experienced and felt at all times, can be reborn within life. Those who love or suffer or are courageous can recreate, as though 'on the first day', the living situation which is the gift for the poet to interpret in his poem.

David Jones' soldiers walk in light:

> Every one of these, stood, separate, upright, above ground,
> blinkt to the broad light
> risen dry mouthed from the chalk
> vivified from the Nullah without commotion
> and to distinctly said words,
> moved in open order and keeping admirable formation
> and at the high-port position
> walking in the morning on the flat roof of the world
> and some walked delicately
> sensible of their particular judgement.

Reading recently in *The Hudson Review* a selection of letters from German soldiers in Stalingrad, I had again the impression that where men are made aware of the extremes of the human condition, in many cases the values whose loss the intellectual critics have so long deplored emerge. For those values are, at least in part, not institutional and doctrinal, but potential in human individuals. What, more than values, we lack is awareness, when we are not by nature serious, or made serious by being thrust into extreme situations, of what it means to be alive. But we can have faith that people are capable of being made conscious of this. I cannot believe that the decay of the 'organic community' has deprived people of the potentiality to be awakened to the fact that they are living individuals. A poet should believe that others are potentially alive as he is, in the moments of his poetry.

By this I do not mean that the creative imagination must work upon that kind of chill contemporary humanism which is sometimes served up as the lowest common denominator of science and lost beliefs. What I do suspect, though, is that dogmas and orthodoxies are no way round the fact that in modern conditions all we can be sure of *knowing* is the common humanity of those who consider themselves civilized and those who 'howl and make faces on the shore'. Beyond this, every 'belief' is 'deliberate' and deliberated. If it rests on institutions and dogmas, then those only divide it from the modern environment. Where it links up with others is in the common human need for affirmation from which it derives. That this is so, is demonstrated, I think, not by current critical attitudes but by the greatest poetic achievements of our time, which in spite of dogma and orthodoxies have rested on the idea of the liberated, unconditioned imagination.

I suggest that Yeats and Eliot and Lawrence and Faulkner, in spite of the fact that they themselves were traditionally-minded artists who deplored the breakdown of tradition in the life around them, nevertheless clung to the idea that the imagination must in modern circumstances reinvent values. It is the contradiction between an eighteenth-century, almost classical critical awareness and artistic self-consciousness, and this trust in the miracle-producing resources of the individual imagination, to which we owe the great achievements of modern art. There is danger today of the paradox being forgotten and of us relying too much on intellectual attitudes.

THE ORGANIC, THE ORCHIDACEOUS,
THE INTELLECTUALIZED

WE can hear through poetry and criticism of the past 150
years a note of regret already poignant in Wordsworth
and Coleridge. It is in Wordsworth's *Intimations of Immortality*
Ode in lines such as:

> What though the radiance which was once
> so bright
> Be now for ever taken from my sight,
> Though nothing can bring back the hour
> Of splendour in the grass, of glory in the
> flower. . . .

For Wordsworth this hour belongs to the poet's childhood.
But we feel that before Wordsworth's day it belonged to a life in
harmony with poetry.

The note is taken up by Coleridge, replying to Wordsworth,
in *Dejection: an Ode*:

> But now afflictions bow me down to earth;
> Nor care I that they rob me of my mirth;
> But oh! each visitation
> Suspends what nature gave me at by birth,
> My shaping spirit of Imagination.

The regret is for a period of innocence in which environment,
existence, and poetic expression formed a single harmony.

This vision of childhood is celebrated, also, in Blake's *Songs of Innocence* in poetry of a spontaneous, seemingly still childlike kind. It is significant that the *Songs of Innocence's* 'opposite' (to use the word in the Yeatsian sense), *The Songs of Experience*, embraces evil as the price paid in order that the poet may continue to experience life at its most real:

> Love seeketh only Self to please,
> To bind another to Its delight;
> Joys in another's loss of ease,
> And builds a Hell in Heaven's despite.

It is as though Blake thinks that for the adult the childhood immediacy can only be retained by seeking evil in experience where the child found good. The view was expressed, with a sophistication which Blake would probably have disliked, by Baudelaire in *Les Fleurs du Mal*. The world which Blake saw emerging, of Newtonian science and 'the dark satanic mills', abstracts the qualities that are personal and immediate from human relationships. Instead of innocent contact with good, or guilt-ridden but still personal contact with evil, there is, like the fogs of that black country of industrialist barracks which Blake saw covering the green English countryside, the screen between man and man of depersonalized values of power and materialism. Later poets have felt envy for poets before the industrial revolution whom they believe to have lived in the presence of those forces of nature which are today screened from us as much by the inner processes of abstract thinking as the outward appearances of industrial civilization.

Twentieth-century criticism is full of sophisticated attempts to explain what has been lost—the once associated forms of a sensibility now become dissociated, the pattern of living of the 'organic community'. But there is the possibility that the sophistication hides a nostalgia just as heavily romanticized as that of Thomas Carlyle for monastic life in the eleventh century, or William

Morris for Merrie England. Eliot looks back to the Elizabethan age as 'a period when the intellect was immediately at the tips of the senses. Sensation became word and word sensation.'

From Carlyle, Ruskin, Morris and Arnold, to T. E. Hulme, Ezra Pound, Yeats, Eliot, Lawrence and Leavis, there is the search for a nameable boojum or snark that can be held responsible for splitting wide apart the once fused being-creating consciousness. The Renaissance, the puritan revolution, the French Revolution, the industrial revolution, have all been named as villains. There runs through modern criticism the fantasy of a Second Fall of Man. The First Fall, it will be remembered, had the result of introducing Original Sin into the world of Man, exiled from the Garden of Eden, and knowing good and evil. The Second Fall seems to result from the introduction of scientific utilitarian values and modes of thinking into the world of personal choice between good and evil, with the result that values cease to be personal and become identified with the usefulness or destructiveness of social systems and material things.

★   ★   ★   ★

Just as I tried before to separate the romantic concept of the power of the sovereign imagination from the picture given by critics and sociological analysts of poets writing in a society where their works are conditioned by modern circumstances, now I want to consider the idea of organic poetry separately from the conditions which are held to have produced the dissociation of sensibility.

I do not know whether it is possible to define organic poetry. But it should be possible to cite examples of poetry in which 'sensation became word and word sensation', and to indicate the tendency of poetry to be organic in the work of poets who aim at this quality. Poetry tends to be organic when the words and form of the poem seem to grow out of the poet's experience of his environment, particularly I should say when that environment and experience seem 'natural'. There is the idea of a continuous process as from environment, through the poet's sensuous nature, into words and form. This is surely what Keats means when he says that poetry should grow as naturally as the leaves of a tree. By growing he does not mean that poets should not work, but that the work itself should resemble the process of diligently growing rather than of being intellectualized.

Organic poetry is, then, that in which there is identification of the poet's experience of nature (meaning by this the life around him sensuously apprehended) with the words used, without there being the feeling that mental activity falls like a shadow between the experience and the realized words and form. In such work, sensibility is sensuous, and if there is idea, then it, also, is experienced sensuously. In the poetry, the reader feels himself present with articulated life realized as earth and movement exactly through the words.

It is the quality in the speeches of Shakespeare's characters which caused Dryden to comment: 'All the images of nature were still present to him, and he drew them not laboriously, but luckily; when he describes anything, you more than see it, you feel it too.'

The simplest and clearest examples of organic poetry are perhaps to be found in certain passages of Shakespeare's sonnets, for example, Sonnet 12:

> When lofty trees I see barren of leaves,
> Which erst from heat did canopy the herd,
> And summer's green all girded up in sheaves,
> Borne on the bier with white and bristly beard. . . .

It is impossible, I think, to apprehend these lines except as the identification of nature with the feeling growing through the language. It is as if one were standing in a harvest field with great trees very close, and felt within the ripeness of the single moment the turning of all the seasons of the year and as if at the same time this sensation was clothed in words directly springing from it. Intelligence and feeling are realized in sap and leaves.

Nineteenth-century attempts to produce a similar effect show the contrast between organic poetry and writing which, marvellous as it may be, springs not from immediacy but from the straining of memory after immediate effect. An example is the justly famous stanzas of Tennyson from *In Memoriam*:

> By night we linger'd on the lawn,
>   For underfoot the herb was dry;
>   And genial warmth; and o'er the sky
> The silvery haze of summer drawn;
>
> And calm that let the tapers burn
>   Unwavering: not a cricket chirr'd:
>   The brook alone far-off was heard
> And on the board the fluttering urn:
>
> And bats went round in fragrant skies,
>   And wheel'd or lit the filmy shapes
>   That haunt the dusk, with ermine
>   capes
> And woolly breasts and beaded eyes;
>
> While now we sang old songs that peal'd
>   From knoll to knoll, where, couch'd
>   at ease,
>   The white kine glimmer'd, and the
>   trees
> Laid their dark arms about the field.

This certainly paints a picture in the mind's eye. It is, indeed, a word painting: that is to say, it attempts in words what a painter does in his different medium. One art is skilfully used to suggest another. The words are chosen with conscious aesthetic precision and put on the paper at the brush's tip. 'Underfoot the herb was dry.' One savours the choice of *herb*. It is distinguished from *grass*, and at the same time contains the French word for grass. One may wonder whether in the recollected instant of regret for Hallam there is not too much observation in the 'woolly breasts and beaded eyes' of the bats. The fact that the scene is dusk when one could not see 'beaded eyes' suggests that the visual mind is working too hard. Too much meticulously detailed emotion seems to have been recollected in too much tranquillity.

If, indeed, there is organic poetry in the nineteenth-century England, it is to be found perhaps not in the poets but in painters such as Samuel Palmer in his early water colours and drawings, Constable in his sketches, and, above all, Turner.

The lines from Sonnet 12 which I have quoted might be taken as purely descriptive. It could be argued that they have something of the Wordsworthian approach to nature in that they are, perhaps, recollected from childhood: in the most English of meadowy tree-weighed river-woven landscapes, one imagines the boy Shakespeare standing in the ripe fields. But Sonnet 26 has the same quality of potent innocence, here embedded in thought removed from immediate observation:

> Till whatsoever star that guides my moving
> Points on me graciously with fair aspect,
> And puts apparel on my tatter'd loving,
> To show me worthy of thy sweet respect. . . .

In some of his later poems, Yeats celebrates the purity, strength, and sweetness which seems inseparable from lives lived passionately, in surroundings identified with vision handed down from the past. He praises those who have the aristocratic view, who live in the country, in great houses, inherit ancestral properties, ride to hounds, fish, are not 'intellectuals'. But he does so out of an awareness of his own divided being, torn by regret, filled with remorse:

> Through intricate motions ran
> Stream and gliding sun
> And all my heart seemed gay:
> Made my attention stray.

> Repentance keeps my heart impure;
> But what am I that dare
> Fancy that I can
> Better conduct myself or have more
> Sense than a common man?
>
> What motion of the sun or stream
> Or eyelid shot the gleam
> That pierced my body through?
> What made me live like those that seem
> Self-born, born anew?

Yeats makes a sharp distinction between the life that is a poem, and the sedentary, reflective, remorseful, and nostalgic life which is that of the poet writing poetry. The life that is a poem unreflectingly fuses environment with living. It is the life of people who have not thought and who therefore, if they are privileged, can go on living as their forbears did. But this is impossible for the modern poet who must needs be reflecting, responsible, remorseful, conscious of a fate of the world wider than the sphere of life he might sensuously apprehend. There is much regret in Yeats for a time when, as he thinks, it was possible to be poet, scholar, and gentleman. So where in Shakespeare there was the unity of unconscious being with conscious creating, in Yeats there is an almost bitter admiration for the 'dumb' life of uncreative full-blooded action, bitter regret that the poetic occupation has barred him out from poetic existing:

> I leave both faith and pride
> To young upstanding men
> Climbing the mountain-side,
> That under bursting dawn
> They may drop a fly;
>
> Being of that metal made
> Till it was broken by
> This sedentary trade.

*   *   *   *

What is called Nature poetry began with the industrial era. With the covering over of the countryside with the industrial slums, untouched nature became a spiritual value. The deeper significance of Nature poetry is surely that it was the attempt of certain poets to return to organic poetry by placing themselves within a setting from which they rejected the values of their contemporaries, those of the town. Nature put them back into the period of history which belonged to the countryside. The movement from London to the Lake District was not just a geographical withdrawal. It was also a retreat into a fortress of past time. It is significant that Wordsworth, in the Introduction to the *Lyrical Ballads*, is not just concerned—as the Wordsworthians sometimes seem to think—with natural scenery and picturesque peasants. He was also concerned with *natural* people—those who lived in Cumberland, their behaviour and view of life, and the language which they used, which he felt should be the idiom of poetry, because it was the idiom of lives in contact with nature. They were not the lives of the town.

Wordsworth identified the nature of Windermere and Derwentwater with his own childhood. He sought to recover a fusion of nature and being he once enjoyed, by reliving those surroundings in his poetry. His greatest descriptive passages have kinetic energy: 'Kinetic' is defined in the *Shorter Oxford English Dictionary* as 'the power of doing work possessed by a moving body by virtue of its motion'. When Wordsworth is actually walking, in motion, literally with muscles and mind going over the territory of his childhood, his memory functions intensely, and his poetry communicates relived physical sensation and spiritual exaltation with correspondence of word after word to footstep after footstep. *The Prelude* is the first great *Recherche du temps perdu*. What is being recaptured is not just the poet's own past but the past relationship of English poetry to the natural environment. And if the Nature poetry of the lake poets is a reaction against industrialism—against the nineteenth century—it is also a reaction against the urban poetry of Pope—against the eighteenth century—whose poetry, in its ideas, was the instrument of a rationalist aristocratic élite.

Augustan poetry was illustrative, then, of attitudes to life, theses, rationalism, social hierarchy, fashions, belonging to that age, to the mentality and intellectual life of the town. Wordsworth turned away from the town to seek out the sources of being and feeling as against those of will and reason. This choice is clear enough. The child cannot distinguish between its own body and its mother's, inner self and outer world. It is this sense of returning to an almost pre-conscious level which results in an ambiguous vagueness when Wordsworth attempts to restate his sensations as a philosophy of the unity of being and experiencing:

> a sense sublime
> Of something far more deeply interfused
> Whose dwelling is the light of setting suns,
> And the round ocean, and the living air,
> And the blue sky, and in the mind of man.

Here is the *idea* of the organic, but it is not organic in expression.

The *Ode on the Intimations of Immortality* is one of the great poems in the English language. Having said this, one might well add that it is both profoundly unsatisfactory as communicated innocence and profoundly unconvincing as philosophy. It opens with the poet's recollections of the time that was when the earth seemed 'apparelled in celestial light', the light of a glory which has now passed away from the earth. In his childhood, the poet both saw and was one with what he saw. Today, he looks, and things are as beautiful as they were, and yet they remain outside him, they are not an inseparable part of his own being. The being-creating fusion has been split apart. He attributes this calamity to his exile from his own childhood. The view of life he offers to justify the intensity of childhood experiences seems taken for granted by Wordsworthians. It has not always aroused sufficient amazement. It is usually accepted, I think, as belief in reincarnation, and Indians are pleased to think that it provides one of those occasions when English poetry links up with Oriental philosophy. Actually, it puts forward a theory of pre-incarnation in which we are invited to look backward to a state of existence precedent to birth, but not forward to later incarnations. The title, indeed, fits strangely with this view which suggests that impressions grow ever fainter as our days remove from the mystical state before birth. There is no indication that posthumous intimations will be stronger than the pre-natal ones, unless perhaps we are to suppose that they precede later births. But this is unlikely, as the pre-natal experience is not represented as being posthumous to a previous life. In fact, any given moment of consciousness is the faintest, because the last, in a series of impressions ever weakening as they grow further away from pre-natal bliss:

> Our birth is but a sleep and a forgetting:
> The Soul that rises with us, our life's Star,
>   Hath had elsewhere its setting,
>   And cometh from afar:
>   Not in entire forgetfulness,
>   And not in utter nakedness,
> But trailing clouds of glory do we come
>   From God, who is our home. . . .

We are asked here to share the feelings of a consciousness which laments the loss of its unconsciousness but which at the same time romanticizes unconsciousness, as a peculiar and intense state of consciousness, of organic union with the mystical sources of nature. The objection to this is obvious: that unconscious bliss only exists at the moment when it becomes conscious and that Wordsworth never entered into the full innocence of being a child until he wrote this poetry. All the same, this answer does not entirely cover the case. For childhood in his poetry is also a metaphor for a world in which there is no divorce between feeling and seeing.

Coleridge in his *Dejection: an Ode* analyses more rationally the split between childhood joy and adult awareness, between

consciousness and unconscious nature. He admits that it is our
own consciousness which gives unconscious nature its attributes:

> O Lady! we receive but what we give
> And in our life alone does Nature live:
> Ours is her wedding garment, ours her shroud!

What is true of nature is also true of childhood fused with its
surroundings. Wordsworth 'received'—to use Coleridge's word
—his childhood because he realized it through his adult consciousness by means of the poetic gift in which that memory was aware.
Coleridge goes on:

> And would we aught behold, of higher worth,
> Than that inanimate cold world allowed
> To the poor loveless ever-anxious crowd,
>   Ah! from the soul itself must issue forth
> A light, a glory, a fair luminous cloud
>   Enveloping the Earth. . . .

Here the accusing finger points, the villainy is named. It is the
'inanimate cold world' with its 'loveless ever-anxious crowd' and
its material goals and debased values, the urban consciousness,
which has set a barrier between the abstract aims of living and
'joy', the shaping spirit of imagination. It is this which has thrust
the poets and 'the happy few' (as Stendhal named them) back
upon their own resources, so that they must create out of
themselves the luminous values which may still envelope the
earth.

Coleridge thinks that he might—as he believes Wordsworth
succeeded in doing—win back that unity of inward being with
outer nature which makes it possible to write organic poetry, the
line that springs directly from 'the shaping spirit of imagination'
which is the result of world-excluded 'joy'. And certainly the
characteristic of the greatest passages in *The Prelude* is that
the language and the thought expressed become one with the
sensation experienced.

For later poets, what may seem enviable about the lake poets is that they were living in an early phase of modern history when it was still possible for them to reject industrial civilization and choose natural scenery as though it were an alternative which met the life of the town on equal terms, without too much sacrifice of significant expression. Of course, there have been poets since, who have rebelled against industrial society—D. H. Lawrence did. But despite his hatred of the towns, Lawrence thought in the idiom of the Nottingham of the coal mines and the chapels in which he had grown up; and the 'nature' which he invoked against the industrial urban consciousness had much more of rebellious instinctual human nature about it than of natural scenery, the moods of the weather, and the annals of the peasantry.

Historically, Wordsworth was the last poet who, making such a choice, could write great poetry. This is perhaps to put the matter too starkly—but at the stage of the industrial revolution which was Wordsworth's youth the country and the town life might seem still in balance: just as Blake's protests against science and rationalism still had the force behind them of a time when it might have been possible to choose another path than the one that led to the 'dark satanic mills', to reaffirm the England that was Blake's Jerusalem. But, already in mid-nineteenth century, for a poet to have devoted himself to writing about the scenes and experiences of his childhood in the countryside, would have been to write poetry about things that no longer seemed 'important' experience in the history of modern civilization.

The scene of the larger battle for writing poetry about the human condition in modern times had to be transferred to the towns and the preoccupations of people living in the world of industry and science. Yet, the lake poets defined a choice which still remains between organic, imaginative writing and that which Lawrence called 'cerebral', but for which—since cerebral seems denigratory—I prefer to use the term 'intellectualized'.

*   *   *   *

That which to Wordsworth was nature, to Keats was the poetry of Chaucer, Spenser, and Shakespeare, his deliberately sought out environment. His was a life lived as far as possible as poetry. Everything in his letters points to his intention of living in the world as though it were palpable poetry; everything in his poetry, to his determination to regard his poetry as surrounding life. 'Oh, for a life of pure sensation!' he cries, meaning by this not what the editor of the *Daily Express* or of the *Chicago Tribune* might mean, but that he wished to live in a continuity of a sensuously apprehended experience which was one with the sensuous experience of the poetry he read and wrote. In his poetry there is a tendency to identify experienced sensation with sensation imagined, to think that if he could not live a life that was poetry, then he could inhabit a poetry that was life. He recounts the experience, apparently frequent with him, of being rapt from the actual world—the anatomy lesson at the medical school where he was an apprentice—to a far realer world of poetic imagining. What he expected from his friends—Reynolds, Hunt, Shelley, and the others—was that they should form a magic circle which excluded nearly all experience except the life of the imagination. The kind of reality which makes us call certain novelists realists was to Keats a stiletto pointed at the ruby jugular vein of lived dream. His identification of beauty with truth was simply a way of stating his lived identification of imagination with a passionately sought out reality. In the context of his poetry and letters, what he meant by 'Beauty is truth, truth beauty that is all / Ye know on earth and all ye need to know' is so clear that it is difficult not to suspect critics of bad faith when they pretend not to understand what it means.

In his uncannily perceptive *Keats and Shakespeare*, Middleton Murry shows the extent to which Keats identified his poetry with the Shakespeare of *Romeo and Juliet*, *A Midsummer Night's Dream*, and *King Lear*. What corresponds in Keats to the pre-natal Wordsworth 'trailing clouds of glory', is a pre-natal Keats who was the young Shakespeare. We are often told that Keats wrote 'pure poetry'. This is true if we mean by it that he invented lines which, while remaining original to him, were yet a concentrated essence of Chaucer, Spenser, Shakespeare, and Milton become his own spiritual habitat. But such quintessentialized poetry is not the same thing as what I call organic poetry, which springs directly from nature and life. Murry almost convinces himself—as he convinced me when I was 17—that through identification the 23-year-old Keats *was* the young Shakespeare. Beware! such identification results in extreme dissimilarity to the person identified with. Shakespeare, himself, was Shakespeare and not identifying with, say, Chaucer. Keats' poetry, like the poetry of Walter de la Mare, fed off other poetry and the idea of poetry. It is exotic, parasitic, orchidaceous. However sometimes, through the veils of his own and other men's dreams, experience poignantly personal to him— a real anguish, a real love—which refuses to be fobbed off with the poetic, breaks through and becomes disturbing autobiographic poetry.

*   *   *   *

What I have been trying to show is that at the beginning of the Industrial Revolution and until our own day, two things which are interconnected have happened which have had revolutionary effects on imaginative writing. One is that poets have felt threatened by a change in consciousness from organic and concrete to scientific and abstract thinking. This has cut them off from a past when poets were intimately and, as it were, immediately in touch with the sacramental, the personal, and the natural forces that were once the ritual of living. The other is that as a result of this sense of an irremediable change, there began to be an examination and re-evaluation of the once primary place of imagination in life as in poetry. Although there has been a reaction against the Romantics, there has been no return to the idea that the imagination could or should be put at the service of a rationalistic or politic view of life. But there has, I think, been a tendency, over-looked by most modern critics, to regard the power of the imagination as religious.

In an essay *Rilke among the Critics*,* Mr. Michael Hamburger cites several authorities to show that Rilke did in fact attempt to make his poetry a substitute for religion. To F. R. Leavis there is no question but that D. H. Lawrence's message is 'religious'. Yeats makes a mosaic of fragments of Oriental and Western beliefs and varieties of mysticism, a religion as eclectic as the picture of art selected from all times and places, which André Malraux in his *Musée Imaginaire* supposes modern men and women to carry round in their heads.

So although Arnold's idea is in disrepute among critics, it is to some extent prophetic of the development of modern poetry. When Arnold wrote that religion had 'materialized itself in fact' he was doubtless thinking of the Victorian controversy between the religious and the evolutionists of his time, about the origins of man. What has happened later is that the exaltation of the act of the creative imagination as a visionary or intuitive judging of the values of life in a civilization of fragmented values, has, as a first stage, separated the imagination from current orthodoxies, and brought it back to the idea of religion as imagination in action, creating the world. That 'art creates values' was an idea frequently expressed by writers at the beginning of the present century. And the point I want to emphasize is that although the view of poets become dogmatically religious seems completely opposed today to that of the heretically undogmatic, in fact the disagreement is of a kind more apparent in their critical prose views than in the works of their poetic imagination.

Michael Hamburger gives some striking quotations from the *Opus Posthumus* of Wallace Stevens to show how close his attitudes are to those of Rilke:

* *Encounter*, 103 (April, 1962), 'Rilke among the Critics', by Michael Hamburger.

The poet has 'immensely to do with giving life whatever savour it possesses. He has had to do with whatever the imagination and the senses have made of the world.'

The world about us would be desolate except for the world within us.

The major poetic idea in the world is and always has been the idea of God.

After one has abandoned a belief in God, poetry is the essence which takes its place as life's redemption.

This expresses the loneliness of the artist with his creation. It is the attitude of Henry James and of Joseph Conrad, which greatly influenced the early Eliot, and what I am suggesting is that it still remains the attitude of modern poets in the actual creation of their poetry. If they have reintroduced the idea of dogmatic religion, it is as corrective to what is dangerous and nihilistic in such an isolated imagination; but their reintroduction of dogma into their thinking is not a return to the kind of religion for which Arnold thought poetry might become a substitute, the religion materialized in fact. Dogma acts in their work as discipline to the imagination.

In the same article, Michael Hamburger observes that 'religious faith is one thing, poetic imagination another', and the distinction he makes is that 'faith demands a concentration of the will, whereas will is the enemy of the imagination'. This seems a bit baldly stated, since there have been, without their suffering inner contradiction, religious imaginative poets. Perhaps, though, in ages of belief the inner imagining of poets is corrected by the sur-rounding discipline of an external will to believe. Thus when Coleridge writes of the imagination as though it were a com-pletely self-sufficient mediator between different faculties of the soul, he takes for granted that in acting thus it has already been influenced by ideas of 'worth and dignity'. In a time of disbelief, there is a danger of art resulting from altogether uncontrolled imagination, a surrender of the poet to his perhaps destructive and diabolic fantasies. For this reason Eliot and Auden distrust the heresies of the imagination become a law unto itself. Nevertheless to say that the religion of T. S. Eliot and W. H. Auden is the contrary of the irreligion of Lawrence and Rilke, is to set up a false opposition. Religion in Eliot's poetry may involve insistence on dogma and traditional attitudes, but it is not a return to the religion 'that has materialized itself in fact' which seemed unacceptable to Arnold. Indeed in its imagining of mystical situations outside the temporal order it might appear, to Arnold, to have some of the characteristics of poetry substituting for religion. In Eliot, imagination remains the primary activity, just as it is in Yeats, or Rilke. Dogma has been introduced not at the centre of the inspiration but as a principle of correction of extravagant despair, or eclectic invention.

Nostalgia for organic poetry, in which the poetic flows, as it were, in an interrupted continuum out of living experience, causes perhaps the bitterest reaction of the modern poet to life as it has been since the industrial revolution. It may seem curious that this is so, since organic writing makes up only a small proportion of past literature. It is rare even in Shakespeare's sonnets. Shakespeare usually uses the devices of intellectualized poetry, in the way in which a modern poet would do. He constructs, for example, metaphors from the machinery of the law to demonstrate his complex feelings about the relationship with the friend. The irony with which in Sonnet 90 the friendship which is of feeling, without calculation, based on genius, nature and generosity to the poet, is recognized as being calculated and contractual on the part of the young man, is also modern:

> Farewell! thou art too dear for my possessing,
> And like enough thou know'st thy estimate:
> The charter of thy worth gives thee releasing;
> My bonds in thee are all determinate.
> For how do I hold thee but by thy granting?
> And for that riches where is my deserving?
> The cause of this fair gift in me is wanting,
> And so my patent back again is swerving.

Organic poetry, as I have attempted to describe it, arises out of an assumed harmony not just between man and his fellow-beings, not just between man and social institutions, but between man and the forces in physical nature, perhaps the nature round him, perhaps his own instinctual nature. The supposition is that the powers, deriving from the stars, the sap, the soil, reaffirm the natural order of society, the naturalness of human love. The feeling of nature moving with the forces of stars and weather and beasts magnetically through individual life and through the social hierarchy is very strong in *King Lear*. Re-reading the play recently, I noticed how it is underlined by the character of Albany, husband of Goneril. He is, militarily speaking, on the wrong side in the conflict between the forces of Edmund and those of France. But it is he who abandons the cause of his wife when he sees that her behaviour and her sister's is not just wrong, but against nature:

> That nature which contemns its origin
> Cannot be bordered certain in itself.
> She that herself will sliver and disbranch
> From her material sap, perforce must wither
> And come to deadly use.

*   *   *   *

So passionate regret is expressed by Eliot for the period before the dissociation of sensibility, and by Yeats for a life in which there is no division between the 'wise and simple man', 'A man who does not exist / A man who is but a dream'—the fisherman—and the poet with his sedentary trade, which cuts him off from that time when he himself was one of those who 'drop a fly' 'under bursting dawn'. The bitterness is the sense that he is cut off because of the poetry; and yet he feels that in differing circumstances, the poetic imagination would have been a key to that very sensuous being of which the poet doomed to intellectualization is now deprived. It seems impossible today to think of the poet as Marvell did when he wrote in *The Garden* of a correspondence between being and creating, like intellect complementary to nature:

> Meanwhile, the mind, from pleasure less,
> Withdraws into its happiness:
> The mind, that ocean where each kind
> Does straight its own resemblance find;
> Yet it creates, transcending these,
> Far other worlds, and other seas;
> Annihilating all that's made
> To a green thought in a green shade.

What seems to have been disrupted, then, is the being-creating fusion, where in participating in the resemblances which are nature the poet also comes into possession of his own mind, and makes a fusion which transcends both nature and intellect.

The bitterness at the splitting of the being-creating fusion is, in Yeats, peculiarly personal, a special grudge which the poet bears against his time. The reason for this grudge may be that poets not only want to make poetry, they want to enjoy the nature of a poetic kind of being—Yeats' fisherman—they want experience of poetic living to be realized in the lines of their poetry, poetry and life at times to be one, in the writing of the poetry. They do not want to be 'intellectuals'. Poets can spend nine-tenths of their time 'making' their poetry—the Victorians did—but at some point they want to be their poetry, and one feels doubt whether even in his lines of purest and most magical poetry, Tennyson is ever being his poetry.

The bitterness of which I am speaking takes the form in Lawrence of rage against what he calls cerebral writing, and the programme he set himself for being himself in all he wrote. 'I write with everything vague—plenty of fire underneath, but, like bulbs in the ground, only shadowy flowers that must be beaten and sustained, for another spring.' (Letter to Edward Garnett, 29 January 1914.) Lawrence—if any modern writer—is organic, but that is both his strength and his weakness. There is something about his work, even at its best, which is like material splitting at the seams. And the split is caused, I think, by the separation of his view of what is life from his practise of literature. His philosophy of living through the senses and through instincts suppressed in the modern age leaves little room for art, because it is a revolt against the aesthetic consciousness, a return to more primitive poetic existence. It is an attitude which can be preached but which cannot attain an expression in which the forces that realize the famous Laurentian sense of life and full artistic awareness of problems of form are fused. Thus in certain passages about the dark gods, phallic consciousness, sex, etc., Lawrence gives the impression that the life realized does not lie in the artistic form but in the physical body or the instinctual life of the reader; and even more disconcertingly sometimes the printed page as it were sacrificially or sacramentally represents the physical or the instinctual and sexual body of Lawrence himself. He makes it clear that by phallic consciousness he means only his own particular variety of blood consciousness and sexual feeling, and that he disapproves of behaviour which does not accord to the models he lays down.

Thus where there is modern organic poetry it is the result of a fusion which seems forced, and this is felt in a certain jarring quality in the technique and form. In a way different from Lawrence (but which leads me to think that he would have preferred Lawrence, as he did Walt Whitman, to many of his contemporaries) Gerard Manley Hopkins is organic: his poetry seems always the result of the fusion of the external experience acting directly upon his sensibility and producing language and form. But the identification with external circumstances is either the result of deliberately willed involution with nature—what Hopkins called 'inscape'—or of great anguish. One may much prefer the poetry of Hopkins to the literary flow of Tennyson— and, still more, of Swinburne—yet the anguish makes for forms of unbearable strain, and the suffering seems at times the perverse result of Hopkins' violation of his own poetic nature. Just as the

organic in Wordsworth seems the kineticism of muscular movement across a childhood scene returned to by the poet, producing
a kinetic poetry, so with Hopkins there is the kineticism of willed
visual concentration, grinding despair.

We have the sense then that modern circumstances have set up a
screen between nature and man so that the harmonious relationship realized in organic poetry in which the soul sees itself reflected
in the physical environment, is prevented. The only way of return
to the being-creating fusion is through spiritual or physical violence, tearing down the screen and forcing the inner sensibility
into contact with the external.

What I have called intellectualized poetry is that in which the
critical attitudes which determine the attitude of what is said and
the technique of the poem, are an inseparable part of the consciousness which the poem conveys. In reading much modern poetry,
especially that in which the poet seems preoccupied with the
modern situation, the reader is aware of critical choices being
made, which are embedded in the poetry. The technique of poets
such as Eliot, Pound and Auden persuades because one feels that
the right choices have been made by powerful critical intellects.
Yeats, on the other hand, was never quite 'modern' in the sense
of having a technique which expresses a kind of intellectual self-
consciousness. Lawrence simply evades the issue by either having,
or pretending to have, no awareness of the intellectual problems
of form.

In Yeats there is not intellectualized form, but Yeats himself is
aware of the sadness of having belonged to the 'last romantics'—
that is to say the last of the generation in whom forms and language seemed spontaneous. Yeats felt that the exigencies of his
art had cut him off from the deepest sources of his natural being,
in order that he might write the poetry which realized that being.
Yet he also felt that in an age not ours it had been possible for a
poet both to 'be' that which the fisherman symbolizes for him
in sensuous living, and in exactly the same way to 'be' in his

poetry. Mellors, the gamekeeper, is, surely, to Lawrence what the fisherman is to Yeats: an image of a nostalgically viewed, outside-our-time projected Lawrence who would both live and create with all his senses. And Lawrence's 'dark gods' are a more recent version of the unconscious childhood bliss, the 'shaping spirit of imagination', regretted by Wordsworth and Coleridge. Intellectualized writing, as distinct from that which I have attempted to describe as 'organic', is penetrated by conscious strategy in meeting contemporary experience, conscious intent in realization. A peculiar modern phenomenon is the resentment many writers seem to feel that their art does not grow 'like the leaves of a tree', is not, in some sense which would be full of meaning to them, spontaneous. The nostalgia is expressed in a short poem of Gottfried Benn, *A Weightless Element*. The English version which I quote here is by Christopher Middleton.

WENN ETWAS LEICHT

Wenn etwas leicht und rauschend um dich ist
wie die Glyzinienpracht an dieser Mauer,
dann ist die Stunde jener Trauer,
dass du nicht reich und unerschöpflich bist,

nicht wie die Blüte oder wie das Licht:
in Strahlen kommend, sich verwandelnd,
an ähnlichen Gebilden handelnd,
die alle nur der eine Rausch verflicht,

der eine Samt, auf dem die Dinge ruhn
so strömend und so unzerspalten,
die Grenze ziehen, die Stunden halten
und nichts in jener Trauer tun.

A WEIGHTLESS ELEMENT

When like wistaria against this wall
around you rings a weightless element,
then is the time that you lament
being not rich and inexhaustible,

not like the blossom or not like the light:
in rays arriving, changing its design,
acting on forms akin to it
that ringed in single ecstasy entwine,

the single velvet ground where things repose,
so lush, so undivided, and
with time according, self-confined,
go not the way lamenting goes.

Ultimately the ground of this lamenting—this hatred even—is that, in the world of industrialization and science, of measurements and reason, poetry has been forced to become an intellectual discipline in order to confront the modern reality on its own terms, its own symbols. Poets accept the fact that they must work, be analytical, etc., but their profoundest wish is to be in their nature different from the modern world which they regard as denaturalized. They admire classic periods of the past, envy perhaps the order and enlightenment of ages of reason (which after all were not so reasonable), but, though condemned to use its intellectual weapons, they do not want to fit into the context of our age of calculations producing monstrosities of good and ill. Their intellect is used to bring past tradition into present consciousness, their techniques are intellectualized, but their hearts belong to a time on which their dreams concentrate, some moment of past history, when 'sensation became word and word sensation'.

Criticism is traditionalist, analytic, scientific even. Poets accept the necessity of being critics in their poetry, but in the deepest centre of their being they know this is a trap, that they have been forced to accept a logic which may enable them to write poetry, but which cuts them off from the sense of being it.

III

IMAGINATION IS PERSONAL

MODERN poets cannot be taken simply as reacting against Romanticism and returning to tradition and orthodoxy. On the surface it would, of course, seem that the most obvious characteristic of the movement in poetry initiated by Hulme, Pound, and Eliot, early in the present century, was a revolt against Romantic standards. And it is true that the mountain range of the Romantics (shutting out the view of everything beyond the early nineteenth century except the highest peaks of English poetry—Shakespeare, Chaucer, and Milton) has been removed. Today, students realize that Shelley, Keats, and Byron were extraordinary men with extraordinary gifts living in an extraordinary time, but they know, also, that these poets had little time in which to mature, and that the collected works of Shelley are a wild, exotic, and unweeded garden.

With the Romantic range removed, words concretely used, metaphors that are coherent and not vague, have, as it were, surged forward, passed through the undisciplined Romantic lines and joined hands with present poetry. Marvell, Dryden, and Pope have become accessible to us in a way that perhaps they were not to Victorian readers. *I read Othello's visage in his mind:* a generation, which began by learning the calm and beauty realized in the surface of seventeenth- and eighteenth-century poetry, stayed to prefer them to the Romantc disorder.

However, this cutting of Romantic poetry down to size did not lead to the new classicism which T. E. Hulme predicted in his *Speculations*. What it did initiate was a revolution in method, in technique, in spreading the idea that writing poetry was deliberate and conscious work and not a matter of entering into an effluvial state of self-intoxication. Yet against this picture of return to a pre-Romantic consciousness of the intellectual problems of writing poetry, we have to bear in mind that, by and large, the criticism of the Augustan poets by the Romantics has, with certain qualifications, been accepted by the anti-Romantic moderns, perhaps on the grounds of its *historic necessity* rather than its critical justice, but accepted nevertheless. When Eliot retracted some of his early attack on Milton, he gave as his excuse that, as a young man, it had been necessary for him to attack Milton for the sake of the development of his own poetry, just as it had been a poetic necessity for Wordsworth to attack Pope.

So we are confronted with the paradox that although there has been a reaction against the Romantics and back towards the poets who preceded them, nevertheless, the same poet-critics who made this revolt have taken over the subjective view of the imagination which was Romantic. Joyce, Yeats (in his later work), Eliot, and Pound combine critical consciousness in the *act* of writing, with instinctive subjective consciousness in their use of material from dreams, as well as in their fragmentariness, obscurity, mysteriousness, and the like. They are objective in being extremely aware of what they want to say and how to say it; they are subjective in their realization that everything said has to be reinvented from the deepest and most isolated centre of individual imagination. They are aware of the importance of contemporary idiom; but they are also aware of the greater importance of the magic of language which is 'rich and strange'.

There could not be a return to eighteenth-century classicism— to the idea of the unified intellectual culture of an élite, exercising reason to reconcile science, God, and the aristocracy, and sublimating the arguments in transparent poetry. The Romantics are of our modern world, and modern poetry comes out of their situation. When we uphold Pope against the Romantics we, after all, are only expressing the view that Byron also expressed—despising the works of himself and his contemporaries, and advocating Pope, but having to be Byron.

There has been talk, on and off, ever since T. E. Hulme's *Speculation*, of a new classicism. Hulme thought that a movement of Cubists and Vorticists in painting and of imagists in poetry could be founded on a synthesis between the tradition of pre-Renaissance non-individualist Byzantine art, and the cold abstract forms of the dehumanized modern age of machinery. But classical revivals cannot be based on dubious historic analogies. Interpreted into political action, Hulme's wish to put the clock back to an authoritarian age indifferent to human values was Fascism. His aesthetic ideas became economic theory and Fascist ideology in the *Cantos* of his admirer, Ezra Pound. The obvious objection to a classical revival is that there is no unity of outlook in our modern age divided between science and the humanities. The only unity we can have is of a kind forced upon us by State-directed politics. A willed and forced parody of modern classicism is that branch of propagandist advertising extended into art which is called social realism.

So, in a civilization split in its allegiances between scientific scepticism, specialization, rationalism, utilitarianism, and the surviving religious and cultural traditions—more powerful than is generally admitted—there can be no classical revival. What we have, instead, is the setting up of outposts of orthodoxy and dogma in the modern waste land. Eliot, Auden, and others have established fortresses of past tradition, reimagined, reinvented in the contemporary idiom of their poetry. But just because terms like tradition, orthodoxy, and dogma are employed, we should not confuse the comparatively isolated position of the orthodox with a time when whole societies were orthodoxies. A dogma today remains sectarian in a society of sects, religious and secular. Orthodoxy today is not that of society but of the orthodox only.

I am here considering literature and not religion. For I well understand that from a religious standpoint it is not very important whether there are few believers or many. Faith may burn more intensely in the day of outcasts than in that of complacent establishments. But for literature, the question whether the religious symbolism and tradition of poets corresponds to those in the minds of their readers matters. For non-believing readers I do not think that there is a great difference between the orthodox symbolism of writers like Eliot and Auden, and the heterodoxy of Rilke, or the eclectic religion of Yeats, as realized in their poetry. Moreover, I think this is recognized by Eliot in his poetic practice. For he does not write so much as one conforming to a doctrine already present and accepted in the mind of his reader, as like one who invents (just as much as Rilke or Yeats) his symbols and values.

There is every difference, of course, between religious faith and poetic imagination. But the modern poet may have to reinvent his faith as poetic imagination; and so to the common reader the difference between the dogma of Eliot and the private religions of Rilke or Yeats may not seem apparent or to matter to the poetry.

This brings us back to the central rôle of the imagination in modern as in Romantic poetry. In a world of fragmented values the imagination cannot illustrate accepted doctrines, cannot refer to symbolic meanings already recognized by the reader, symbols of the faith he believes in, and imbibed with his education. Everything has to be reinvented, as it were, from the beginning, and anew in each work. Every position has to be *imagined* in the poem. The imagining cannot be left to the social environment.

But if there are not ceremonies, symbols, sacraments, generally accepted by the community, within the ritual of living—if society offers no face but the mere machinery of receiving work and giving pay, and providing amusement and distractions—and if beyond this there lurks only the life-or-death, promising-or-threatening abstract hopes and fears of the machines—then, nonetheless, the artist has to find references of human consciousness on which to work. These references are inevitably the elemental qualities of the individual's experience of life—his inescapable awareness, after all, that he is alive and situated in a time and a place, his hopes and fears, his loves and hates. He is capable of being shown of what consciousness consists.

There is in much modern literature an evocation of compensatory depths in individual human life. Everyone carries round an infinity, if not in his head, then in his sex. If his thoughts are cupboard-size, nevertheless, his dreams open on to prairies, constellations. Art invokes the subconscious world to counterbalance the conscious results of materialism. The most potent and awesome lesson of Joyce's *Ulysses* and *Finnegans Wake* is that an eyelid, open or shut to let in the light of consciousness, the dark of sleep, can explore in every direction into memories which, through chains of association, would traverse the whole past and future of humanity. Sometimes Lawrence seems convinced that the forces of the unconscious released by the sexual act might transform the whole world, make men and women become gods instead of being social units.

It is this appeal to forces stronger than those in conscious individuality but which yet *are* the individual, and of which he can be made conscious, that writers as opposed as Lawrence and Joyce, movements as divergent as futurism, dadaism, surrealism, and existentialism, yet have in common.

In times when there are no generally shared religious or societal interpretations of experience, the artist may take over the task of inventing his own references, or of reinforcing past ones as though they were reinvented for his poetic purposes. There is the idea of a burden, a task, a pressure of disparate outer things seeking to realize themselves as inner significance, running through the history of poetry during the past hundred and more years. One may, of course, resent this burden, on the grounds that it puts responsibility of a too vast and altogether too public and impersonal kind on the artist, who can only retain his integrity by limiting his experience within the scope of that which he can personalize. The objection to Shelley's 'we must imagine that which we know' is on these grounds. A history of poetry during the past hundred years and more could be written relating it to swings between the pole of the idea of the imagination as a task imposed, and that of it as strictly limited to the poet's most inward personal awareness.

As so often, there is no real contradiction here—for in fact nothing is artistically significant unless it has become personalized. But there are, nonetheless, pressures and tensions from the outside life upon the inner consciousness. Social conscience can easily work a destructive effect upon artistic conscience, which is not a duty towards society at all but a duty of being conscious as an individual and as an artist. And those who are aware of this danger may insist too much that consciousness can only be about things that are private.

The ideal and often evoked task for the poet in society is to personalize in his work the greatest possible amount and intensity of interest outside his private concerns. A world of external impersonal forces must be sacrificially reinvented as the poet's inner personal world, so that, for his readers, the impersonal modern world may be personalized in poetry. To avoid misunderstanding, I repeat that I do not mean that a poet has to become a public figure or that—to use Keats' phrase—the shadow of public life must fall across his work. What I am concerned with is his awareness of a contemporary situation which affects personal relations and art itself, and which is different from past situations.

The great example of an attempt to personalize the contemporary situation was, of course, Walt Whitman's, especially in *Song of Myself*. Walt Whitman took upon himself the task of imagining the America of his day, and seeking to invent in his poetry the geographical and historical concept of America which his contemporaries and future generations of Americans might themselves realize in their feelings and attitudes. In order to accomplish this, Whitman had not only to invent a kind of poetry different from European models, but he had to become America, as America had, in a sense, in his own imagination, to become Whitman. A great deal of his poetry is about this process, about how Whitman became the wounded of the Civil War, how the continent entered into and absorbed the consciousness of Whitman (just as in *Finnegans Wake* the landscape becomes the consciousness of Joyce's dreamer). Whitman summarizes himself:

Immense have been the preparations for me,
Faithful and friendly the arms that have help'd me.

Cycles ferried my cradle, rowing and rowing like cheerful
    boatmen;
For room to me stars kept aside in their own rings;

They sent influences to look after what was to hold me.
Before I was born out of my mother, generations guided me;
My embryo has never been torpid—nothing could overlay it.

For it the nebula cohered to an orb,
The long slow strata piled to rest it on,
Vast vegetables gave it sustenance,
Monstrous sauroids transported it in their mouths, and
    deposited it with care.

All forces have been steadily employ'd to complete and
    delight me;
Now on this spot I stand with my robust Soul.

Everything has to become thus personal and individuated to be imagined because there is no such thing as a public imagination. Imagination means individuation. What is imagined may be a world as large as that of Shakespeare or Dickens; but it is imagined by one person, the writer. And it becomes part of the life of one person, the reader.

The kind of communication that is art rests on the truth that individuation is the basic pattern of all experiencing—that everyone, in his view of everything outside him, in his knowledge of past and present, in his relations with other people, even in what he has read, makes, and is, his own world. He may be influenced by others, he may be unoriginal, and be scarcely conscious of having an identity separate from that of colleagues, or tribe. But the fact remains that he is irreducibly himself, filling a body and occupying a time and space no one's but his own, and perceiving things through his sense organs that are no one else's. The 'truth' of poetry is that it discourses on this just assumption that poet and reader are unique. Every poet begins again from the beginning that is himself, and outside experience meets in the centre that is his unique sensibility.

Poetry is, then, not a co-operative effort leading to collective results, like science, in which the personal contribution becomes absorbed into the body of collected impersonal knowledge, and the personal quality of the scientist disappears. There is, of course, in each country, a 'sum' of poetry which consists of all the poems written in that language; and they add up to more than any poem or poems. But, supposing that the total of the poems in the language could be signified by the figure 100, then it is a total in which each figure remains, as it were, separate, a sum of 1 and 1 and 1, each retaining its uniqueness though a fraction of, and contributing to, the whole. Through the fusion of the imagination of the writer with that of the reader, the reader is able to hear with the ears, see through the eyes, feel with the feelings of the writer, the world which becomes that of both. This is possible because the outward forms and techniques of art imitate—as the leaf the seed —the inner mode of perception of the poet, a person, experiencing through his unique mind and body the world outside himself. The poet is writing as one person for the reader reading as one person.

A situation which holds true of poetry in all its communication is that expressed by Housman dramatizing to the person he loves (who certainly will not understand) that ideal communication which is simply that of one life speaking to another also uniquely situated within existence:

> From far, from eve and morning
> And yon twelve-winded sky,
> The stuff of life to knit me
> Blew hither: here am I.
>
> Now for a breath I tarry
> Nor yet disperse apart—
> Take my hand quick and tell me,
> What have you in your heart.
>
> Speak now, and I will answer;
> How shall I help you, say;
> Ere to the wind's twelve quarters
> I take my endless way.

It is extremely important, I think, to insist that the poetic imagination is centripetal, a bringing together of experiences from a circumference which could theoretically be enlarged to include all pasts and presents, all things known and experienced into the centre of the artist's individual sensibility where they are the projected patterns which can also be the consciousness of readers.

* * * *

The view has been put forward by C. P. Snow, in a famous and much debated essay, that there are today two cultures, a scientific and a literary. It is clear that what Sir Charles means in this context by 'culture' is the ideas and *mores* of scientists, and those of writers. He is concerned with what is being discovered, and with what is being imagined. He reproaches scientists for their ignorance of literature and writers for their ignorance of science. He wants there to be bridges between the so-called two cultures. He tries to apportion blame equally to both sides in the alleged controversy, but it is evident that his sympathies are really with the scientists: he enters into their reasons for not appreciating the poets. He does not enter into the reasons of the poets for not appreciating the scientists. For he bases his whole case on the question of ignorance and knowledge. The scientists do not *know* literature and the men of letters do not *know* science. Put like this, obviously the writers are the more to blame, for science is knowledge, whereas literature is creating art from that which can be imagined. On grounds of knowledge, the scientists are not to be blamed for not knowing works of the imagination which from their point of view offer little to know. The members of the literary culture have, in his view, ignored a renaissance taking place in science; all that the scientists, on their side, appear to have ignored is the medieval ideas of antiprogressive men of letters.

As a thesis, a good deal of this seems open to dispute. I happen to know that the favourite reading of one of the most eminent physicists, J. D. Bernal, is *Finnegans Wake*. In itself this may not be statistically significant. Yet one can see why a physicist might be interested in Joyce, whose novels are just as much an invention of the modern mind as is a jet aircraft, whose technique has resemblances to work in the laboratory, and whose intelligence expresses a new kind of sensibility. It would be crude, surely, of scientists to think that novels, to be scientific, have to be about scientists, or about matters of social administration, and poems, about social progress. A scientist would surely agree that if literature is scientific it is nevertheless dealing with special kinds of material, and uses special techniques. An argument defending poetry on the ground that poets employ extremely subtle and complex techniques for expressing the psychology of individuals, has been put forward by I. A. Richards, and should rightly have been considered by C. P. Snow if he wished to avoid the charge that what he really meant was that literature should reflect scientific progress, and so earn the interest of scientists.

Sir Charles raises important points which have not, perhaps, so much to do with culture as with education. But he blurs the distinction between the world viewed by scientists and the world viewed by poets. Restricting even the distinction to the level of Sir Charles' argument (that the scientists are progressives, and the writers reactionaries), it is apparent that science is concerned with the extension of the resources of materials and power which can be put to general use; literature is concerned with the meaning which individual life has in the world in which these resources have been made available.

It may be true that certain modern writers—poets, especially— have shown too great antipathy to the progressive aspects of science. But the reason they have done so is because they are concerned not with science but with the world which is so largely the result of science. It is a world in which past values have been fragmented, in which the constructive powers of science are cancelled by its powers of destruction, in which the forces of human personality have broken down, and men and women have come to think of themselves as 'social units'. Of course, to blame scientists, in their disinterested pursuit of knowledge, for this world, would be as unwarranted as to blame writers for delivering their warnings against progress. On the whole, it would seem that it is right for the so-called literary culture to be critical of the so-called scientific. As Wilfred Owen, the most interesting poet of World War I, wrote in the Preface to his poems: 'All a poet can do today is to warn.'

The literary culture is essentially critical of the contemporary world which is the result of the scientific. This criticism may be expressed explicitly in critical works or imaginatively in poetic ones. It keeps alive the sense of the past as living thoughts and feelings crystallized, and in this way it judges present values by the values of past life.

Science is not, then, like literature because it is, as method, concerned with knowledge and truth and technology, not with aesthetic and moral judgements. Sir Charles Snow attacks the representatives of the 'literary culture' (he means Ezra Pound and T. S. Eliot) for their hostility to progressive ideas, and he argues that to take sides against progress today means letting large numbers of people starve. But even while he is making it, the moral bias of this attack does not come out of the methods of science, which are conducive equally to killing large numbers of people as to feeding them. The idea of progress itself derives from the literary culture. It is one of those ideas with roots in primitive Christianity, humanism, and the French Revolution which are one aspect of a long debate that is an important part of Victorian and twentieth-century literature. Scientists who support progress do not belong to a special scientific culture, but to that of Dickens, Shaw, and Wells.

Progress produces material benefits but it is only through the alive intelligence of the imagination that these can be related to significant values. And although the great material needs of the world can and should be satisfied by progress, there is the great spiritual danger of judging individual lives as units in the progressive society: that is, as social units which ought to be statistically happier and to live statistically better lives because statistically they are better fed. But perhaps a parallel problem with undernourishment is that people are not automatically better or even happier as a result of social improvements. For example, it is notorious that in England the real benefits accomplished by the Welfare State have produced an unprecedented spiritual malaise. If there were danger of progress being stopped as a result of the 'reactionary' attitude towards it of T. S. Eliot, there might be justification for the charge that the supporters of the literary culture are in favour of taking potential bread out of the mouths of the starving. But since this is not the case, they are surely right in drawing attention to the spiritual crisis which results from beneficial materialism.

Though I do not agree with the formula of the Two Cultures,

I think that within the 'literary culture' itself, it may well be just
to criticize poets for their ignorance of the great advances made
by science. But this leads back to the problem of the imagination. For there are examples enough to show—the effect on
Coleridge's poetry of his delvings into abstract philosophy is one
—that the poetic imagination is harmed by absorbing more intellectual knowledge than it can digest. The poet can use no more
knowledge than he can transform into his poetry, the novelist no
more than he can make the behaviour and dialogue of realized
action and characters.

What writers may fruitfully know is that which they can experience with their sensibility. And it is not so important that they
should know the second law of thermodynamics as that they
should perceive the subtle changes effected in the rhythm of
language by the environment resulting from inventions, their
influence on human behaviour, and modes of feeling. It is not
scientific knowledge but its effects which become part of the
experience of modern life. Joyce, Eliot, and Lawrence certainly
reflect in their works the results of science. In his own novels even,
C. P. Snow is creating a fiction about the results of science and
power, not about scientific theories and abstract policies. And
if one were to defend the two-dimensional characters in these
novels, one might argue that these embodiments of ideas and
petty ambitions are studies of the effect on human beings of
working in laboratories, colleges, and corridors of power. It may
be that, without knowing it, with his imagination Sir Charles
creates a picture which is critical of progress, and that as an
artist he agrees with the T. S. Eliot whom, as a critic, he dismisses
as reactionary, that 'we are the hollow men'. In this case, a
criticism of Snow the novelist would be that, like Galsworthy,
he writes unconscious satire.

The position of the literary culture is that it is a different mode
of interpreting experience from organizing, inventing, statistical
procedure. The 'literary intellectuals', unless they betray their

task or are conscripted into doing so, cannot assume that because there is the knowledge and the technology to improve the situation of millions of people who are hungry, people will necessarily be better or even happier as the result of those means being used. They cannot accept the concept of social man as a unit among many units who will improve because his material conditions improve. They think that human life is made up of individuals, and that the present situation of the life that has taken up its habitation in the bodies of the living (as it previously did the bodies of the dead) is reflected in the minds of the most aware, most fully conscious, and most able to compare the condition of life in the present with that of the past. 'Belonging to a tradition' means simply living spiritually on a chart where you are aware that your physical existence is but a small point in the whole of the life that has reached us from the past, and being able to have a realization of the equal intensity of past living with present existence, so that you can measure present life against the lives of the dead. Unless the sense that flesh and blood are just the outposts of a continuity of living is maintained, there is a considerable chance that material improvements, however beneficial and welcome, will lead to a loss of consciousness of the whole significance of life. To be as aware as the most aware minds were at other times is surely an indisputable aim, a responsibility, of being alive. To measure genius in our time against its achievements in the past is therefore also a way of seeing whether our ways of living are not weakening the consciousness which can be thought of as timeless, carried on for a moment within eternity, by ourselves.

If the literary intellectuals seem sceptical of the benefits produced by science, one reason may be that so many scientific advances seem to result in a deadening of consciousness. I mean by this, they destroy life-memory, which is not mechanical memory, but is memory of the kind that can retain significant experiences—can cultivate awareness of consciousness before our day. Such judging and comparing and savouring memory is the essential quality of full and complex consciousness. Instead of our living in an extremely complex present moment, packed as it were with experiences of the past related to immediate ones, technology enables more and more people to live in a single-strand moment, receiving the latest sensation, which obliterates previous impressions. The literary intellectuals are, it is hoped, those who have attained the greatest degree of that subjective or self-awareness which is also awareness of the potentiality of such mental and spiritual living in others, so that in being most individual it is most representative of human consciousness.

The poets and creators are as it were separate witnesses, each reflecting his world, and in an interrelationship in which each corrects the vision of the whole. Without them we might have a great deal of information about people's analysable capacities and needs, and broad pictures, based on statistics, describing their material and perhaps also their psychological condition. But we would not have those voices which express the subjective and spiritual reactions of the most perceptive recording instruments in a civilization.

The responsibility of saying 'this is how I see things', and 'this is how they happen to me', is entirely different from the responsibility of scientists. Their responsibility is to make their minds the instruments through which objective truths add to the sum of disinterested knowledge, and inventions advance according to the logic of preceding processes.

Technology can of course be put to beneficial ends, and is being so. But it can also be put to totally destructive ones. And 'Science', as such, is that system of truth and discovery which is indifferent to the results. If there is any morality of the scientist injected into science, if there is any 'spirit of science', it is expressed in the phrase 'the truth at any price and without regard to the results'.

The man of literary culture is, in a very complicated way, responsible for the effects of his work. Thus it is arguable that some of the writings of Nietzsche were in some way responsible for that demonstration of the vision of the superman which was Nazi Germany. The poet infuses into the pattern which he makes from his experience his view of life, for which he is responsible. But the last person who is responsible for his own inventions is the scientist. If the world were all but destroyed by atomic war, it would be possible—according to our present way of thinking—to blame philosophy, politics, religion, poetry, which could all be seen as leading to this result. The one person who would not be to blame would be the scientist who invented the bomb, because he is regarded as the mental instrument which invented the physical instrument. If blame ever were attached to science it would be on account of this very lack of responsibility to anything except objective truth and technological performance. But for the scientist to be held responsible for his science would require a revolution in our thinking.

The different responsibilities of the 'scientific' and the 'literary culture' can be demonstrated, I think, by considering a passage in an essay by Snow which appeared some years before *The Two Cultures*. It is from the volume of essays by various hands, called *The Baldwin Age*, and is on Rutherford and Cavendish:

> The scientists were themselves part of the deepest revolution in human affairs since the discovery of agriculture. They could accept what was happening, while other intellectuals shrank away. They not only accepted it, they rejoiced in it. It was difficult to find a scientist who did not believe that the scientific-technical-industrial revolution, accelerating under his eyes, was not doing incomparably more good than harm.
>
> This was the characteristic optimism of scientists in the 'twenties and 'thirties. It still is. In some ways it was too easy an optimism, but the counter-attitude of the non-scientific intellectuals was too easy a pessimism. Between Rutherford and Blackett on the one hand, and, say, Wyndham Lewis and Ezra Pound on the other, who are on the side of their fellow beings? The only people who would have any doubt about the answer are those who dislike the human race.

We are told here that the scientists made revolutionary discoveries, and this is doubtless true. We are told that they rejoiced
in the discoveries, and it is quite natural that they should have
done so. 'Other intellectuals', we are told, 'shrank away'. By
them is meant the writers, and two writers, certainly unrepresen-
tative in their views, are mentioned, in order to emphasize the
burden of implicit complaint against the literary culture for not
rejoicing in the scientific revolution.

Next we are told that Rutherford and Blackett were confident
that their 'scientific-technical-industrial revolution' was doing
'incomparably more good than harm'. But everything we know
about the development of technology in the scientific age warns
us that this subjective reaction of theirs has no connection with
the actual results of their revolutionary theories or discoveries.

Belief in progress simply reflects an optimistic view of human
nature: that on the whole, perhaps as the result of the pressures
of various conflicting self-interests, the means put at the disposal
of the politicians and managers of the world by science will be
used for good rather than bad ends.

So progress is nothing more than a general hope which has
been attached to the certainty that knowledge and invention will
advance. It is a mistranslation of the concept of material advance-
ment into the concept of human improvement.

One thing we cannot escape from is the qualities of the human
beings who use the knowledge and forces put at their disposal by
science. If the scientists can be regarded as simple midwives of
technological progress, the political leaders, the managerial class,
the bureaucrats, cannot. They are in a directive position in which
the complexity of their nature counts; and in a technological
society in which the endeavours of the inventors are directed to
alleviating the condition of the people, and the demand is made
that all the writers and artists should share in the enthusiasm for the
technological revolution, and in which those who express reactionary views can be silenced: in such a society, where no poet is

allowed to say he is unhappy in case his doing so hinders the great processes of amelioration, a Stalin is liable to assume control. And although, as decent human beings, the scientists may be dismayed at the emergence at the top of society of such a miscalculation, where all their mechanical calculations have been so exact, there is nothing in their culture of objectivity to prevent a Stalin, who, after all, in his way, is the direct result, in a given set of circumstances, of the scientific culture. Defending the study of literature, Matthew Arnold observed in his Rede lecture on *Literature and Science*: 'At present it seems to me, that those who are for giving to natural knowledge, as they call it, the chief place in the education of the majority of mankind, leave one important thing out of their account: the constitution of human nature.'

To the reader of Matthew Arnold's lecture, as to that of Peacock's *The Four Ages of Poetry*, it may seem that the controversy started by Snow is familiar. It is like a volcano, supposed to have become extinct a century ago, suddenly erupting in the mid-twentieth century.

The reasons for the excitement are several. Firstly, there is a real debate going on all over the world today about technological education. In the conflict between East and West, Soviet successes in rocketry have produced a panicky feeling that we must train more and more scientists.

But deeper than this, the proposition suggested perhaps even more by the title than by the content of Snow's lecture, that there are two cultures, and that the one of knowing and technology is on the defensive against the other of imagining and creating, stirs up fears which reach to the subconscious. Indeed one way of restating the argument might be to say 'there is a responsible culture of the conscious, and an irresponsible culture of the subconscious. The subconscious is ignorant and reactionary, and does not appreciate the great public benefits being achieved by science. The subconscious must learn the lessons of progress.'

We should have learned by now that it is dangerous to attack the subconscious on grounds of public morals and public works. Moreover we are today uncomfortably aware of the existence of a vast threatening world not of the unconscious, but of reason and logic, whose inventions we fear—despite the optimism of the members of the 'scientific culture'—may destroy our civilization. And we know that somewhere the destructive-constructive powers are after all not just works of pure reason to be used in purely beneficial ways by officials who are not appreciated by reactionary poets: we know that they are the terrifying expression of alternatives of good or ill, now realized externally on a colossal scale, of human nature.

The author of *The Two Cultures*, with his dislike of the literary culture, and his simple trust in optimistic scientists, does not understand this. We are driven to the conclusion that it requires imagination to do so.

Here we are brought back to Shelley, and to that time when the Romantic imagination became released from the enlightened views of the rationalist eighteenth century: released, because it was cut loose, and was left with no view of the world outside its own power of continual subjective interpretation to which it could remain attached. The old systems had ceased to explain the terrible forces brought into the world.

Shelley had an idea, which was perhaps wrong, that poetry had a task, which was to imagine the world of concrete realizations by abstract processes. It is easy enough to see that the moment you have named a task—of imagining that which we know—you call upon poets to write out of intellect and conscious will—just that which is impossible. At the same time, the nightmare remains, that without such imaginative comprehension of the powers released by the 'sorcerer's apprentice' we are at the mercy of those powers.

*　　*　　*　　*

Two types of procedure have been discussed here as 'cultures', and although one may not be happy with the word, one can see what is meant. The people who know and the people who imagine are in their opposite ways both interpretors of contemporary reality. The behaviour of scientists or writers—what sociologists would call their cultural pattern—is indeed only a red herring drawn across the controversy. What is really the matter of debate is that research, specialization, analysis, statistics, are supposed to be 'progressive', whereas the imagining, picture-making faculty of communicating in visions the understanding by individual internal life, the spiritual condition of our time, our life, in relation to past times and past life, is held to be anachronistic, negative, reactionary.

Science, as it is understood by most people, and certainly by Sir Charles Snow, is, as I have explained, the realization of objective processes of theory and invention that transform the material environment, and multiply immensely man's power over nature. We are told that the second law of thermodynamics is 'beautiful'. This means that the operation of natural laws is in itself beautiful and that their exposition and demonstration by a human mind is also beautiful.

Part of the beauty of this, however, is that the human mind does not 'interfere' in the demonstration. When one is talking about the beauty of a poem, one means something quite different from the beauty of the second law of thermodynamics.

For the beauty of the poem consists of the fact that when the poet operates upon the object of his experience to make the poem, the poem is penetrated with the subjective qualities of his being. When we say that Keats' 'Ode to a Nightingale' is beautiful we do not mean that it is a beautiful demonstration of a particular nightingale, we mean that in treating of the object of his experience, which was (perhaps) listening to the nightingale, Keats revealed qualities of his sensibility which we intensely admire.

Precisely what is beautiful about the scientific law is that if another scientist had discovered it, it would have been the same law. It is objective truth. Precisely what is beautiful about the poem is that if another poet had written about the same subject, it would have been entirely different.

The 'literary culture'—if one can admit such a term—is a culture because it cultivates the object with the qualities of human personality. There is no such thing as a 'scientific culture' (apart from, perhaps, the group behaviour of scientists) because science does not, as such, cultivate objective reality with subjective states of mind which are the results of a long history of civilization. Science simply realizes the true nature of the object, it releases into the stream of life discoveries and inventions which, although they may be chosen for utility or destructive purposes, in themselves incorporate no subjective vision of the individual who discovered or invented them.

PART TWO

THE OBSESSIVE SITUATION

I

MODERNS AND CONTEMPORARIES

THERE is art which is modern, different from several movements grouped approximately under the heading 'modernism'. Modern art is that in which the artist reflects awareness of an unprecedented modern situation in its form and idiom. The quality which is called modern shows in the realized sensibility of style and form more than in the subject matter. Thus, early in the scientific and industrial era, the age of Progress, I would not call Tennyson, Ruskin, Carlyle moderns because although they were aware of the effects of science, and most contemporary in their interest, they remained within the tradition of rationalism, unshaken in the powers of what Lawrence called the 'conscious ego'. They had the Voltairean 'I', the confidence that they stood outside a world of injustices and irrationality which they judged clearly with their powers of reason and imagination. They regarded themselves as in a line of writer-prophets. Their sensibility was not the product of the times that they deplored.

They did not feel that they had been conditioned in their own natures by the values of a materialist society, and that they had somehow to reflect and respond to the effects of such conditioning in their art: perhaps by allowing unconscious forces to erupt through its surfaces; or perhaps by the cultivation of an extreme critical awareness, as it were an uninterrupted stream of communication with the values of the past, in what they wrote. The Voltairean individualists, most of them influenced by socialist ideas, and believers in progress, regarded contemporary society from a point of view stemming from the French Revolution. They judged the world in which they lived by the most up-to-date developments of materialist thinking.

What I call the 'Voltairean I' participates in, belongs to, the history of progress. When it criticizes, satirizes, attacks, it does so in order to influence, to direct, to oppose, to activate existing forces. The 'Voltairean I' of Shaw, Wells, and the others, acts upon events. The 'modern' 'I' of Rimbaud, Joyce, Proust, Eliot's *Prufrock* is acted upon by them. The Voltairean 'I' has the characteristics—rationalism, progressive politics, etc.—of the world the writer attempts to influence, whereas the 'modern' 'I' through receptiveness, suffering, passivity, transforms the world to which it is exposed. The faith of the Voltairean egoists is that they will direct the powers of the surrounding world from evil into better courses through the exercise of the superior social or cultural intelligence of the creative genius, the writer prophet. The faith of the moderns is that by allowing their sensibility to be acted upon by the modern experience as suffering, they will produce, partly as the result of unconscious processes, and partly through the exercise of critical consciousness, the idioms and forms of new art. The modern is the realized consciousness of suffering, sensibility and awareness of the past.

The Voltairean egoists are contemporaries without being, from an aesthetic or literary point of view, moderns. What they write is rationalist, sociological, political and responsible. The writing of the moderns is the art of observers conscious of the action of the conditions observed upon their sensibility. Their critical awareness includes ironic self-criticism. 'No I am not Prince Hamlet nor was meant to be,' thinks Prufrock, who in his doubting self-awareness certainly reflects the sensibility of early Eliot. But Prufrock's contemporaries—Shaw, Wells, Bennett—

had not the least doubt about themselves. In a world of confusion they were clear-sighted social prophets.

*　　*　　*　　*

The attitude of the latterday Voltairean egoists is amusingly demonstrated by a now almost forgotten episode of the late 1920's. I remember it, because when I was a boy it fascinated me. The firm of Harrods invited H. G. Wells, Arnold Bennett, and Bernard Shaw to write articles as publicity, dealing with such aspects of Harrods as might appeal to them. Harrods of course took the honest dealer's risk of offering them a free hand to be appreciative or critical, as they chose. All three refused, but in letters of sufficient length to fill up a whole page of advertising taken by Harrods in several newspapers. All the parties concerned seem to have had their cake and eaten it. Remembering the episode, I wrote recently to Harrods and asked for copies of the published texts, with which they have kindly provided me. It seems to me that the reason why the memory of them has remained in my mind is because the replies reveal the fundamental attitudes of writers in a radical rationalist tradition, with a developed sense of responsibility towards their public, better than considered declarations of faith might do.

Shaw, after animadverting on 'puffery', argues that for him to give his signed statement in support of a commercial house would be like his paying critics to approve his plays. Theatre critics

> write in a judicial capacity. But so do all authors whose work is of sufficient weight and depth to have a formative effect on the public mind. For such an author to accept payment from a commercial enterprise for using his influence to induce the public to buy its wares would be to sin against the Holy Ghost. . . . By all means let our commercial houses engage skilled but nameless scribes . . . to write their advertisements as such. But a writer who has been concentrated by Fame to the service of the public, and has thus become prophet as well as author, must take wages in no other service.

Arnold Bennett admits that he has no objection to the proposal:

> I see no possible reason against my acceptance, except one. The reason is that public opinion is not yet ripe to approve the employment of responsible imaginative writers to whom it has granted a reputation, in any scheme of publicity for a commercial concern. Personally I differ from public opinion in this matter; but the opinion exists and I will not flout it. In flouting it I should certainly lose caste, and I do not intend to lose caste by creating a precedent which could result, for me, in a dangerous notoriety. The time must inevitably come, sooner or later, when the precedent will be created, and after it is established people will wonder why it should ever have met with opposition.

The attitude of Bennett is not, like that of Shaw and Wells, that of the prophet, but more like that of the reluctant public servant. One recalls that such poetry as there undoubtedly is in his novels is of the department store—the shop windows alight at dusk, stuffed with merchandise displayed like tropical fish in their illuminated tanks:

> As a writer I have always been keenly interested in the very impressive phenomenon of the big departmental store, regarded either as a picturesque spectacle, or as a living organism, or as a social portent.

H. G. Wells declares

> I have to rout about in my mind, to discover the hidden almost instinctive reason

for refusal. Of course, when found, it turns out to be that

> rightly or wrongly, the writer takes himself more seriously than that. In his heart he classes himself not with the artists but with the teachers and prophets.

He adds that apart from this objection the

> project is most attractive. I can imagine nothing more amusing and exciting than to study your marvellous organization closely and explain its working. Some day I shall do something of the

sort and come to you for particulars. But you will pay me nothing
for that. I shall do it because it will interest me and because I think
it will interest my readers. Facts you may give me with both hands,
but not money. . . . I have already sketched the appearance of your
type of business in *Clissold* and of something distantly akin in
Tono Bungay.

*   *   *   *

I think these unguarded self-revelations are interesting, not
because of something innocently disingenuous about refusals which
are really disguised acceptances, but because they show how
wholeheartedly Shaw, Wells and Bennett accept responsibility to
the world of public interests and materialist values even if they
opposed the economic system as such. In fairness one should add
that the principles of Wells and Shaw were not the same as those
of Harrods—and perhaps it was only politeness that prevented
their saying so here—but they were those of business (if publicly
owned), just the same. All of them plead a sense of responsibility
for the writer which is nevertheless not that of the artist—it is,
responsibility to be a social prophet. It is interesting to recall that
in the famous epistolary controversy with Henry James, after the
publication of his novel *Boon*, containing a parody of James'
later manner, Wells describes himself as a 'journalist' rather than
an artist. To Henry James—the journalist; but to Harrods 'teacher,
priest, or prophet'.

What would have been the answers of James Joyce, D. H.
Lawrence, T. S. Eliot or Virginia Woolf if they had received the
proposal from Harrods? At least one of them might have been
more tempted than were Wells, Shaw and Bennett. But I can't
feel the temptation would have been of the same kind. They
would not have thought that their business—producing literary
consumer goods—was after all a branch of Harrods—the book
department; that their success, like that of the other departments
in a store, was judged by their capacity to sell their particular
literary article. They would not have described themselves as

'prophets'—at least not in any religion known to Harrods. They would have regarded advertising as the most questionable activity of commerce. James Joyce might have taken the offer as a joke or treated it as an exercise and therefore have gone in for it. To guess what he might have replied would make an amusing literary competition.

It may have been a virtue in Bennett, Wells and Shaw that they could take Harrods' offer 'on the level'; and it may have been a failing in the moderns that they would have treated it snigger-ingly if they did not repudiate it disgustedly. I have winkled this odd episode from my memory. Perhaps it throws light on why a younger English generation of writers such as Kingsley Amis and John Wain, reacting against the modern movement, prefers Arnold Bennett to Virginia Woolf. The candid response of Bennett might appeal to them.

The episode draws attention to the division between what I call 'contemporary' and 'modern'. Shaw, Wells and Bennett thought of themselves as prophets of a materialist society. The way in which the kind of life they describe in their works is up to date, is the way in which Harrods is enterprising. Wells and Bennett indeed go out of their way—as we have seen—to insist that they have described just such a 'living organism' and 'socio-logical portent' in novels which were by no means social satire. If Joyce had boasted that there was an apparition of Harrods in *Ulysses* the irony would have been apparent. The appeal of Harrods is rejected by Shaw, Wells and Bennett on account of a responsibility towards the same public with the same interests as Harrods. But the 'moderns', Joyce, Lawrence, Eliot, Woolf, would, as literary artists, feel an entirely different kind of responsi-bility. They would feel responsible to a past which had been degraded by commerce, a past of realer values betrayed by adver-tising. They would feel that their responsibility towards them-selves was as artists, and not as money-makers producing a consumers' product.

It makes no difference to my argument that Eliot was at one time a bank clerk, that Joyce regarded himself as a good business man, and even as a socialist, that Lawrence was only too glad to sell articles to the popular press. These things only emphasize that the life and feeling out of which they wrote was different from that in which they made choices when voting in an election, or fighting in a war, or supporting themselves and their families.

*   *   *   *

The contemporary belongs to the modern world, represents it in his work, and accepts the historic forces moving through it, its values of science and progress. By this I do not mean that he is uncritical of the world in which he finds himself. On the contrary, he is quite likely to be a revolutionary. For the social scene is one of conflicts, and in reflecting its events and values the contemporary will be taking sides in these conflicts but doing so on terms — of whichever side — laid down by society. The contemporary is a partisan in the sense of seeing and supporting partial attitudes. However, in a world torn by passionate conflicts, he cannot have a contemporary attitude which sees modern life as a whole. The modern tends to see life as a whole and hence in modern conditions to condemn it as a whole. When writers become engaged in conflicts — as some did, for example, during the 'thirties when they supported the cause of anti-Fascism which seemed that of freedom and humanity, and as some do today when they represent the interests of an emergent working class — they tend to be 'contemporary' rather than 'modern'.

The contemporary is involved in conflicts, but fundamentally he accepts the forces and the values of today which are fighting one another, with the same weapons of power, ideology and utilitarian philosophy, for different goals. Thus the socialist Wells accepts the same values of distributing consumer goods as the department store, but he thinks that the store should be owned by the government, and that goods distributed should be different.

And when he says that he is a prophet he means that he looks
forward to the distribution through a socialist society of better
consumer goods among a population of enlightened utilitarians,
through the directed efforts of scientists. The extent to which
Wells himself has lost interest in the past tradition reflects that to
which the world made by science has outdistanced the past.

*   *   *   *

The modern is acutely conscious of the contemporary scene,
but he does not accept its values. To the modern, it seems that a
world of unprecedented phenomena has today cut us off from the
life of the past, and in doing so from traditional consciousness.
At the same time it is of no use trying to get back into the past by
ignoring the present. If we consider ourselves as belonging not
just to our own particular moment in time but also to the past,
then we must also be fully aware of our predicament which is
that of past consciousness living in the present.

The modern is the past become conscious at certain points,
which are ourselves living in the present. Hence we find that the
modern in his work is occupied with trying to bridge a gulf
within his own awareness, of past from present. With his sensibility he is committed to the present; with his intellect he is
committed to criticizing that present by applying to it his realization of the past. The great fusions of present and past are works
such as Joyce's *Ulysses* or Picasso's *Guernica*. In *Ulysses* an attempted realization of the whole of contemporary life at a particular
time and place is brought into collision with the Homeric epic
interpreted into the terms of that present. In *Guernica*, by a process
the opposite of this, the terror of a modern air raid is translated into
the imagery of classical Greek or Mithraic tragedy—the sacrificial
bull, the sword, the flaming torch.

II

THE MODERN AS VISION OF THE WHOLE

(A) THE ADVANCE

'THE modern is the past become conscious at certain points, which are ourselves,' needs qualifying. In a survey of every aspect of the modern movement, the modern art that expresses tension between past and present would only represent a few of many tendencies. However, in literature, with which I am here mostly concerned, it is this which today still challenges the reaction against the modern movement. I consider that early in this century, and perhaps up to the 1930's, the best work of the modern expressed this tension between past and present, which could only be expressed in a revolutionary kind of art. What Joyce, Eliot, Lawrence, Pound, Yeats, Virginia Woolf were doing could only be done in ways which are today sometimes dismissed as 'experimental'.

I have distinguished what I here discuss as 'modern' from the 'contemporary' which I considered characteristic of Shaw, Wells, and Bennett. At the other end of a scale, I should also distinguish it from futurism, the attempt to regard the present as though it were a line completely dividing past from future, and to base art on phenomena, supposedly unprecedented, on the side of that line which represents the future. This is, of course, to include under the heading futurist more than the movement of Marinetti and his followers. But to see the term futurism in this way is,

I think, correct, because far more artists are futurist than those who call themselves so. Like most movements the name of the movement—futurism—represents a tendency wider than the movement itself.

Futurism is, in any case, inevitably a misnomer. We do not and cannot know what the future will be. By futurism is meant concentration on those aspects of the present which seem least related to the past, most prophetic of the future. Presentism would be a more accurate, though less glamorous term.

Whatever excludes the past and concentrates on the present has therefore the futurist tendency. It does not rely on tradition, for subject, treatment, or to find an audience, Hence unless it is only of instantaneous interest, it must be invested in the future. The dadaists, Gertrude Stein with her 'continuous present', and today's activists and tacheists are thus futurist unless, indeed, their works are immediate gestures against art meant like some dadaist manifestations intended only to last for as long as the few seconds they take to make.

*   *   *   *

The confrontation of the past with present seems to me therefore the fundamental aim of modernism. The reason why it became so important was that, in the early stages of the movement, the moderns wished to express the *whole* experience of modern life.

The feeling that the modern world, even if its values are fragmented, nevertheless shares a fate that in being modern is whole, is important. It results doubtless from contrasting the European past, as consisting of many different traditions, and the present, as an all-embracing fatality which is progress. The present is looked upon as knowledge, and the results of true knowledge that has overtaken the whole of civilization and has broken the line of tradition with the past. This situation can therefore only be apprehended as a whole, as tragedy or overwhelming disaster, unless indeed it were possible to consider it optimistically.

If the concept of wholeness is abandoned then at once work becomes fragmentary, the parts cut off from the whole. This is the characteristic of futurism, that it separates the future finally from the past. It is also the characteristic of the reaction against modernism, which accepts the idea that there can only be 'minor' fragmented art. Thus today when poets and critics say that they aim at elegance and correctness of form, they reveal that they have accepted the idea of writing within a fragmentary part of the fragmented situation, instead of trying to comprehend the situation itself in a single vision that restores wholeness to the fragmentation, even by realizing it as disaster, as the waste land, or night-town.

Of course, a reaction against the modern movement was inevitable, and I am not arguing that it should have continued until the present time. It demands respect however when it lingers on in the work of that heroic survivor, Samuel Beckett.

When we read the following by Miss Pamela Hansford Johnson on Literature in *The Baldwin Age* we ask ourselves whether it is not Miss Johnson who is 'in retreat':

> The full retreat began in the years between 1922 and 1925, the years that saw *Mrs. Dalloway* and *Ulysses*. It was the retreat into perimetal experiment in verbal and oral techniques: and it pretty well dominated the English novel for the next thirty years . . .

After a paragraph in which she concedes that the influence of 'Woolf and Joyce' has been 'aural and visual', Miss Johnson continues:

> What shrivelled away in their work was any contact between man and society. 'Bloomsday' is Bloom's alone and no-one else's: Mrs. Dalloway, if she is anything at all, is merely herself, walking in her own dream of a private world. Everything dropped away from the novel but Manner: all that counted was how the thing was done, and never the thing itself. We must blame no writer for the influence he exerts on his successors: to have been an influence at all is a seal of achievement. Yet the followers of Virginia Woolf and James Joyce began to lead the novel into

sterility. And nobody saw anything wrong in that inexorable and dangerous process. Why not? Because life was growing too hard for writers to face, and quiet lay in impotency alone.

It is difficult to disentangle this. It reads like lines deliberately crossed in order to confuse and mislead. For example, in the muddling up of Joyce and Mrs. Woolf as though they were one flesh like Hamlet's uncle and his mother; and in writing that no-one 'saw anything wrong' in these writers—as though polemicists as vociferous as F. R. Leavis and Wyndham Lewis had not spent years of their critical activity in attacking Virginia Woolf and James Joyce.

The passage confuses two important issues. For while on the one hand it is untrue to imply that there was no contact between man and society in James Joyce, it is true that the method of the interior monologue (which in *Ulysses* was a technique for presenting not just his main characters but also a whole society as a state of consciousness) became in Virginia Woolf's work largely an instrument for projecting her own sensibility; and in that of other writers, for subjective outpourings, which were indeed perhaps cut off from the outside world.

The important point which becomes suppressed in Miss Hansford Johnson's essay is that, although Joyce employed a technique of subjective monologue in his work, the intent of his writing was to achieve an almost total objectivity. *Ulysses* and *Finnegans Wake* may not be complete successes. It is difficult to imagine how they could be, considering that the aim of Joyce in *Ulysses* was to invent an imaginative form which would express the whole experience of modern life, and in *Finnegans Wake*, the whole of history. They were gigantic achievements which include elements of gigantic failure. But to dismiss them as mere 'experiments' whose discoveries have been usefully absorbed into the novels of C. P. Snow, is to overlook what remains truly important and challenging about them: that they attempt to envisage the past as a whole complexity enclosed within a consciousness conditioned by circumstances that are entirely of today. They state a challenge which perhaps they did not meet and which perhaps cannot be met, although they indicate the scale of the challenge. And what has come after the works which Miss Hansford Johnson so easily dismisses is fragments of a fragmented view of civilization, and is on an altogether lesser scale.

★   ★   ★   ★

The movements of modern literature and art—the 'isms'—are programmes of techniques for expressing this whole view of the past-future confrontation. There are different types of programmes which might be analysed as establishing the following categories:

1. *Realization* through new art of the modern experience.

2. The invention through art of a *pattern of hope*, influencing society.

3. The idea of an art which will fuse past with present into the modern symbolism of *a shared life*.

4. The *Alternate Life of Art*.

5. *Distortion*.

6. The *Revolutionary concept of Tradition*.

1. *Realization* is the primary gesture of modernism, the determination to invent a new style in order to express the deeply felt change in the modern world. Industrial towns, machines, revolutions, scientific thinking, are felt to have altered the texture of living. Everyday language and taste reflect these changes, even though the image they mirror is ugly. It is only art that remains archaic, forcing its ideas into forms and manners that are outmoded. Therefore artists have to learn the idiom of changed speech, vision and hearing, and then mould the modern experience into forms either revolutionized or modified.

The outstanding characteristic of realization is, then, the great attention paid to inventing an idiom which responds to the tone of voice of contemporaries, the changed vision of a world of machines and speed: the rhythms of an altered contemporary tempo, the new voice of a humanity at times when the old social hierarchies are breaking down.

The street speaks the idiom and the idiom, in the mind of the artist, invents the form. Eliot and Joyce in their early work are realizers of the modern idiom in their poetry and their poetic prose. In music Alban Berg's *Wozzeck* is a classic example of the realization of the 1920's in Germany as idiom. In his Blue Period, Picasso had supremely this quality of realization, as did Eliot in the *Preludes*:

> I am moved by fancies that are curled
> Around these images, and cling;
> The notion of some infinitely gentle
> Infinitely suffering thing.

The human element is often reduced to pathos, clownishness, in *Wozzeck*, Blue Period Picasso, the early Eliot, *Petroushka*. In Apollinaire as in some of the German Expressionists, this clownishness acquires a quality of touching and nobly absurd heroism, a gay despair.

2. By *the pattern of hope*, I mean—and this certainly will seem an unfashionable view today—the idea that modern art might transform the contemporary environment, and hence, by pacifying and ennobling its inhabitants, revolutionize the world (there is, surely, a pun on this idea in the programme of Eugene Jolas in his magazine *Transition*—'the revolution of the word').

The word *hope* has to be understood seriously, as Malraux still intended it when he entitled his Spanish civil war novel *Espoir*. Early in the century, hope was based on the international inter-arts community of the alliance between the ballet, architecture, furniture design, painting, music and poetry, all of them partici-pating in the movement to revolutionize taste, and at the same time make it an operative acting and criticizing force in modern life. The way in which art might revolutionize the environment

and hence, by implication, people living in it, is explored in many
of the manifestos of poets and painters early in the century. The
famous *Der Blaue Reiter* (1914), the anthology of the group of
painters which was founded in Munich in 1909, is prefaced with
remarks of which these are characteristic:

> 'Everything which comes into being, on earth can only have
> its beginning.' This sentence by Daeubler might stand written
> over all our inventing and all our aims. A fulfilment will be
> attained, some time, in a new world, in another existence (*dasein*).
> On earth we are only able to state the theme. This first volume
> is the prelude to a new theme. . . . We wander with our passion-
> ate wishes through the art of this time and through the present
> age.

This is touching, innocent, mysteriously exciting. The same
dream of transforming the world—but this time the world of
actuality in which we live—is expressed by Wyndham Lewis, a
decade later, in *The Tyro*:

> Art, however, the greatest art, even, has it in its power to
> influence everybody. Actually the shapes of the objects (houses,
> cars, dresses and so forth) by which they are surrounded have a
> very profound subconscious effect on people. A man might be
> unacquainted with the very existence of a certain movement in
> art, and yet his life would be modified directly if the street he
> walked down took a certain shape, at the dictates of an architect
> under the spell of that movement, whatever it were. Its forms and
> colours would have a tonic or a debilitating effect on him, an
> emotional value. Just as he is affected by the changes of the
> atmosphere, without taking the least interest in the cyclonic
> machinery that controls it, so he would be directly affected by
> any change in his physical milieu.
>
> A man goes to choose a house. He is attracted by it or not,
> often, not for sentimental or practical reasons, but for some reason
> that he does not seek to explain, and that yet is of sufficient force
> to prevent him from, or decide him on, taking it. This is usually
> an example of the functioning of the aesthetic sense (however
> underdeveloped it may be in him) of which we are talking. The

painting, sculpture and general design of today, such as can be included in the movement we support, aims at nothing short of a physical reconstructing and recording of the visible part of the world.

The basic reason for hope is that art might re-connect the life, which has been driven inwards into the isolated being of the artist, with the external world, by accomplishing a revolution in the lives of people converted to share the visions of modern creation. In being victimized, oppressed, and in having dreams, the artist already meets half-way the insulted and the oppressed who fight for change, although their aspirations may be far removed from his visions. But it is important to him that his visions are nevertheless closer to the poor and the powerless than to the rich and those who enjoy power. Hence the current of revolutionary feeling which runs alike through dadaist, expressionist and surrealist manifestos. Each group claims to be the true revolutionaries, and that the life-force which it represents would join with the force of the social revolution. If only the revolutionaries were not too philistine to realize that modern art represents the democracy of the unconscious forces which should be equated with economic democracy! Hence the surrealists were later to insist that they were communists. Some of them—Aragon, Tristan Tzara—even, as surrealists, joined the communist party, later to renounce surrealism as bourgeois.

3. Art which will transform reality into *shared inner life*, is the converse of (2) which would transform inner vision into outer social change. It is the idea that the images of the materialist modern world can be 'interpreted', made to become symbols of inner life where they are reconciled with the older things symbolized by words like 'jug', 'mountain', 'star', 'cross'. This process was the infinitely patient research of experience of Rilke. It finds its completest realization in the *Duino Elegies*, where the Angels are set up as almost machine-like figures over the human landscape in which there is the fair, the world of values, that are money.

The angels are perpetually occupied in transforming the world of outward materialism back into inner tragic values.

The connection of poetry here with iconographic modern painting is evident. One of the *Duino* Elegies is inspired by Picasso's *Les Saltimbanques*, in which Rilke sees the method of interpretation of the performers in the fairground who are at once traditional and contemporary.

4. The *Alternate Life of Art*. By this I mean something different from (2), the hope that art might become the agency for inspiring a transformed society, and (3) the use of art to interpret the external materialism into the language of inner life. The Alternate Life is when it is intended that the processes of art are brought close to borderline ecstatic or sexual experiences. I am thinking here of the exaltation of violence, sexual relations, madness, drugs, through art which is regarded by the artists as a transition towards the actual experience of these states. Lawrence surely often regarded his writing not as an end but as a means of inducing in the reader a state of feeling which would release in him the 'dark forces' or 'phallic consciousness', or the approach to the mystic-physical sexual union which were more important to him than that he should create literature.

The tendency here is to regard writing as hallucinatory: that is to say as a literary technique for inducing non-literary sensations. The poet, supposedly, has a peculiar insight into life-sensations which he upholds as more real than the externals which are everyday reality. The surrealists used poetry as a technique for inducing states of mind supposedly super-real. It might be said that surrealist writing is itself the super-reality, but if this were true, it would only be in the way that incantation may itself be what is invoked: a strangeness of feeling induced by the language that lies beyond the threshold of the words.

However much one disapproves of non-literary aims in literature, nevertheless it is easy to understand the temptation today for modern artists to use art as a modern kind of magic. Two

definitions of surrealism, by André Breton, which I quote from
David Gascoyne's *Surrealism*, are relevant:

'SURREALISM, n. Pure psychic automatism, by which it is
intended to express, verbally, in writing, or by other means, the
real process of thought. Thought's dictation, in the absence of all
control exercised by the real reason and outside all aesthetic or
moral preoccupations.'

'ENCYCL. *Philos.* Surrealism rests in the belief in the superior
reality of certain forms of association neglected heretofore; in the
omnipotence of the dream and in the disinterested play of thought.
It tends definitely to do away with all other psychic mechanisms
and to substitute itself for them in the solution of the principal
problem of life.'

Just as futurism is the expression of an impulse to repudiate the
whole of the past which is common to several movements called
by different names, so surrealism has features in common with
quite other movements. All the 'alternate life of art' movements attempt to discover through art, or to use art to discover,
spiritual, sensual, or esoteric forces, which restore the balance of
inner life against industrialized societies.

The tendency to seek such a compensation of life through art,
and of art through life, was already present with Byron and
Keats. Sensuality tinged with despair and anticipation of death
produced a mood in which Keats regarded the taste of a peach or
rose, with its further suggestion of a drug, as lines of poetry.
Keats was tasting, I suggest, at these moments the sensation of
his own being as a poet. Today at a later stage of individual
despair there is a meeting ground in drugs, violence, sexual
relations, hallucination, madness, between poets and non-poets
who live the life of poetry regarded as experienced sensation.
Not the poets who are influenced by Dylan Thomas, but the
hangers-on who imitate his life, think they ARE Dylan Thomas.
The 'dark forces' released through sexual passion or through
'phallic consciousness', the mystical-physical sexual union, surely
suggest in Lawrence a meeting in which the art-sensation is

transformed into the life-sensation. The reader is recommended
to have sex in the way which will identify for him the sensation
described in the words. Significantly, Lawrence disapproved of
all sex which is not experienced exactly in the way that he
describes, or prescribes it. And the purpose of this is not, of course,
pornographic. It is to assert the proximate reality and force of
experienced sensation against the abstract supra-personal forces
of machinery and social organization.

Here, the confusion of art-experience with life-experience seems
dangerous. The example of movements like that of the Beatniks
in America shows the degradation of life, through art and of art
through life, which follows from the substitution of what is
supposed to be the life of the artist for the discipline required to
create art.

5. *Distortion* is much more obviously an element in modern visual
art than in literature. One has only to call to mind Picasso's
women's faces with features pulled about, displaced, rearranged,
of the bulges and holes in Henry Moore's sculpture, and most of
all, of the paintings of Francis Bacon, who in an earlier age might
have been described as the Master of the Distortions, to realize
this. And in fact I owe most of what follows on this subject to
remarks made to me by Francis Bacon and Henry Moore.

For Francis Bacon, distortion is an essential development of his
art, and perhaps of all modern art, and in it several distinct aims
coincide. In the first place, modern distortion is the last phase in
interpreting, selecting and changing the image at the end of the
line of the tradition. It is the new twist given to the game of art,
the something which the modern artist can do with the material
he handles, to the nature he sees, which has not been done before.

But arising from this, secondly, distortion is a way of expressing
the felt truth of the relationship of the subjective artist to the
objective reality in this time. Consider for instance the implications of a statement: 'A portrait is always also a self-portrait.'
This means that the painter regards the image of the model he

sees as fused with an image of himself which he carries round in his mind, and which, for the sake of describing the truth of his own limitations, he has to project into the portrait. The fusion here is, to the spectator, evidently distorting. But one must add to this account that this way of looking at things, of regarding the artist's self-image as the prime factor of his consciousness which affects his vision of everything, and which cannot be evaded, is a result of our time. Moreover, if the artist is thus a prisoner of the moment, the subject is also. One might say that the element of distortion is the factor of the relationship of subjective self to objective reality multiplied by the present moment in time.

I remarked to Henry Moore one day that I was particularly struck by his 'three quarters figure' 1961, a distorted figure with a lumpy grotesquely shaped torso and a head half bird-beak, half hippopotamus. He said he was glad I liked it because a good many people had not seen the point of it, and it was one he liked himself. The next time we met I could not resist asking him what the point he had in mind was. He answered that what he was trying to do was pull the human body about as much as possible, distending it here, pushing it in there, and putting on to it a non-human head, but nevertheless retaining its recognizability as a human figure.

Thinking this over, and having the experience of the 'three quarters figure' much in mind, I began to notice, in this my middle age, that what Moore was doing to this figure, distending it here, pushing it in there, time was palpably doing to my own body! It seemed to me then that the 'three quarters figure' was full of dark references to the sculpture which is of time upon flesh, the subjective experience of growing old, whereas the beaked or trunked head referred perhaps to the depersonalizing objective forces of the time in which we live. These last sentences are my interpretation, not Henry Moore's.

It may seem from what I have written above that distortion is a factor in painting and sculpture but not in writing. On reflection I do not think this is so. I think that the interior monologue, as it is used in *Ulysses*, for example, is a technique of distortion, employed very much in the manner of Picasso or Francis Bacon. The character of Bloom is created for the reader by Bloom's thoughts. These thoughts, which are represented to us as the result of the action of events in the environment upon Bloom's sensibility, are distorted by his sensibility. Moreover the context of Bloom's environment is distorted by the forcing against it of the Homeric parallel of the Odyssey. Thus not only is Bloom's vision distorted but the world he sees is also one of distortion.

In later Yeats the imagery that most suggests the present, although it may be derived from the past, is of some inhuman distorted half-bird half-beast:

> Here at right of the entrance this bronze head,
> Human, superhuman, a bird's round eye,
> Everything else withered and mummy-dead.

Obviously the scene here is a museum, but the horrific force of the grotesque head is that it is seen through—invented by, one might say—contemporary eyes. Yeats in putting the Egyptian statue's head into his poem is doing what Moore does when his inhuman superhuman heads of human bodies recall some shadowy night of past statuary and architecture.

6. By the *Revolutionary concept of Tradition*, I mean the introduction, into certain works, of critically selected traditions. Often such use of tradition seems outrageous to those who regard themselves as traditionalists, but who are better described as academics or conventionalists. A famous example of the transformation, distortion and even perversion of a tradition into modern expression that seemed to contemporaries its opposite, was Baudelaire's *Fleurs du Mal*. The traditionally catholic consciousness of Baudelaire realizes itself in the pursuit of evil. Grace is discovered in damnation, and the only part of the faith that does not seem to have undergone a terrible transmutation is the doctrine of Original Sin. The process by which the little flowers of St. Francis become in the late nineteenth century the

flowers of evil is, as it were, sometimes reversible. Intensity of corruption or debauchery can be taken as a sign of grace. Claudel was converted to catholicism by reading the poems of Rimbaud, *poète maudit par excellence*, and one can imagine readers being converted to religion by Dylan Thomas' poetry.

The idea of tradition as an explosive force, an unknown quantity almost, an apocalyptic mystery, something sought out from the past and chosen by the modern artist, perhaps in a spirit of grotesque mimicry, something disturbing and shocking, belongs to the early phase of modernism in poetry and fiction. In painting it still retains the enormous eclecticism of Malraux's *Musée Imaginaire*, the whole of visual art contained within the walls of the contemporary skull, and in one timeless moment.

(B) THE RETREAT

In an important paper on 'The Spirit of Modern Art' (published in *The British Journal of Aesthetics*, Vol. I, No. 3, June 1961) J. P. Hodin, discussing the visual arts, offers a definition of the modern:

> Modern Art is cognition, the findings of which, often highly specialized and elaborated on an analytical basis, are organized into a new visual order. Linking up with a tradition of its own choice, of universal significance and without limitations in time and thus breaking with the chronological tradition generally acknowledged in art history, it strives for a synthesis in the work of the individual artist and through the mutual influence of its different trends upon one another; a many-faceted process moving towards a new unitary concept, a new artistic tonality, in other words, a style.

This would not apply to poetry and criticism in England since the 1930's. It has ceased to do so because of the breaking up of the once single modern movement into different tendencies in each art. The break is clearly shown in the development of T. S. Eliot's poetry and criticism. *The Waste Land* admits of a complete eclecticism in the choice of tradition. But with *Ash Wednesday* and *Four Quartets* the choice has been narrowed to the Christian tradition and, more specifically, to the English Church. Parallel with this, there is in Eliot's criticism a corresponding narrowing down of the concept of tradition. When Eliot defended *Ulysses* and the early work of Ezra Pound, his concept of tradition surely extended to the pagan. He greatly admired Frazer's *The Golden Bough* and I surmise that he thought that whatever could be used as a myth was also tradition.

In Yeats' *A Vision*—a book in which he considered that he had compiled the storehouse of symbols, myths and imagery for his poetry—there is also freedom of choice in tradition. And of course Pound, in the *Cantos*, is as eclectic as a painter like Picasso in his wide wandering over all history and all mythology.

Although the reputation of Yeats is unimpaired, and although Pound's cantos are vigorously defended, nevertheless the tendency of recent poetry and criticism is against the freedom of choice of tradition which Yeats, and Pound, and Joyce (and Eliot, in *The Waste Land*) shared with the painters, and with Stravinsky. The modern painter, according to Mr. Hodin's account of what makes him modern, might be seen as asking himself 'What tradition should I choose, that would best serve my purpose in inventing my own new style?' But the attitude which has more and more divided the poets from the painters is that poets have been influenced by critics to ask themselves 'what tradition am I already *in*?' And the critics have also pressed upon them that the correct answer to this question is the answer discoverable to criticism. They have argued, against Mr. Hodin, that there is no such thing as freedom to choose a tradition which at the same time breaks with the 'chronological tradition'. There is—they have insisted—only a choice between true tradition and no tradition. True tradition is that past which survives in a continuous—if very fragile—line into present life, so that if you apprehend it with critical intelligence, it can put you into contact with some pattern of living in the past. Thus it might be said that although we do not live in a Christian society, nevertheless, there is a lifeline of Christian tradition which will lead us back imaginatively and intelligently to true Christian communities. But, in this sense, there is no pagan tradition. There is just a pagan past.

The prevalent argument is more and more to maintain that so far from there being a freedom of choice among traditions, there are extremely few lifelines leading back into past traditions. From this there naturally follows the idea that there is only one true tradition anyway, and debate in America and England becomes more and more concentrated on discussing which is the true line of the tradition. The tradition is in the Church, say some. Others, embarrassed by the fact that it is difficult to agree to this without having to accept the Church's creed, argue that the tradition is in the 'organic community', or New England, or the South; and since there is no question of being able to revive these communal patterns, they conclude that the tradition exists simply in the library of works written by the best writers who were privileged to belong to a place and time when the tradition flourished as actual living.

These lines of thought have disrupted, in literature, what was essentially modern: the vision of the present confronted by the past as a single total experience. The vision of a whole modern world—a whole fatality—related to a past which is also whole, if only in not being modern, is, let me emphasize again, essentially the characteristic of the modern. As Rilke writes in the letter already cited: 'We let it be emphasized again, in the sense of the Elegies WE are the transmuters of the earth; our whole existence here, the flights and falls of our love, all strengthen us for this task (besides which there is really no other).' What I call neo-traditionalism is the reversal of the modern.

The connection of the idea of wholeness (the past as a whole, the task of the artist to interpret it into the wholeness of the present fatality) with freedom of choice to select any part of the past as tradition, should be apparent. The attitude of some recent critics to tradition in the work of D. H. Lawrence demonstrates the way in which a partial interpretation can be superimposed on what in the life and work of the writer himself was the pursuit of wholeness. F. R. Leavis, Richard Hoggart and others acclaim Lawrence as the great exemplar of the alternative tradition: the chapel-going, Bunyanesque, proletarian. In doing this they make him the champion of what is hopefully looked forward to as a new socialist puritan revolution, with roots in Cromwellian England, and spear-headed by *Lady Chatterley's Lover*, against the upper class public school Oxford and Cambridge and Bloomsbury culture. It is of course quite possible to quote from *Fantasia of the Unconscious* and several of his essays to make him fit such a rôle. On the whole, Lawrence was probably more of a socialist than a Fascist or the blood-and-soil race-conscious Nazi whom Bertrand Russell saw him as. But even though the socialist and puritan working class sentiments he sometimes expressed may prove that he was capable of playing the kind of part that is now being written out of his own books for him, in fact he refused it while perhaps writing some of its speeches. His actions and the greater part of his writing show that he was largely concerned with getting away from the very tradition which he is now being written (or analysed) into. And those who put him back in this tradition ignore the fact that he left Nottingham and England and wandered over the earth in search precisely of a tradition which he felt to be lacking as much among his 'own' people as among the Bloomsbury intellectuals. Moreover the traditions—whether of Italian peasants, Etruscans, Aztec or pueblo Indians—of which he went in search were precisely those which, from the point of view of the literary traditionalists who are concerned with establishing effective connections between past and present, were most illusory and useless.

The reason why Lawrence in fact refused the rôle now being thrust on him, of leader of an English alternative-tradition puritan revival, is, surely, that he rejected the idea of being that kind of partisan. Although he was as much against the English upper class and the Oxbridge common rooms as any inmate of a Red Brick University common room could wish, he was not *for* Nottingham and the mines either. He had virtuous weaknesses which made partisan action impossible for him—a complete inability to co-operate with sociological types, and professors: above all a blind, hysterical hatred of industrial ugliness, and an utter unwillingness to work for any cause with which he would have had to deal in realistic social-political action. But the real objection is that he was, despite his contempt for all the literary sets, in the most essential respect a modern: that is to say, he saw contemporary civilization as a whole catastrophe which would eventually engulf all the future and which already had only left in primitive civilizations those pockets of uncontemporary existence which he sought out. And in thinking that hope for the future could only begin by a change of consciousnesss occurring within the individual, and between individuals in their mutual spiritual and physical awareness, he was committing his trust to individuals in their living and behaving.

*   *   *   *

What I have described here as the revolutionary concept of tradition was, then, of fundamental importance to the modern movement, because it permitted creative minds to view the whole significant past of art at all times and in all places as an available tradition out of which modern forms and style might derive. The reversal to the idea of institutionalized or continuous tradition, probably contributed more than any other cause to the collapse in literature of the modern movement. It may well be that the change was, in literature, at all events, inevitable. All the same the price that is paid for the present reaction is the abandonment of the aim of representing a whole modern situation, which produced the greatest works of the modern movement.

Withdrawing into the limited fortified area that is the out-post of what remains of the continuous line of the tradition, poets turn away from the vast areas of the modern world where these connections no longer count, critics use the communicating lines as a means of getting back into the works of the past, and they condemn modern and unprecedented forms of experience. Myth becomes split from tradition, mere illustration for academic poems by academic poets. Inevitably, poetry seems as an art to have receded, and while painters digress into futurism, the most hopeful tendency in literature is the realism of novelists and play-wrights oblivious of the aims that were modern, but who are at least contemporaries in the manner of Arnold Bennett, and ener-getic propagandists of an impassioned argument that they are in the line of the true tradition. In place of the upper class tradition—universally admitted to be in decline—they have set up their standard of insularity.

III

THE MODERN NECESSITY

THE modern arises from the need to express a situation outside and beyond the present time in imagery which is of the time. This necessity is better illustrated in the works of writers who write out of the pressure of their experience and not because they are conscious of themselves as enclosed in a literary situation—than by those who more obviously express tendencies or belong to movements.

Gerard Manley Hopkins and D. H. Lawrence were moderns without their being literary aesthetes. In their work one can see in a pure form the pressures that drove them to employ a modern idiom.

Gerard Manley Hopkins was forced by the intensity of his lived experience and the pressure of surrounding life to invent new forms and a highly individual idiom. It is the very force of his sense of belonging to the tradition of the Roman Catholic Church which compels him to find only in phenomena which are specifically modern an imagery powerful enough to express his spiritual predicament:

> The world is charged with the grandeur of God.
> It will flame out, like shining from shook foil;
> It gathers to a greatness, like the ooze of oil
> Crushed. Why do men then now not reck his rod?

These lines spring from ideas which might seem to belong to the past, but which for Hopkins are of the present, immanent in the modern environment. God fills the world which seems alien to Him, is felt most in those forces of the industrial scene which appear most empty of Him. The process involved in the world being 'charged' with God suggests the world-mass charged with electricity. The metaphor of the metal foil, and still more, that of the slightly repulsive oozing action of oil crushed under a skin which has formed over it, insists on the presence of God in the 'progressive' world, refuses to accept the idea of His retreat to the temples and places and language associated with His biblical past. He has advanced and is present in those very machines from which nature has been banished.

I am not here concerned with analysing the whole of this sonnet, which returns to the idea of nature being the force underlying the industrial life which is denatured. So that God is both present in the denatured world, and hidden in the nature which is only driven back and which still persists 'deep down things'. The point I want to make is that Hopkins, convinced of the immanence of God in the present moment, is driven to use the imagery of those things which strike the reader as above all contemporary. Poets like Hopkins' friends Coventry Patmore or Canon R. W. Dixon, to express the same thought, would have turned to Biblical imagery, and used the conventional reverent utterance of pieties, creeds and institutions in retreat in the advancing industrial world. The very use of such imagery and conventions of language would be to make the poetry occupy the restricted area and the recessive time, which was the position conventional religion had been driven into by the advances of science. Hopkins took the battle of his faith into the enemy's camp by using its imagery. His writing was advanced not because he had attached to himself the label 'modern', but because the world was advanced and he wanted to plant the banner of his poetic-religious principles into the heart—or the lack of heart— of this world. He is as serious and if necessary as ugly, in his imagery, as the industrial scene is oppressive and grim.

The need for Hopkins was essentially the need to bear witness to the truth, which was more important to him than poetry even, and had therefore to be expressed in the strongest and most vigorous terms. For him religion was the truth, but to James Joyce for whom irreligious truth was religion, the dislike of literature as such, the passion to say real things with as much force as the world around him offered, even if the result was ugly and brutal, resembles the passion for truth of Hopkins. His brother Stanislaus writes in *My Brother's Keeper*:

> In our world today, serious literature has taken the place of religion. People with liberty of choice go, not to the Sunday sermon, but to literature for enlightened understanding of their emotional and intellectual problems. And it answers in parables. My brother held that these parables for the most part falsified men, women and issues—all life, in fact, as it is lived every day or as it is lived in the imagination, and that at best it was a literature of entertainment, the province of men of letters. . . . Falsity of purpose was the sin against the Holy Ghost, and he was vigilant to detect it. In his fashion not unlike Carlyle's ideal of the poet as priest, he watched, though he did not pray.

It may be that Joyce's passion for truth, his contempt for the world of letters, his deep conviction that he must write about modern life, in all its aspects, and that he had to weave his stories into an entirely modern form and idiom, derived from the same missionary Jesuit spirit which was his early training as that of Hopkins the Jesuit priest.

*   *   *   *

D. H. Lawrence, writing to Edward Garnett in 1914, justified his novel *The Rainbow* on the grounds that he was not concerned with creating the pattern of the 'old stable ego of character', but 'another ego, according to whose action the individual is unrecognizable, and passes through, as it were, allotropic states which it needs a deeper sense than any we've been used to exercise, to discover are states of the same radically unchanged element'.

Lawrence was concerned with what he took to be instinctual human nature which has, he thought, been driven under the surface in the life of the individual in modern society. Life could, Lawrence thought, only break forth within new patterns of behaviour which must be realized in a different kind of art. He objected to Edward Garnett's idea of the novel as a vehicle 'for creating character'; for the very concept of a novelistic 'character' had become a literary convention which he regarded as inhibiting to an imaginative realization of the state of life in modern times. To Lawrence the problem of creating new forms in fiction for the expression of life was inseparable from the problem of life itself in the modern world.

Both Hopkins and Lawrence were religious not just in the ritualistic sense but in the sense of being obsessed with the word—the word made life and truth—with the need to invent a language as direct as religious utterance. Both were poets, but outside the literary fashions of their time. Both felt that among the poets of their time was an absorption in literary manners, fashions and techniques which separated the line of the writing from that of religious truth. Both felt that the modern situation imposed on them the necessity to express truth by means of a different kind of poetic writing from that used in past or present. Both found themselves driven into writing in a way which their contemporaries did not understand or respond to yet which was inevitable to each in his pursuit of truth. Here of course there is a difference between Hopkins and Lawrence, because Hopkins in his art was perhaps over-worried, over-conscientious, whereas Lawrence was an instinctive poet who, in his concern for truth, understood little of the problems of poetic form, although he held strong views about them. Oddly both stood in a certain relation to Walt Whitman, of whom both disapproved, but for whom each felt an affinity. This scarcely needs illustrating in the case of Lawrence in whose poetry the influence of Whitman is evident. But it is as surprising as it is revealing to find Hopkins writing to Bridges (18 October 1882) when Bridges had charged him with being Whitmanesque:

> But first I may as well say what I should not otherwise have said, that I always knew in my heart Walt Whitman's mind to be more like my own than any other man's living. As he is a very great scoundrel that is not a pleasant confession. And this also makes me the more desirous to read him and the more determined that I will not.

Hopkins' awareness of the divorce between manner and matter among his contemporaries, his suspicion that perhaps the professionally poetic manner of the late Victorians concealed an emptiness, are revealed in his comments on the outstanding poets of his time:

> (to Bridges, 22 April 1879) Lang's . . . is in the Swinburnian kind, is it not? (I do not think that kind goes far: it expresses passion but not feeling, much less character. This I say in general or of Swinburne in particular. Swinburne's genius is astonishing, but it will, I think, only do one thing.)
> (ditto, 22 October 1879) Tennyson ('s) . . . gift of utterance is truly golden, but go further home and you come to thoughts commonplace and wanting in nobility (it seems hard to say it but I think you know what I mean.)

Perhaps the most important statement of the necessity of a modern idiom is that made to Bridges in the letter of 14 August 1879:

> . . . It seems to me that the poetical language of an age should be the current language heightened, to any degree heightened and unlike itself, but not (I mean normally: passing freaks and graces are another thing) an obsolete one. This is Shakespeare's and Milton's practice and the want of it will be fatal to Tennyson's Idylls and plays, to Swinburne, and perhaps to Morris.

The correspondence of Hopkins with Bridges and Dixon is

rather painful, because, as the reader cannot but feel, Hopkins' friends are, poetically speaking, incapable of salvation, or of understanding at all profoundly Hopkins' point of view. Thus here (26 October 1880) Hopkins' remarks on Browning are a courteously disguised affectionate criticism of Bridges' own failings in his famous poem *On a Dead Child*:

> The rhythm (of *London Snow*) . . . is not quite perfect. That of the child-piece is worse, indeed, it is Browningesque. . . . '

Hopkins' attitude to all these contemporaries is summed up in his comments on Swinburne in a letter to Canon R. W. Dixon (1 December 1881):

> The Lake School expires in Keble and Faber and Cardinal Newman. The Brownings may be reckoned to the Romantics. Swinburne is a strange phenomenon: his poetry seems a powerful effort at establishing a new standard of poetical diction, of the rhetoric of poetry; but to waive every other objection, it is essentially archaic, biblical a good deal, and so on: now that is a thing that can never last; a perfect style must be of its age. In virtue of this archaism and on other grounds he must rank with the mediaevalists.

So on the one hand, Hopkins realized that 'a perfect style must be of its age', on the other hand, that this style must be extremely concentrated, have the quality he called 'inscape', and be in 'native rhythm'.

Lawrence had, as I have pointed out, far less sense of the problems of art in writing poetry than did Hopkins. A letter to Edward Marsh (19 November 1913) shows that his feeling for metre was instinctive and that he did not really think about it at all until challenged: 'You *are* wrong. It makes me open my eyes. I think I read my poetry more by length than by stress—as a matter of movements in space than footsteps hitting the earth.' But although his justification of his own ear is vague and rather unconsidered, he sees that there is something wrong with the accustomed literary ear of his time:

If your ear has got stiff and a bit mechanical, *don't* blame my poetry. That's why you like *Golden Journey to Samarkand*—it fits your habituated ear, and your feeling crouches subservient and a bit pathetic. 'It satisfies my ear,' you say. Well, I don't write for your ear. This is the constant war, I reckon, between new expression and the habituated, mechanical transmitters and receivers of the human constitution.

He expresses the other essential which he feels to be necessary to modern poetry in his criticism of the writers for the war number of *Poetry*, in a letter to Harriet Monroe: 'Your people have such little pressure: their safety valve goes off at the high scream when the pressure is still so low.'

So Lawrence, like Hopkins, is not a vocational 'modern'. He does not belong to any school or movement, and he lacks a quality which seems essential in Joyce, Eliot, and Virginia Woolf, that of being preoccupied above all else with problems of inventing new forms. He judges himself and wants to be judged by the feeling for life which is the ebb and flow of the writing.

> Primarily I am a passionately religious man, and my novels must be written from the depths of my religious experience. That I must keep to, because I can only work like that. And my cockneyism and commonness are only when the deep feeling doesn't find its way out, and a sort of jeer comes instead, and sentimentality, and purplism.

Essentially, Lawrence thought that a novel or poem should realize through the form the same kind of wavering but organic existence as a human being. For Lawrence art was the imitation of man and woman as they are with their intensities and their imperfections. For the aesthetic moderns art was the redemption of life-experience through perfection of form. Putting the matter in a more literary way, the great difference between Lawrence and the others is that what he regarded as the essential of art was the line and rhythm, and if these were moody and irregular, then so also is life; and pattern should not be willed on to them by conceptual form. What they cared about was relating every part of a work to the architectural whole. The difference is that which Lawrence would have described as between the movement of the blood, and the willed act of cerebration. 'But you should see the religious, earnest, suffering man in me first, and then the flippant or common things after,' he writes to Edward Garnett (22 April 1914). A James, a Flaubert, a Joyce, could never have written this because he would have considered the novel as a work of art separate from the writer, something into which the writer had poured his whole experience and skill but which should then be judged as an object, not as a flow of life blood or subconscious forces.

These remarks apply less to *The Rainbow*, and *Women in Love*, in which he was struggling to achieve unity of pattern. But after *Women in Love*, his most successful book, the novel ceases to concern him as form. It becomes a vehicle to convey the most recent developments in his relationship with Frieda and with the people they encountered in whatever part of the world they happened to be, and his philosophy of life.

Lawrence was not an artist in the sense that Joyce and Eliot were. Nevertheless as between Galsworthy and Bennett, and Joyce and Eliot, his work shares the positive characteristics of the latter and has nothing in common with the former, though he himself lumped them all together, as the cerebral stuff he disliked.

What Lawrence shares with the moderns, and what Galsworthy and Bennett, with their acceptance of business, and their belief in reformism, lacked, is the awareness of the whole modern industrial predicament as a universal greyness and doom (6 October 1912—to A. W. McLeod: 'I hate Bennett's resignation. Tragedy ought really to be a great kick at misery. But *Anna of the Five Towns* seems like an acceptance—so does all the modern stuff since Flaubert. I hate it. I want to wash again quickly, wash off England, the oldness and grubbiness and despair'). It is an awareness of life as it was, and is not, and still should be. From the modern point of view, as I have described it, the divorce between past and present is so complete that to express the feeling for the past it is no good using past conventions and forms. The hankering for the past is merely archaic unless it can be expressed in a contemporary idiom. The past has to be absorbed into the struggle that goes on within the present, the sense of it be re-invented.

*   *   *   *

Lawrence did not have worked-out aesthetic principles, but he made up rationalizations for his way of writing, which he produced to correspondents. He had feelings rather than ideas about his artistic procedure. Essentially, he thought that form should imitate or spring from some kind of instinctive life-feeling of which his art was the expression. A work of art should be the external form of a living impulse as is the behaviour of an animal or the growth of a plant. His writing 'grew', and if it was sometimes inspired, sometimes dull, sometimes great art, sometimes ephemeral opinion or daily record—well that was like life. He wanted art like a butterfly along a country lane, sometimes settling on a flower, sometimes on horse dung.

Although this view of his art had its successes, it also resulted in his glaring defects. The successes were that his stories and poems do have a deeply lived carelessness, at best achieving unity in a pattern which gives the reader the feeling about the work which one has about the pattern of behaviour of people one knows. Though he is sometimes boring and tiresome, in a novel such as *Aaron's Rod*, sometimes perversely inartistic, as in *Kangaroo*, his books do not suffer from the pedantry of theories of art ruthlessly carried out, as do passages of *Ulysses*.

The most obvious defect which mars his poetry is the strange mixture of free verse formlessness and searchings after forms that he perhaps remembers from hymns and the Bible. But that scarcely matters since he did not consider himself a poet, and his poems give more to be grateful for than those of most professionals. Yet his lack of interest in artistic form prevented him from achieving a most serious aim. This was to convey the idea of a dialogue carried on between people who are in a relationship on more than a conscious level; the dialogue of their truth, which cannot be expressed in words, because it concerns scarcely conscious feelings.

Women in Love has two or three sets of relationships of this type: notably, that between Rupert Birkin and Hermione, and that between Birkin and Gerald. This is the novel in which D. H. Lawrence made the most sustained attempt to write the dialogue as symbolic action. For example, there is the scene in which Hermione hits Birkin on the head with a lapis lazulae ornament, and there is the naked wrestling, late at night, between Gerald and Birkin.

Memorable as both these scenes are, they are a bit absurd, and they do not succeed as symbolic action. In fact they give rise to the suspicion in the reader's mind that they are partly obtrusive autobiography: strange absurd scenes from Lawrence's life which get into the novel because he does not fully understand them. They fall midway between expressing the 'true' feeling of the characters, and between being true in the sense of 'truth is stranger than fiction'. One is not sure whether Hermione really wishes to murder Birkin or whether the wish to go through an act of symbolic murder is not part of their relationship, and satisfactory to both of them. Both things might be true, but the symbolic language does not reveal this, and it also comes too close to the kind of crude melodrama, or the novelettish writing which Lawrence sometimes lapses into through his failure to find a medium to express the semi-conscious relationship (or the relationship between two people's unconsciousness) which was so important to him. There is doubt again whether the Birkin-Gerald wrestling match is meant to express a homosexual relationship; and a further doubt whether it expresses this, without its being what Lawrence really intended (again as the result of obtrusive autobiography—his relationship with Middleton Murry). Probably though, Lawrence did not intend the wrestling to be open to homosexual interpretation. It was meant to be symbolic of the inner dialogue between Gerald and Birkin at the stage it had then reached in the novel.

The failure of Lawrence to invent a language for this kind of dialogue is most evident in *Lady Chatterley's Lover*, when Mellors and Lady Chatterley fall into a mixture of baby talk, on her part, dialect on his, in those passages where the consciousness of each is supposed to be most revealingly close to the other.

Lawrence regarded Joyce as cerebral and despised him accordingly. Joyce used to talk about 'Lady Chatterbox's Lover'. But if Joyce carries out his theories to the point of fictional pedantry, Lawrence's refusal to think intellectually about the language he undoubtedly needed, to express the deepest interrelationship of people, results in his worst lapses, and in an incompleteness even in his greatest achievements. Joyce invented a special imagistic poetry for his interior monologue. Lawrence, a poet in his descriptions of nature, failed to invent a special poetry for his interior dialogues.

* * * *

Another difference between Lawrence and his contemporaries is that he came passionately to think that the struggle against the modern world had to be carried out within life, could not be confined to art. This is important, because some critics deny that there is any such distinction between literature and life.

The reason for denying such a distinction is that philistines talk as though there were something called life which is 'real', as distinct from something called literature which is unreal: non-readers are in contact with direct experience, whereas readers only know things at second hand. This is a shabby argument, unlikely to be true in a complex society. The truth is that 'life' without literature is unreflecting, uncritical activity, the exercise of physical reflexes, and indulgence in social prejudices. Reading does not mean leading a substitute life (though some readers might live this) but exercising judgement about experience, entering into conversation with the dead, criticizing the values of the society around one.

All this may be true, and yet there remains the danger to which the aesthetically minded are particularly prone—that of treating the art-object as if it not only created life but actually was life. Lawrence was opposed to the idea that art created values. He thought rather that it should direct people back into the values of living. Yet no one felt the temptation to despair of real living more than he did; when, for example, he wrote to Dr. Trigant Burrow:

> Myself, I suffer badly from being so cut off. But what is one to do? One can't link up with the social unconscious. At times one is *forced* to be essentially a hermit. I don't want to be. But anything else is either a personal tussle, or a money tussle: sickening: except, of course, just for ordinary acquaintance, which remains acquaintance. One has no real human relations—that is so devastating.

Of two opposite dangers, Lawrence thought that the one of becoming obsessed with problems of form was greater than that of directing his novels away from literature into life. He regards his reader not as one for whom the words on the page become more significant than surrounding conditions but as one whose life and relationships with other people should be changed by reading him. One way of putting this is to say that he was a preacher, and this has been said. I do not think it quite covers his case. It would be truer I think to say that he was a poetic writer who trusted in the genius of his line and who distrusted the kind of effort which consists in turning the experience which is art into the enclosed world of a form.

IV

THE SEMINAL IMAGE

THE modern, as I discuss it here, involves the stripping away of previous assumptions about form, manner and subject and returning to the most elementary operation of outer event upon poetic sensibility. And this unit of inspiration, the initial creative moment, has to be accepted without prejudice. The modern poet does not assume that what strikes him immediately is unsuitable for the poem. Prejudices arise from assumptions about form and manner and therefore exercise a selective influence over the subject. Refuse to be directed by these, and the subject is free. And to the extent that the poet's own sensibility is contemporary his work will be significantly modern.

The aims of the imagist movement in poetry provide the archetype of a modern creative procedure. The fact that the imagists themselves did not achieve very much does not affect this. Purists are often too pure to be anything but pure. But the imagists made a new start. They stripped writing poetry back to the primitive situation in which the outer experience produces a poetic reaction on the sensibility. This is when it strikes off an image, like a spark. The image is the basic unit of poetry, preceding even the metaphor, unless, indeed, one argues that it is already an implicit metaphor.

The essential principles of the famous imagist manifesto from

which the aims of idiomatic language, verbal exactitude and free
rhythms derive, are 'absolute freedom in the choice of subject'
and the aim 'to present an image'. But the image which demands
exact language, concentration and complete freedom is the basic
element from which all else springs. The image is the charter of
freedom.

The image is the immediate visual reaction of the sensibility of
the poet to an event which strikes him with felt force. Hit me on
the head and I, presumably, see stars. The liberating impulse of
the imagist was the idea that any image was authentic to the
extent that it realized itself in the mind of the attentive and aware
reader. Here there was the example which gave authority not
only to the outrageous imagery of Joyce and of the early Eliot
('her drying combinations touched by the sun's last rays') but
also to a new idea of what was meant by 'work' in poetry.
Work was not hunting around for rhymes and filling up metrical
lines, but the kind of concentration in performance which remains faithful to the moment in which an idea, visualized,
first purely occurs and asserts its claim that it is capable of further
definition.

When I ask myself the question: 'Is this image suitable for
poetry?' the answer I give is revealing of my innermost convic-
tions about the nature of the kind of poetry I believe I ought to
write. I might say, for example, 'Yes, if it is beautiful or if it can
be conveyed in words which are poetic, or if it fits into a stanza
form which I already have in mind.' The imagists insisted that
the answer should be simply: 'Yes if I feel the force of an image.'
And if I then protested: 'I do see an image, but I don't feel it
suitable for a poem.' They then replied: 'There is no such thing
as unsuitable.' 'Yes but I can't see this image as music or pattern.'
'Well then, do without music or pattern, simply use the best
words in the best order to realize the image.'

Indeed, the less conventionally suitable, the more the image
was likely to please them. Diction need only make the image as

clear and simple as possible. Music and form were mere auxiliaries.

The imagists left out too much (for instance, that poems can be statements, and that pattern can realize and not impede imagery) and they made things too easy for visualizers who had no ear or sense of form anyway. The imagist poems of T. E. Hulme read like notes for longer poems, and those of H. D. and Amy Lowell are as conventionally nostalgic, as, say, the neo-classical poetry of Landor, but less interesting. A great deal of interest, after all, is in the form.

There is a further reason why imagism although it had a revolutionary influence—the revolution being of a kind which was particularly effective as polemic against the poetry of writers who held different theories—achieved such thin results where the poet remained completely true to its precepts. This is that although the verbalized image may with excellent poets be the flash-point from which the poem starts, it does not have that richness and strangeness which enables poetry to 'arrive'. Departures but few arrivals. The image seems unique to the poet and personal, but in fact what is finally and decisively distinct in poetry is the ear not the eye. Rhythm carries the tone of the inner personality. It is the least analysable element in a poem: the invisible quality in which the poet exists. Although the imagists sought new rhythms, actually often this meant having no rhythm at all, or reducing it to the mechanical monotony of chopped up lines: that is, the rhythm not of the poet's ear but of the phrases into which any writing or speaking falls through the exigencies of grammar and meaning.

But Pound and Eliot constructed on the uninhibited not-by-any-means-poetic image, music and forms which provided conjunctions with other images, bore up the images on language rich and strange, connected them with symbols and myths. When the imagistic seed was planted in soil which was not dry it produced plants that were mutations of poetry. They led on the image to that point where it created its own form.

The value of imagism as example was, as I have said, that it provided a literary technique for releasing experiences which occurred as suppressed images in the minds of poets—suppressed because they did not seem 'poetic'. They seemed unpoetic because they had not been used in previous poetry. The reason why they had not been so used was because they belonged to the area of things modern and unprecedented.

*   *   *   *

Imagism was then, as I have said, in its programme for de-inhibiting poets from poetic conventions, in its opening up of all subject matter sufficiently felt as proper for art, in its beguiling false offer of an easy way for every man to be a poet, its pseudo-democracy, the archetype of other movements. But it released into poetry material which, before imagism, poets themselves would have rejected. Yeats learned from the imagists, by way of his secretary, Ezra Pound, to reconcile images which at first seemed unsuitable to him for his way of writing, with traditional forms. The imagists recognized the merits of the poetry of D. H. Lawrence in which they saw the image breaking through the forms. Lawrence, although printed in imagist anthologies and in *Poetry* (Chicago), did not return the compliment. He said nothing good of them.

Different though surrealism may seem to intellectualist imagism, it is only an extremer technique of de-inhibition, of flooding the poem with a previously suppressed imagery. The differences, which are of extremes, between it and imagism, are significant. Imagism makes admissible the rejected conscious images of current writing, and makes these the goal of a new poetry. In fact most imagist poetry is notable not so much for the audacity of the images, as for the use of word and form to do nothing except create the image. Mostly the imagists were men and women of refined literary sensibility and what was released into their poetry was bric-a-brac of past literature and classical scenery.

As these lines of H. D.:

> Your insight
> has driven deeper
> than the lordliest tome
> of Attic thought
> or Cyrenian logic;
> O strange, dark Morpheus,
> covering me with wings,
> you give the subtle fruit
> Odysseus scorned
> that left his townsmen fainting on the sands,
> you bring the syren note,
> the lotus-land . . .

Surrealism adopts non-literary techniques in order to stimulate a stream of images, coming, supposedly, from the subconscious mind. The surrealists wished to break down the boundaries of literature altogether, and make poetry a machinery for drilling through the surface of consciousness into the world of passions and fantasies below. Surrealism was the attempt to liberate among the sane the forces of insanity, to construct a world after the pattern of man's most hidden dreams and desires.

Imagism, as we have seen, isolated the basic unit of the modern poem, the image sprung from, and acted upon by, critically conscious sensibility. Eliot wrote in his *Criterion* Commentary in July 1937:

> What was needed was a critical activity to revise creative writing, to introduce new material and new technique from other countries and other times. The accomplishment of the Imagist movement in verse, seems to me, in retrospect, to have been critical rather than creative; and as criticism, very important.

It made possible that fusion of the creative and the critical impulses which was so formidable in the modern movement. It resulted, during the '20's and the '30's in the view that the truth not only of poetry but also of fiction was poetic: that

Virginia Woolf and not Arnold Bennett understood Mrs. Brown. The famous interior monologue of James Joyce was the method of the image resulting from the immediate impact of outer event on inner sensibility projected into the consciousness of invented characters.

V

POETIC MODERNS AND PROSE
CONTEMPORARIES

ONE reason why imagism remains historically important,
despite the slight productions of the imagists, may be
that as a method, a *modus operandi*, it demolished a frontier between
poetry and prose. For if nothing except the image matters, and
form, music, rhythm, rhyme, are of secondary importance, then
there is no boundary dividing imagist prose and imagist poetry,
except perhaps the degree of concentration of the imagery.
Imagism finally removes the kind of distinction which people
have in mind when they doubt that the psalms or the Book of
Isaiah are poetry. The answer of the imagists is that they are,
on account of the images.

By imagist standards, a great deal of *Ulysses* is poetry. The
famous interior monologue is, as we have seen, the method
of imagist poetry; and Leopold Bloom, Molly Bloom and, to a
lesser extent, Stephen Daedalus (whose mode of thinking is not
so entirely imagistic) are imagist poets, of a higher order than
H. D., Richard Aldington and the anthology imagists. They are
imagists because the interior monologue is the method of revealing sensibility acted upon by outward events, which produce
images: the smell of frying kidney, the sun shining on the pavement, memories of Molly Bloom's lovers.

This is important to my argument because from it there

follows a consequence of the distinction I have been making between contemporary and modern. The contemporaries use a realist prose method, whereas the moderns use an imagistic poetic one.

The imagistic poetic method derives from the action of the external world upon inner sensibility. Individual consciousness is the centre which is acted upon by the environment. Contemporary economic conditions, politics, etc., affect it as discords in music, screaming colours, distorted form or lack of form. These conditions, that affect sensibility, form a 'climate' or 'atmosphere' — moral, intellectual or aesthetic—which is the complex result of material and social circumstances, seen by the mind's eye, just as the physical eye sees the colours of the sunset which result from the precipitation of dust in the air.

The conditions that affect sensibility are themselves the result of other conditions, far and near, past and present. The impression of a moment intensely recorded may be the crystallization of a whole history, a wide geographical area. In the ideally perceptive inner sensibility there is contained the image of the whole condition of the world.

While, from the outside, the centre of consciousness is acted upon by impressions attacking it from the circumference of the environment, reaching into the whole world, it also contains within itself another universality, that of subconscious life, childhood, personal history, sleep, dream, the subjective ego which moves into pasts and depths beyond individuality, where it is pure existence and no longer knows its name.

This attitude to writing, whether prose or verse, fiction or poetry, is essentially poetic, because it apprehends the real by way of feeling, intuition. The writer has faith in the potentiality of the most individual or subjective experiences and feelings, to be, if they are truthfully realized, representative of the state of existence.

Henry James in his last novels, James Joyce, and Virginia

Woolf, used a poetic method. And for two or three decades their manner and approach were extremely influential. It was a tidal wave coming out of poetry and flowing into the novel. It may have arisen partly as the result of the lack of poems with great themes, perhaps because poets found it impossible to write poetry on an epic scale. The poetic novel stimulated poetry, and *The Waste Land* can in a way be regarded as a by-product of *Ulysses*. I. A. Richards called it a compressed epic. Well, *Ulysses* was an extended epic. The epic poems of our day, Edmund Wilson suggested, were written by Flaubert, Henry James, and James Joyce.

The term the 'poetic novel' has befogged the discussion between the supporters of the poetic, and those of the prose, principle in fiction. A presentation of the discussion must start off by stating that the rationale and justification of each method are that it is an attitude towards, and a means of grasping, reality. It is absurd to make one list consisting of Henry James, James Joyce, D. H. Lawrence, and Virginia Woolf, who are supposed to have written novels which are experimental, about poetic experiences, or art, and contrast it with another of H. G. Wells, Arnold Bennett, C. P. Snow, Kingsley Amis, Alan Sillitoe, who are supposed to be writing about 'real life'.

A more useful distinction might be to say that the poetic method is seismographic, barometric: the prose method is sociological and cataloguing.

I have compared the poetic method to a centre of sensibility, which is also a point with depths reaching to unconscious life. The prose method might be described as that where the writer provides a complete description of all those material factors in the environment which condition his characters. The poetic method sees the centre of consciousness as the point where all that is significant in the surrounding world becomes aware and transformed; the prose method requires a description of that world in order to explain the characteristics of the people in it. The hero of the poetic method is Rimbaud; of the prose method, Balzac.

Three famous disputes between novelists in the present century are really between the supporters of the poetic, and the supporters of the prose method. These are the quarrel between Henry James and H. G. Wells; the attack on Arnold Bennett by Virginia Woolf, in her pamphlet entitled *Mr. Bennett and Mrs. Brown*; and the quarrel between D. H. Lawrence and John Galsworthy.

Wells, Galsworthy, and Bennett were for prose. They see their characters as being formed by their social environment, having its aims, ideas, dreams, whether they are directed against it or towards it. The Forsytes want to get rich, they want to conform and be respectable, or else to get away with their adulteries without offending society. The Pollys, Kippses, Annas of the Five Towns, etc. are characteristic emergent figures coming out of social conflicts and aspiring to better social conditions. And today in the same way, the characters of C. P. Snow's novels are the results of their mixed social and educational conditioning; their individuality is realized by their positions in a hierarchy of academic or bureaucratic power. But these positions—which of course make them different from one another and provide their interest for themselves and the readers—measure them only by the external social values of the power conflict. They lack the inner life which separates people from social values.

To Henry James, Wells seemed, with all his immense gifts of enjoyment and vitality, lacking in the consciousness of that separateness which alone can create individual values. To Lawrence it seemed that Galsworthy in his novels invented nothing but social units, described a life which had none but social standards. And to Virginia Woolf it seemed that Arnold Bennett saw his characters only from the outside, and when he attempted to describe what went on inside Mrs. Brown saw only a wall:

> I have formed my own opinion of what Mr. Bennett is about—
> he is trying to make us imagine for him; he is trying to hypnotize
> us into the belief that, because he has made a house, there must be

a person living there. With all his powers of observation, which are marvellous, with all his sympathy and humanity, which are great, Mr. Bennett has never looked at Mrs. Brown in her corner. There she sits in the corner of the carriage—that carriage which is travelling, not from Richmond to Waterloo, but from one age of English literature to the next, for Mrs. Brown is eternal, Mrs. Brown is human nature, Mrs. Brown changes only on the surface, it is the novelists who get in and get out—there she sits and not one of the Edwardian writers has so much as looked at her. They have looked very powerfully, searchingly, and sympathetically out of the window; at factories, at Utopias, even at the decoration and upholstery of the carriage; but never at her, never at life, never at human nature.

The moderns felt that the realistic method of describing characters as the results of their environment and their social or familial relations, ambitions and aspirations, could no longer create the essential truths of individual life. Lawrence does not dispute that people like the Forsytes existed, but he regarded them as abstractions and corpses; if there are such people, he pointed out, then they are the subject not for sympathetic realization but for malicious satire. As Lawrence wrote in his essay on John Galsworthy:

> When one reads Mr. Galsworthy's books it seems as if there were not on earth one single human individual. They are all these social beings, positive and negative. There is not a free soul among them, not even Pendyce, or June Forsyte. If money does not actively determine their being, it does negatively. Money, or property, which is the same thing.

The same criticism, that life is evaded, that the writer, despite his discontent, has the same grey devitalized values as the world he describes, is made by Lawrence of Wells in *The World of William Clissold:*

> His effective self is disgruntled, his ailment is a peevish, ashy indifference to *everything*, except himself, himself as the centre of the universe. There is not one gleam of sympathy with anything

in all the book, and not one breath of passionate rebellion. Mr.
Clissold is too successful and wealthy to rebel and too hopelessly
peeved to sympathise.

This line of criticism leads back into modern society. What
Lawrence is saying—and what James perhaps came to think—
was that living had become separated from the social environment. Therefore it could no longer be conveyed by realistic
descriptions of characters and social values. The traditional novelistic character is a person described through his or her relations with
other persons, family, or community. In the past vital characters
could be portrayed from such material. Consciousness was shared
because moral values were shared. But today the individual who
is fully conscious is aware of having values separate from those
of the society in which he lives.

The last of my three examples of the quarrel between poetic
and prose novelists, is that between Henry James and H. G. Wells.
It arose as the result of the publication of Wells' novel *Boon*,
which contained a parody of Henry James' final manner.

In July 1915, James picked up in his club the copy of *Boon*, the
most recent novel of Wells, which the author had sent there for
him. On reading it he was to discover that it contained a parody
of a novel written in the manner of the late James. 'Poor H. J.'
in his letter to 'my dear Wells' grapples with the blow received:

> I have more or less mastered your appreciation of H. J., which I
> have found very curious and interesting after a fashion—though it
> has naturally not filled me with a fond elation. It is difficult of
> course for a writer to put himself *fully* in the place of another
> writer who finds him extraordinarily futile and void, and who is
> moved to publish that to the world—and I think the case isn't
> easier when he happens to have enjoyed the other writer from
> far back—

Pursuing his theme in his inimitable way, he goes on to explain
that he cannot completely enter into Wells' view of him, however hard he tries:

For I should otherwise seem to forget what it is that my poetic and my appeal to experience rest upon. They rest upon *my* measure of fullness—fullness of life and the projection of it, which seems to you such an emptiness of both . . . I hold that interest may be, *must* be, exquisitely made and created, and that if we don't make it, we who undertake to, nobody and nothing will make it for us.

In a second letter, James sums up his aesthetic credo:

It is art that *makes* life, makes interest, makes importance, for our consideration and application of these things, and I know of no substitute whatever for the force and beauty of its process.

So James' attitude to his writing, and to all art, is that of a poet who creates the values of life in his poetry, rather than of a novelist who applies the traditional values of the society in which he lives to the reality he describes. This, one sees on reflection, is not just his philosophy, nor even the architectonic principles on which he constructs a novel. Poetry is the secret of his style in its rhythms, its evocativeness, its use of symbolism, all of which invent the atmosphere and the inhabitants of a separate world. Clearly the misunderstanding between James and Wells is about the poetic or prose nature of the novel. To James, Wells' parody of his manner and his satiric attack on it for excluding life, must have seemed like parodying poetry on the grounds that people did not talk in verse.

Wells' defence is of prose, the prose method, the attitudes of the prose novelist against the novelist who in his novels invents a new poetry. He answers James:

To you literature, like painting, is an end, to me literature like architecture is a means, it has a use. Your view was, I felt, altogether too prominent in the world of criticism and I assailed it in lines of harsh antagonism.

Wells here puts into opposition two kinds of criticism, and in doing so, puts his finger on what is one of the underlying causes of disagreement between the poetic and the prose schools of fiction. By 'literature like architecture is a means' it is clear— from the context of every line he wrote—he meant that his novels were to him social criticism, his purpose being to describe the life around him, and to use the novel as a means of improving society. The word 'architecture' probably has a special relevance to him, because he was thinking of abolishing the slums, building the new cities of a socialist Utopia. He is defending himself as a social critic against what he discerns in James as a sinister alliance between the poetic artist and the literary critic, enabling litera- ture to withdraw into its own values of life created by art.

In a further letter he significantly adds:

> When you say 'it is art that *makes* life, makes interest, makes importance,' I can only read sense into it by assuming that you are using 'art' for every conscious human activity. I use the word for a research and attainment that is technical and special.

Wells is right. James does, of course, think of art as completely realized consciousness. It is, indeed, exactly the lack of such a consciousness that James in an earlier letter, about Wells' novel *The Passionate Friends*, has, in an aside, noted in the younger writer, 'I find you perverse and I find you, on a whole side, unconscious, as I can only call it . . .'

The debate is inconclusive partly because it arises from the reaction of different temperaments with different gifts to the modern situation which can be viewed in two ways. On the one side there are artists who are conscious above all of art and who therefore feel overwhelmed by the conditions which have up- rooted from society the values from which art, in the past, derived. On the other, are those whose values are not so rooted to cultural achievements of the past, institutional beliefs, and a classical education, and whose work is based not on the values of literature, but on what, as social optimists, they take to be the potentialities of society.

It is significant that those who feel isolated within the values enshrined in art are for the most part those who judge the state of civilization by the values of a classical education and the Christian establishments. This is, of course—or was—often the case with expatriate Americans who came to Europe, envisaging it as a historic culture still having a precarious flickering existence in the lives of decaying aristocracies and heroic bohemians. The process which one watches in Henry James is of the belief which was once attached to an aristocracy, gradually becoming transferred to the creating and transmitting power of art.

But what is important is not temperaments, but reality. Is either side justified in claiming that it·represents what is real, and in its frequent dismissal of the other as superficial or merely experimental?

An incomplete answer to the question is that in its approach to reality, each is conditioned by circumstances, temperament, and generation.

The novelists with the prose approach tend to be those who are crammed with news, information. They have a lot to tell us about the circumstances of their childhood, before they knew or were known to literary circles: the mid-West, the northern industrial town, the slum, the kitchen sink, the back parlour. They have a background of poverty and perhaps they have matured in harsh circumstances of hard unintellectual labour, or perhaps they have been conscripted to a war.

They may be—and probably are—egotistic, but they are not introspective, subjective, or aesthetic. They are soaked in experiences which they have been thrust into. They are wet through with contact with the outside world and have little time for inner life.

The poetic novelists are the opposite of all this. They are interesting to others and interesting to themselves. If they come from the English middle class then they grow up bookish, and bored with their surroundings. If they come from the working class, they are abnormal, exceptions like Lawrence: a mother's child, only likely to play with girls and hating his father; or like Joyce, sensitive, proud, short-sighted, isolated. At the same time, they have a passionate grasp of their own kind of reality, which is that of inner life.

There is an inside and an outside reality to be grasped. One modern writer—Joyce—was so conscious of this, that his interior poetic writing is provided with the most elaborate apparatus of external realism.

Why, then, is war between different groups, who regard themselves as having a monopoly of reality, so characteristic of modern literary controversy?

The three polemical debates between the poetic and the prose novelists which I have cited here, indicate, I think, one answer. For in each case the poetic novelist is criticizing the later work of the prose realist where the realism has become a mere convention, or he is attacking one aspect of the work, in which the grasp on reality seems weak. Henry James and—for that matter—D. H. Lawrence both admired the early work of Wells, when Wells was still, as I have described him above, dripping with experience of the outside world. D. H. Lawrence admired the early Galsworthy: he thought that Galsworthy had begun by seeing the real life of the bourgeois Forsytes and had then allowed himself to fall in love with the unreal sentimental image of them.

Virginia Woolf's attack on Bennett seems unfair, if one thinks of the early Bennett: but not so unfair if one thinks of the pontifical reviewer and diner out he had become at the time when she wrote it.

The young in our century have something of a monopoly of reality—whether they are poetic visionaries or realists of the kitchen sink—because they are either victims of external circumstances from which they have not yet been rescued by being discovered and published; or because they are still possessed by that vision for whose virtue they have not yet been taken up, praised, dropped, attacked, by the machinery of the literary life.

Modern conditions tend to loosen the grasp of the writer on the subject matter, the view of life, which is most deeply his. A writer, like any other artist, begins by being his material as well as his work. If he is the mid-Westerner of Sinclair Lewis' early novels, he really belongs to Main Street: his is the miraculous single sense of beauty that has grown in a world utterly materialistic, but convincingly real. The same is true of the early Wells. He is the boy who in the public park becomes lost in contemplation of the bronze statue of a sylphlike naked girl, and whose innocent reverie is interrupted by the gloating laugh of the man sitting on the bench next to him, who can only share his contemplation as a dirty joke. All the same, with its glimpses of a naïve Douanier Rousseau-like beauty, its grubby enthusiasm for spanners and gadgets, its sense of a world consisting of a shopkeeper, a housekeeper and a chemist sitting in the basket of a big balloon which is going to climb into the stratosphere—this is the real Wells in the real environment writing the real fiction.

But when Wells or Bennett or Sinclair Lewis has written a couple of novels, which are critically well received, what happens? His authentic personality which was that of his own place and people becomes dissolved into a new literary personality, with a new social life, taste, ideas to go with it. Everyone here has despised the standards of Main Street all along; everyone knows better than to grunt conspiratorially over statues of nude girls. (They do not even think of them as naked girls, but as art objects which arouse only aesthetic emotions.)

The writer, instead of being the misunderstood boy from Ohio, or Leeds, or Nottingham, finds that the philistinism, the materialism, the coarseness and the vitality of the non-literary world from which he sprang, are all saleable in the world of literature. They are life—real life—and in a world where this has become an increasingly rare commodity, he finds that providence, so far from being unkind in breeding him in one of those insensitive places, was actually in its infinite wisdom nurturing him among nuggets: as though he were some child brought up in a pit among hard stones, who suddenly discovered in himself not only a vocation to be a gold-miner, but that the hard impenetrable stones around him all concealed gleaming ore, which could be melted down and beaten into plate for lords' and ladies' tables.

Unfortunately though, in the process of becoming a writer, he has ceased to be Kipps, or Arrowsmith, or Paul Morel, or Anna, or a Jimmy. He has become a writer, moving in the air-conditioned, morally free, aesthetically wide open, understanding, unconvincing, cynical, liberal, community of writers.

At this point, if he is a cataloguing prose realist, he becomes a professional: no longer one of the people he came from, but an inventor who has taken out a patent in his own background origins, a bit aggressive, as though not only were he determined to be the only writer coming from Nottingham or Leeds, but the only person with a pen who had ever come from those black, dire, gruff, bluff, inexpressive regions.

Bennett, Galsworthy, and Wells were typical of writers who had come out of real situations, but who had gradually become professionals, specializing in their own material. They had something about them strongly reminiscent of Harley Street surgeons. It was this which Virginia Woolf was attacking in her pamphlet.

But of course she was equally open to attack for lack of grip on reality. The writer who relies completely on sensitivity, in the end becomes professionally sensitive, just as Arnold Bennett became a professional writer of the Five Towns.

It is, in short, a problem for the writer in modern conditions of literary life which dissolve his early identification with his own material, to keep a grasp on his reality, whether this is of the prose contemporary or the poetic modern kind. The most serious artists cling to their original vision with tenacity. Thus Joyce never wrote about any scene except the Dublin of his childhood, and, at the same time, clung to this vision, in exile and in isolation. Henry James' immense notebooks contain endless evocations of his art, his sacred task as a novelist, his own ability, through his art, to create his own values, isolated from those of the surrounding society.

There is a distinct thinning of the rather dense texture of real external life in Lawrence's work after *The White Peacock* and *Sons and Lovers*. The reader of Nehls' three-volume composite biography of Lawrence (consisting of memoirs written throughout his life, by almost all those who encountered him on his wanderings) will note that the friends and acquaintances of his youth—those whose recollections fill the first volume—entered into far closer and more perceptive relationships with him than do those later on. The Lawrence literary myth takes over very soon, and his relationships become not neighbourly and normal, but those of people filling roles in a drama written for them by Lawrence himself. On the other hand—this was the real centre to which he clung—he projected into his relationship with Frieda all the visceral passion which characterized his intense feeling, in youth, for his mother.

Thus the basic accusation of each side in the quarrel between the supporters of the poetic, and those of the prose method, is that the other side lacks hold over reality. What is true, is that each has its grasp, but that, for the reasons I have given, in each case the grasp is liable to become extremely tenuous. The bitterness of the pursuit of each for his particular hold over the real, is the cause for the recriminations that are so frequent, and for the violent swing of emergent generations whose members feel themselves to be 'real'—because they are not yet part of the literary conditioning—and an older generation whose hold over its own reality has become relaxed.

*   *   *   *

Just as the reality of the 'contemporary' novelists is open

to the criticism that it does not tell us enough about the inner being of these characters, so that of the moderns is open to the charge that, within the rules of any fiction, we cannot know that these people would think the images that the writer attributes to them. The characters in James' later novels seem to think in a language which is far closer to the rich idiom of the novelist, than any which his invented persons could possibly use. What we expect from the novel is that inner spiritual circumstances are projected by external material and social ones: that the idiom of inner thought of a character is justified by what we know of his outer history—his education, his idiosyncrasies, the things around him that strike into his depths, his emotions, etc. Unless these are provided, we may suspect that the persons in the novel are masks and mouthpieces for a sensibility and view of life which is that of the author. This suspicion, in different forms, arises in the novels of D. H. Lawrence and Virginia Woolf.

James Joyce, in *Ulysses*, provides the imagist poetry of the interior monologues of his main characters with outer novelistic references. Everything that becomes imagery in the thought of Bloom or Stephen Daedalus is supported by the set of circumstances which is the outward events to which it refers. This results in a novel which in one of its aspects is the poetry of inner lives: but in another is a directory providing every scrap of information—every street and name and time—to which the poetry refers.

Today there is a reaction from what is called the experimentalism of Joyce. . . . I think the reaction is inevitable because Joyce embarked on a course which was to combine an infinite exploration of individual sensibility with an infinite cataloguing of the outer events which produce the images that are the language of sensibility. Joyce invented a method for turning all experienced history and geography into an unending stream of idiomatic language. He had a method but he did not have a form: or, perhaps it would be better to say that his form was unendingness. It is significant that *Finnegans Wake* begins again at the beginning with the last sentence, which continues into the first. A form has to have beginning, middle and end. Young writers turn to more limited aims than those of inventing imaginatively the whole of modern life. For the aim of the modern was to create a literature which imagined modern life as a whole.

*　　*　　*　　*

There is an acting and reacting tendency among novelists and poets, for poetry to invade prose and for prose to invade poetry. The novelists who are closest to the poets, and the poets themselves, are greatly preoccupied with questions such as 'What is the real nature of the consciousness of the individual of acute sensibility in the modern world?' and 'What is the modern reality?'

There are also phases in which one or the other, the prose or the poetic, become the dominating mode. After a period of the poetic being in the ascendancy, we seem today to be in a phase when it gives way to the prose. This is obvious enough when one considers the current English novel, weighed down with sociology and written by class-conscious young people concerned not with inventing values of life, but with communicating information about their working-class origins, or the Red Brick University. But what is more symptomatic of the change is that poetry itself is invaded by the prose idea, the reaction against what is dismissed as a period of 'experiment'. The reaction is called 'consolidation' or the revival of traditionalism, or 'correctness' or 'clarity'. But of course behind these labels is the assumption that it is possible to be clear in a period of confusion, that it is possible to be traditional when the line of tradition has been fragmented, that it is possible to consolidate the 'experiments' of Joyce. Indeed, it may today be necessary to do these things, but only at the price of retreating into conventional aims and attitudes in order to relieve the poet of the pressure of the whole

modern experience, which broke through the bounds of conventions a generation ago: only in adopting an attitude towards
poetry which is the method of prose—the selection of outward
events from experience which can be correctly and neatly and
lucidly translated into poems which are paraphrases of the
experiences.

A recent spokesman of this invasion of poetry by the prose
principle is Miss Elizabeth Jennings in her little British Council
Pamphlet *Poetry To-day*. Here we are told that poetry today is

> markedly unlike much contemporary painting or sculpture; it
> eschews abstraction, even meaningful abstraction, and will have
> nothing to do with 'free expression', action painting, or any other
> artistic expression whose dominant element is irrational. It may be
> that poets today have felt the influence of the prevailing philosophy
> of linguistic analysis, that philosophy which works always from
> the principle of verification. Whatever the cause may be, the best
> poems written today abhor confusion and obscurity; they want to
> discover the truth about an experience, an event, an emotion, a
> person. Above all, they respect language, not as a lofty, tran-
> scendant medium but as a tangible vehicle for worthwhile meaning
> and honest reflection.

And later, she writes:

> Elegance and its counterpart, a sense of style, are usually found—
> as we can see even from a cursory glance at eighteenth-century
> verse—where there is also moral concern, a feeling for values.
> This respect for elegance and this feeling for values are to be found
> in all the best poets writing today.

From what I have written above, it will be clear that, to my
mind, this is the reverse of the application of the poetic principle
to the situation of modern writing. It is the application of the
prose principle to poetry. Imagism was the writer's open receptiveness to any experience which occurred to him as an image,
and his disciplining the form he used *by* the image: that is, whatever realized and liberated the image was justified, whatever
subdued it was rejected. But here we see principles of conscious

choice applied. For elegance, correctness, and, above all, reason, require thoughts suitable to go into elegant forms, correctly expressed in rational language. One's suspicion that Miss Jennings' idea of poetry is neatly patterned and rhyming prose is confirmed when one reads that the poets who are her respected contemporaries 'have felt the influence of the prevailing philosophy of linguistic analysis', a philosophy which could render poetry superfluous.

Poets are content not to go beyond what fits into the graceful poetry of intellectual toughness. The modern movement disintegrates with the view that formal poetry is an activity with limits defined by intellectual criticism. The prose consciousness, for the time being, triumphs.

VI

A SHORT HISTORY OF THE PERS. PRON.
1st SING. NOM.

THE modern aim was essentially the re-invention of
reality: re-presentation of the shapes and forces of a new
world, and also of a modern kind of sensibility. Thus Eliot
wrote in *The Egoist* in his review of *Ulysses* when it first appeared
that 'It has the importance of a scientific discovery.' He admired
the parallel of the Homeric myth as a wonderful inventive device
for conveying the chaos and anarchy of modern life which Joyce
set against the foil of an heroic age. He was to use mythology
for the same purpose—of relating the modern to the past—in
The Waste Land.

The moderns considered that sensibility had itself altered as a
result of the obsessive modern situation. Already with the French
impressionists, this double aspect of the modern—that the thing
observed is changed, and the observer also is changed in his
manner of perceiving—begins to appear. Impressionism is not
only a 'more scientific' way of looking at nature in an age of
science. It also suggests the way in which the eye, conscious of the
mechanism of vision, sees light. But to be conscious of the way the
eye sees and to represent this as well as the thing seen is to make
art partly out of the mechanics of seeing.

The mode of perceiving itself becomes an object of perception, and is included as part of the thing perceived. Here again painting provides examples. Cubists do not just analyse the structure of objects, they also impose on the object the simplifying, abstracting, yet multifold way of seeing things which is their own and which they claim to be surely modern because it represents the approach to things of men living in a scientific, analytic, abstracting age, their absorption in the mechanics of things, their alienation from nature, and the simplifying effect on vision of living in an age of speed. Movement flattens out objects, simplifies, and makes forms seem more abstract.

What corresponds in poetic writing, to this representation within the work of the mode of perceiving, is the altered attitude of the modern writer towards the rôle in his work of himself as 'I'. The writer, present within his work, puts himself into a communicating relationship to the reader.

It would be interesting to make a study of the significance of the *pers. pron., 1st sing. nom.* in imaginative literature. Here I can only caricature such a history in order to indicate why the moderns made such a determined effort to disorientate or shatter or replace the 'I'.

Traditionally, this by no means egoistic first person is the 'I' who acting, as it were, on behalf of both poet and reader, falls in love, is filled with wonder before nature, believes, judges, errs. 'I' is, 'I' does, 'I' sees, and 'I' suffers. 'I' has faith by virtue of a mode of being and moral feeling shared with the reader. In literature the 'I' traverses some barrier which divides the indivi-dual—even the communal—mode of awareness from egotism, only when it [the 'I'] insists on the peculiar and separate nature of 'its' feelings or experiences from those which the reader may admire but which cannot altogether be his. The 'I' of the writer is consciousness of beliefs and values, in which the reader participates.

The 'I' then—if it does not go beyond the boundary where it becomes egotistic—is the sign for a fusion of experienceable values shared by writer and reader in a situation in which the writer's consciousness 'stands in' for the reader and enacts experience created in the work. When writer and reader belong to a community which provides as it were a continuous context of values and beliefs enclosing them both within the same symbolic referents, then the 'I' is also 'we,' and 'thou' and 'he'. This may have been how it was in Chaucer's and Shakespeare's times. But in, for example, an aristocratic society of intellectual pretensions, like that of eighteenth-century England, the 'I' may come to represent only the conscious superiority of an intellectual class, or an aristocratic variation of the 'natural man'.

The seventeenth-century 'I' of John Donne seems to us close to the modern 'I'. For what is closer to us than the miracle-producing individualism of Renaissance artists is the multiplicity of persons, of whom Donne is conscious in himself, and which he dissects in his poetry:

> When thou hast done, thou hast not done
> for I have more.

Donne was consciously exceptional, not just through rank or even talent, but through being John Donne. It is true that his poetry is largely autobiographical and is self-analytical. Yet he is all these modern things in ways which are unlike ours today. He is outstanding through the strength and violence of intellect and passions which separate his selves into categories of courtier, wit, lover, philosopher, theologian all in the style and manner of his time. He brings his intellect to bear upon himself as lover, sinner, religious, satirist, splitting the image of himself apart as though it were stone under the hammer of a master sculptor. His self-examining reveals passion and mind belonging to the most energetic life of his own time. His poetry might of course provide plenty of material for a modern psychologist to analyse, but there is nothing of the psychological analyst in Donne himself. He never stops to say 'how strange I am'. Metaphors of charts frequently appear in his poetry, and he can trace the journeys of his soul and body clearly across a world which is mapped by theologians. The 'I' of Pope's poetry, while strongly portraying his intellect and eccentricities, is known to him only in its critical attitudes, reasoned faith, aristocratic and literary alliances and enmities. Pope projects his 'I' as a correct incisive consciousness; intellectual and informed, taking sides with the establishment when its members have the same qualities, deriding those who are fools, poor, or the opponents of his patrons and friends; he transforms into his transparent poetry the attitudes of an intelligent aristocrat, and he extends no charity towards slums and mad-houses. He can strike the note of noble generosity in his friendships, of Baroque piety in his beliefs, and of intellectual beauty in his art.

It is the Romantics who are nearest to the moderns. The Romantic 'I,' reacting against the exalted but limited and transparent intellectual 'I' of the eighteenth-century élite, projects the 'I' from which art has never quite escaped since—the seductive artistic 'I' which suggests that what is art for the artists, might become life for the spectator and reader living out Romantic feelings. Every reader is free to imagine himself to some extent a potential Byron, Keats, Shelley or Dylan Thomas not in writing his Romantic poetry, but in taking over his feelings and behaviour, sharing his self-destruction, loving his women, drinking his drinks.

What Keats called the 'egotistical sublime' that is the 'I' in Wordsworth, is different from the later Romantic's offering of his poetry as the reader's life. Wordsworth has the Romantic solitude, but it is of an exalted, disciplined and severe kind. 'It is', as Keats observed, 'a thing per se and stands alone'. One suspects that it has a lot to do with the will. It is a concentration in himself of Miltonic qualities of moral purpose grandiosely imagined, in which his time appears to him to be deficient, and an Atlaslike determination to use the work of his imagination to support a falling world.

The Romantics fascinate us even when we have ceased to tolerate more than a limited selection of their poetry. When we have criticized and related their achievement to that of earlier and later poetry, it still seems difficult to keep them in their place in a mental picture of the whole of English poetry. Nor can we ever quite dissociate their haunting personalities from their actual work. Perhaps this is because we are so conscious in them of the displacement of the 'I', which in earlier poetry has such a clear position and forms such definite links between the poetry and the reader. The Romantics were forced back on to themselves in the great crisis of the breakdown of eighteenth-century values at the time of the French Revolution, and the beginning of the industrial revolution. So they remain, when all has been said, convincing in the inevitability of their isolation. They provide the first examples of the poet becoming the poetry.

One reason why we cannot really dismiss them—I mean dismiss something about them which remains a concept of the poet inseparable from the poetry whatever selective discrimination we apply to the mass of their works—is apparent I think when we consider the Victorian poets. For the Victorians reversed the Romantic process whereby the poet becomes the poetry. With the Victorians the poetry becomes the poet. When Shelley cries: 'Oh! lift me as a wave, a leaf, a cloud! I fall upon the thorns of life I bleed!' we may smile, but we cannot altogether consider it as Shelleyan self-pity. In the sweeping context of the poem the poet has become identified with the poetry and this 'I' is the spirit of poetry itself within the Romantic situation which is the poet's own life.

In Tennyson the Romantic 'I' ceases to express the potentiality of the reader to become Tennysonian. The superiority of the poet as penetrator with piercing eyes, voice from cavernous throat, is implied and presumably carries over into his excursions into liberal politics and religious doubts: this 'I' disclaims any reader who would identify with it, except when it is the autobiographer's 'I' using poetry to ask the reader for sympathy, as in *In Memoriam*.

If it seems impossible to our sensibility quite to dismantle the Romantics as our intellects may tell us to do, it is, for the opposite reason, difficult to reinstate the Victorians. We are too conscious of the Victorian poet, with his superiority, his sense of high mission, his prophetic voice and solemn appearance, frozen into the poetry.

There was nevertheless, in certain nineteenth-century writers, at times that peculiar sense of the exposure to a reality which is so overwhelming that the conscious ego which holds opinions, which is man of letters, which asserts itself even as 'poet', seems to be shattered. This is the 'modern' note in Arnold, Clough, Hopkins and Hardy.

When Tennyson was concerned with science or religion, he was greatly (and honourably) worried by the question of what attitude he should adopt. There is a lot of Shall I? shan't I? about *Locksley Hall*, *The Lotus Eaters* and *In Memoriam*. Shall I be a liberal and perhaps betray the country to philistine progressive industrialists, or shall I be a conservative, and thus perhaps sacrifice art to philistine lords? Shall I write poetry, or throw myself away and be begetter of a dusky tribe in a South Sea island? etc. . . . But Matthew Arnold strikes the modern note when he stands on the shore of Dover Beach and meditates on the 'ignorant armies' that 'clash by night'. Arnold is there in the poem, of course, but the 'I' has become as it were a conductor between the external terror of modern history and his utterly exposed consciousness to forces he cannot control. The 'Ah, love, let us be true' only emphasizes the helplessness, like a crumbling breakwater against a stormy shore.

What is true of Arnold is still more true of Hardy, whose very self-questioning connects his sense of outward fatality with his innermost dark sensibility. And Hopkins' religion helped him to that destruction of the 'I' in his poetry which made him the first great modern English poet, disapproved of by his co-religionists.

In the sketch I am here roughing out, the development of the melancholic weary-Willy early 'I' of Yeats to that of the man involved in theatre business and politics of the middle years of the great 'I', stricken with consciousness of old age and death and who declared

> I have prepared my peace
> From learned Italian things
> And the proud stones of Greece,

should be revealing of how 'I' was transferred from 'Mask' into acted upon consciousness, in the work of the greatest modern poet in English.

*   *   *   *

By the end of the nineteenth century the 'I' becomes the mask, the persona, which is a projection of the stylized pose of the poet acting a rôle in real life. The drunken, affected, vitiated mask of a Wilde, a Lionel Johnson, or a Dowson, is partly a defence against the public, a refusal to become involved in the self-betrayal of playing an accepted rôle, and partly a sophisticated and self-conscious variation of the Romantic poet becoming the poetry. In ninetiesh poetry the 'I' is both the poet subjectively, and the poet regarded by himself as 'he'. In Wilde and the early Yeats the 'I' is regarded ironically but the irony is at the expense of the public, not at the poet's own expense. The poet deliberately produces before his public an impression of mocking frivolity: but alone, to himself, he is all wearied seriousness rhapsodizing to the moon. Satyr satiric to his public, the 'I' of the 1890's is to himself harlequin, a symbol in a symbolist poem.

Study of the 1st person singular in poetry would make sense of connections which otherwise seem rather obscure: for the 'I' is the connecting link between the poet himself and the responsive personal consciousness of the reader. One cannot write 'I' in a poem without assuming a relationship with a *thou* who reads it, though in some cases this *thou* might be oneself. Thus to trace the use of the 1st person singular between a poet in various phases of his writing is to trace a secret development. In the Eliot of *Prufrock* and the *Hugh Selwyn Mauberley* of Pound, the Prufrock and Mauberley are the 'I-he' figures of the 1890's: only the mask, the symbolism, have become the objects of ironic self-mockery.

I have tried to show that when the poetic 'I' ceases to participate in a living community, that is to say, to be the mouthpiece of a consciousness which is common to people who are close to nature, to heaven and hell, to birth and death, then it becomes alienated from the wholeness of experienced life, and becomes attached perhaps to an intellectual élite, perhaps to an aristocratic cere-monial caste, perhaps to a priestly monkish one: or perhaps the poet is thrust back, as were the Romantics, on to a poetic bio-graphy which imitates the dream and aspirations and despair of the poetry: the poetry became the poet's life so that we can never really separate the strands of the *Ode to the West Wind* from what we feel about Shelley, and perhaps should not wish to do so. Perhaps, like the Victorians, the poet sets himself up as the image of the poet as it exists in the mind of the bourgeois.

The modern imagist attempts to operate upon the 'I' by trans-forming the action of art into acting experience directly upon the sensibility, thus short-circuiting it. This is, I have suggested, what survives from the imagist method, which is more important than its programme of having poetry consist of nothing but images. It is the view of poetry advanced by Rimbaud in his famous letters to Georges Izambard and to Paul Demeny, written on the 13th and 15th May 1871. The justification of the systematic disordering of all the senses in order to attain the unknown, is that it cuts out that which is consciously the poet or man of letters who writes 'I'. Instead, the nerves and brain become mere instrument on which experiences write. 'C'est faux de dire: Je pense. On devrait dire: On me pense.' 'Car JE est un autre.'

So the 'I' undergoes a transformation, a mutation. What is eliminated is the subjective self-consciousness that comes between receptive sensibility and events acting upon it.

Henry James' attitude towards art as an impersonal force creating its own values, his total lack of interest in opinions—his own or anyone else's—his style the responsive instrument of the area of his spread-out sensibility—this is the modern attitude as against the jaunty little contemporary 'I' of H. G. Wells, acting as an interpreter between Wells' often poetic material and the reader.

The contemporary thinks that he must cut his view of life to the measure of his own conscious 'I', which has opinions, beliefs, etc., and a character which goes on defending itself in his works and opinions. Thus the measure of every line H. G. Wells wrote was the temperament, feelings, opinions, *Weltanschauung* of H. G. Wells. The same is true of Shaw, Bennett, Galsworthy, the Georgian poets, and certain recent writers such as C. P. Snow and Kingsley Amis. They have a clear idea what they know, and what they think—of their likes and dislikes. Everything they produce is in the correct proportion to this whole view of themselves as keepers of their own consciences. They are like people who know how much money they have in the Bank of Social Responsibility and Conscious Awareness—whether they are drawing out six pence or five pounds, what proportion this is of the whole of their resources, and how it relates to the surrounding economy.

Leopold Bloom and Stephen Daedalus are instruments of the writer's projected sensibility acted upon by immensely powerful streams of events which they apprehend, giving them a characteristic Bloomian or Daedalian colouring. The interior monologue is not—as I once myself thought—a super-real device for expressing how streams of thinking actually go through people's heads. It is the conductor through which the external world passes in order to realize itself as interior world in Joyce's particular kind

of poetic writing. It is the method of Rimbaud: 'For *I* is someone else. If brass wakes up the trumpet, it is not its fault. To me
this is obvious: I witness the unfolding of my own thought—I
watch it, I listen to it. I make a stroke of the bow, the symphony
begins to stir in the depths, or springs on to the stage.' Joyce
portrays convincingly the way in which Bloom or Stephen might
really have *been* thought by their environments. Their thoughts
are demonstrably within the contexts which act upon their sensibilities. However, no-one could really think like them. Bloom's
and Stephen Daedalus' thoughts have the same kind of relation to
their characters as the blank verse speeches of Shakespeare have
to his heroes and heroines. Shakespeare convinces because these
speeches express the given situation in which his characters act
and are acted upon by events. Joyce realizes through the channels
of his people within their situations the modern world, and
brings it into a striking and critically aware relation with the
ironically viewed world of Homer:

> So warm. His right hand once more more slowly went over
> again: choice blend, made of the finest Ceylon brands. The far
> east. Lovely spot it must be: the garden of the world, big lazy
> leaves to float about on, cactuses, flowery meads, snaky lianas
> they call them. Wonder is it like that. Those Cinghalese lobbing
> around in the sun, in *dolce far niente*. Not doing a hand's turn all
> day. Sleep six months out of twelve. Too hot to quarrel. Influence
> of the climate. Lethargy. Flowers of idleness. The air feeds most.
> Azotes. Hothouse in Botanic gardens. Sensitive plants. Water-
> lilies. Petals too tired to. Sleeping sickness in the air. Walk on
> roseleaves. Imagine trying to eat tripe and cowheel. Where was
> the chap I saw in that picture somewhere? Ah, in the dead sea,
> floating on his back, reading a book with a parasol open. Couldn't
> sink if you tried: so thick with salt. Because the weight of the
> water, no, the weight of the body in the water is equal to the
> weight of the.

VII

THE WORLD OF MECHANICAL
METAMORPHOSIS

THE art of the past is attached to traditions, values, symbols, objects, nature, which had, until modern times, a relative stability. Modern art moves within a world which, in all these respects, is shifting.

★   ★   ★   ★

Many things that formerly signified rootedness and permanence —trees, rocks, the rotating seasons of country life—today have become significant almost of their opposite: the destruction of unspoiled nature by machinery, the breaking of links connecting the present with the past. It is as though what stays still moves backwards, recedes, against the onrush of the transformed world.

Not, of course, that the Nature of 'nature poetry' has ceased to exist. But there is less sense that it is organically continuous with the most perceptive contemporary sensibility. It has become a background for the restlessness of those who are bound to leave it, who may, indeed, be involved in destroying it. In Dorothy Wordsworth's Journal, for the lake poets to live near Derwentwater still appears to indicate their plausible choice of a pastoral life as distinct from an urban one. The country life, although unsophisticated, still bears the stamp of what is in some ways a superior, more permanent civilization. The vagrants, victims of war or industrialism, who play such a rôle in the Journal, and in Wordsworth's poems, are in part emissaries who justify the lake poet's seclusion by telling stories of the corruption and loss of innocence of the alternate world.

But whereas, still in Wordsworth's day, nature was a true alternative to the urban, today the urban consciousness absorbs nature. Even those who live in the country become part of it.

Nature for Lawrence, who hated industrial towns, is not the background of a centennial past older than that of cities, which can be returned to as roots. Nor is the relationship of urban to rural life for him complementary, as of pastoral nature to the cultivated court, nor even one of choice, as with Wordsworth, of steadfast and potent nature against uglifying progress. It is, rather, a drama of life-forces in the individual, in which the impersonal forces of machinery and socialization are destructive to the inhibited life forces still present under the surface consciousness. In this drama, sometimes hopefully, but sometimes pessimistically viewed, Lawrence increasingly puts forward the view that if modern man is defeated in his 'phallic' consciousness then the darker animal and vegetable forces of nature will take their revenge. The machines will wreck one another and the tigers, lizards and ferns triumph over the twisted steeel of their wreckage:

> So mechanical man in triumph seated upon the seat of his
>   machine
> will be driven mad from himself, and sightless, and on that day
> the machines will turn to run into one another
> traffic will tangle up in a long-drawn-out crush of collision
> and engines will rush at the solid houses, the edifice of our life
> will rock in the shock of the mad machine, and the house will
>   come down.
> Then, far beyond the ruin, in the far, in the ultimate, remote
>   places
> the swan will lift up again his flattened, smitten head
> and look round, and rise, and on the great vaults of his
>   wings

will sweep round and up to greet the sun with a silky glitter
   of a new day
and the lark will follow, trilling, angerless again,
and the lambs will bite off the heads of the daisies for friskiness.
But over the middle of the earth will be the smoky ruin of iron
the triumph of the machine.

*   *   *   *

We inhabit a machine of living. We belong to society.

You might divide our mechanical and social environment into
landscape, *house*, *horse*, *church* and *state*. Before, say, the end of the
eighteenth century, of these five, three were, comparatively
speaking, constants. *Landscape*, *house*, *horse*, were centennial,
carrying forward to the grandchildren and their children the
shaped thoughts that poets have from a common enduring
symbolism, as from marble. The fact that symbols of authority
and belief would survive justified the claim hurled to the stars
that the poet's work was immortal. Immortal, because it had the
shape of mortal images that might endure a few generations.
'Not marble, nor the gilded monument / Of Princes shall out-
live this powerful rime.' But rime lasts because it is up-borne on
winged marble, gilded monuments, and the blood of Princes.

Today only a very ruinous old house has any look that it might
—if the authorities were kind—survive for several generations.
The modern house belongs to the mythology of metamorphosis:
it is made of steel and concrete, but it will give birth to a better
job, done in plastic. *Horse*, which had changed into the abstract
horse-power I always imagined when I was a child to be locked
under the bonnet of the Ford Tin Lizzie, has changed since then
into the biplane, the monoplane, the jet aircraft, the rocket that
can shake up the dust on the moon.

State of course, and its values, were nearly always symbols of
the contemporarily inconstant, and only when one looked back
to Rome (so long as one did not look too close) signified permanence of unshakeable power. The dream of a settled society is

always nostalgic and is only realized in the pure fantasy of a Golden Age.

Anxiety about the State is a chronic condition at all times. Often it provides the 'modern' element to be found in much past literature. That is no doubt why we may (perhaps too self-indulgently) find ourselves in sympathy with unhappy periods of history which seem to mirror our own social anxiety. Or, by the attraction of opposites, it may be why we try to attach our intellectual will nostalgically to what seems least our own circumstances: classical styles in settled communities with fixed institutions. But the 'institutions are necessary' of T. E. Hulme, the supporter of anti-Romantic, dry classical modernism reconciling Cubism with Byzantine painting, led to the politics of Ezra Pound.

A simple way of describing the modern situation would be, then, to say that it is one where Nature has become penetrated by the characteristics of human nature. Modern man, with the help of science, has projected the temperamental restlessness, the duality, the ambition, of man-at-any-time, the wars and revolutions and the materialist evolution of his societies, into the animal, vegetable and mineral kingdoms.

As Kurt W. Marek writes in *Yestermorrow:*

> In our technological age, man can conceive of nothing that he might not invent. A magic carpet is no longer a scientific problem but only a problem in construction. All the pipe dreams of the old high cultures can today be made to come true, but some of them are so primitive (like the magic carpet, for example) that it is no longer worth the trouble. The pipe dreams of the men of the old high cultures appear to have been consummated in the same historical period as the old high cultures themselves.

Man's most recent invention, atomic fission, is scandalous to the life of the imagination, because it suggests an obscene union of perverted will with power to disturb the immoveable centres of nature, against which change could be measured. It outrages the imagination by introducing the picture of a world in which there is nothing solid left that, for the purposes of metaphor, can be referred to. The Future allied to the past has been the Promised Land towards which the poets guide their poems. Today, the most potent image of the Future has become the abyss. The imagined has become the unimaginable.

Yet we have to proceed on the hypothesis that the future is solid. We can do so, noting only that what was the staying power of 'marble monuments' has now become hypothetical. Matter itself is hypothesis.

*　　*　　*　　*

Unless our civilization is destroyed, the clearly forseeable future is the continuation, at an ever-increasing pace, of the transformation of the environment by science.

A world, in which the inventions of scientists are realized in the transformation of nature after the image of their utilitarian dreaming, undermines the referents of art, and to some extent parodies artistic processes. Everything that can be changed into machinery, or by machinery, is its medium, and every form it invents expresses the same theme of man's control over nature. And in converting all things into the symbols of this transforming agency, it also undermines their capacity to symbolize anything else. So the metamorphosis of objects in which we live is a kind of parody of individualist art. It expresses wishes, dreams, experiences, visions, but they are both everyone's and no-one's. The inventor, the artist, becomes lost in the realization of function. It may be true that nothing is more beautiful than the most recent jet aircraft, but any desire that the designer may have had to express his own feelings is absorbed into the needs of the aircraft to achieve the greatest possible efficiency in perform-ance, and thus whatever aesthetic qualities it may have are dictated by these impersonal forces, and, in that sense, are accidental. We know that if a very ugly machine was safer and quicker then this aircraft would be very ugly. Moreover, the personal consideration that finally qualifies the impersonal efficiency of the aircraft is the average needs of comfort of the passengers. So what began by the creative insight of Leonardo foreseeing the possibility of a flying machine, ends as an instrument for which the formula of the design is dictated by necessities of forces of nature, qualified by average human needs.

So the world brought into being by science is a simulacrum of human wishes symbolized in the transformation of things. Nevertheless it is one in which the consciousness of the individual scientist is absorbed into the purely objective considerations which govern the form of the product. It has to function, it has to be marketable, it has to be averagely useful. If the Romantic Comedy of the Industrial Revolution, which was supposed, after various unhappy episodes (such as the Babes lost in the Woods of Victorian factories and slums) to end in an earthly paradise, in fact ends in universal disaster, it will not be possible to say who was the author of the tragedy.

The modern world is the expression of human inventive genius stimulated by the irresistible urge of the human dream of Progress. If there were not so much subhuman misery in the world it would be possible to reject progress on account of its impersonality. But in fact progress does offer the means of overcoming poverty, of solving even the problems of its own creating. For a contemporary to oppose it for the sake of the traditions of a personal art is to run his face against three-quarters of humanity for the sake of the monuments of the dead.

Yet the automatism of the world of scientific invention, governmental power, and consumer needs, results in a sense of everyone living amid doomed impersonal, and perhaps self-destructive, forces. In the course of arrogating to himself such immense powers for realizing his vision in steel, concrete, plastics, energy, man has not been able to build into the system of mechanistic wish-fulfilments corrective checks to his own impulses. Thus the machinery of progress, while undoubtedly adapted to diffusing the material benefits which fulfil needs of charity and justice, also multiplies to an almost infinite extent the powers of the forces of self-interest. Both principles, justice and injustice, charity and power, are equally realizable by progress. The individual finds himself an ineffective spectator of the competition between forces of constructiveness and destructiveness within the material achievement of machine-realized wishes.

So early in the industrial revolution there were poets, like Shelley and Blake, who wished to correct the impersonality of science by injecting into the life around them the personal qualities of imagination. Such a wish was expressed in Shelley's assertion that the poets were the 'unacknowledged legislators' of mankind. Shelley's claim contained a grain of truth. His own poetry inspired socialists like William Morris, and perhaps his views on marriage have contributed to the change in the laws of divorce. But in the long run Shelley draws attention to the shrill weakness of the poetic voice raised against the scientific mind, the great inventions and interests of the industrial age. The weakness is that of any voice which speaks against power on human or personal grounds.

On the whole the visual artists have proved sympathetic to progress, while the poets have turned, to an extent which may prove limiting to the future of poetry, against it. Painters and sculptors are Renaissance-minded. Modern poets have a long tradition of opposition (beginning with Baudelaire) to progress, hardening later into dislike of the Renaissance. Poets, like Apollinaire and the surrealists who tend to be most sympathetic to it, are those who are also closest in their relationships to visual artists.

The Industrial Revolution was, as I have pointed out, projected human dream. The Renaissance and the Industrial age both have in common resources of mental energy released in order to make great numbers of inventions streaming from studio or factory. A difference is that the criterion of the industrial age is primarily

utilitarian and only secondarily aesthetic, whereas the order of
these aims was reversed in the Renaissance. Renaissance artists,
even when they were inventing instruments of war, considered
that their works should be aesthetically beautiful. The ideal
of architecture was a house in which no-one could live. The
need for a home for orphans or a hospital was an excuse for
cloisters, statues and towers. Clearly some of the moderns,
particularly those who were visual artists, regarded the world
that had resulted from industrialism, as a Renaissance development which required only to be converted to beauty by art and
architecture. They welcomed the invention of new materials and
techniques and thought that if utility could be ruled by the taste
and creative genius of great living artists to whom governments
had given the means and status enjoyed by great architects and
sculptors during the Renaissance, then they would be able to
build cities more beautiful than any known to any past
civilization.

The breakdown of the modern movement was largely the
result of the disintegration of what was a movement common
to all the arts into the separate elements of each medium. The
literary artists withdrew into the conservatism of language. The
sculptors and painters are still carried on the wave of the technological revolution which proceeds at an ever greater rate within
the media that are accessible for use in those arts. In the book
Yestermorrow from which I have already quoted, Marek suggests
that painting and sculpture are even ahead of science in foreseeing
the shift in the relationship of the scale of man to the world of his
dreams realized by new techniques:

> More clearly than in the sciences the abandonment of man as a
> measure has been discernible in painting. But even in sculpture
> which, from Michelangelo to Maillol and Lehmbruck, was
> exclusively governed by the image of man, the departure from
> this image, begun by Archipenko, is evident. This coincided with
> the conquest of new materials (metal, glass, enamel, wire) which

deprived sculptures of their corporeity and brought them closer to artifacts. In constructions such as Richard Lippold's variations on the sun and moon, gigantic golden structures of brass wire, chrome nickel and stainless steel, the discussion of a possible 'artistic value', such as was sought in the nineteenth century, becomes meaningless. These patterns of metal whose charm cannot be defined by a classical aesthetician, have their counterpart in the lacework of colour with which the American painter Jackson Pollock, in the last years of his life, covered canvases sixteen feet long.

It is clear, I think, that in the early stages of their work, modern poets like Eliot, and, of a later generation, Auden, were nearer to the painter's approach to the problem of modern art, than in their later work. They were fascinated by phenomena which were specifically modern, and they regarded the city and the industrial scene as worlds to be conquered by poetry. In Eliot's poetry up to *The Waste Land* the atmosphere of London streets, fog, the squalor of rooms in boarding houses, wharfsides and the tar-polluted Thames, is everywhere to be felt. There is the pleasure of spiritualizing all this, seeing it as the expression of humanity. In Auden's early poetry there is a parallel attempt to make poetry out of the industrial scene visualized as symptomatic of the decay of society.

There was a possibility, already apparent in the poetry of Apollinaire, of poets converting whole tracts of modern experience into their imagery coloured by their feelings about the modern world, much as Marlowe was a large scale converter of the new world into his imagistic exuberant poetry. Perhaps one reason why there has not been an English language Apollinaire, or a twentieth-century Marlowe (if Dylan Thomas had begun early in his meteoric career to write poetic drama he might have been just this) is contained in the phrase 'an age of criticism' — indeed of philosophizing and theologizing. Poets like Eliot and Auden found quite early in their work that the search on which they were embarked was for significances of a kind which were not simply the conversion of large tracts of experience into poetic paintings. The searching intellectual and critical spirit was too deeply fused with their creativity for them to be content with naïve transpositions. They soon found, I think, that for what they wanted to say comparatively few images captured from the modern world had the symbolic intensity which they required.

It is possible to regret that, parallel with the highly critical searching for significance *within* modern life of Auden, Eliot and Empson, there has been so little poetry of a less critically conscious kind by writers of naïve vitality and brilliant eyes who were content to find significance in all things, as Picasso is able to animate everything his vision lights on. A more animated and naïve poetry might have fed a more searching and intellectual one, as Marlowe's poetry fed that of the early Shakespeare. One can only regret the tendency of some critics to berate Dylan Thomas, who was passionately involved in his own sensations, because he was not intellectually aware and technically strategic.

*   *   *   *

I am brought back to considering once again Shelley's sweeping generalizations. Although the rôle of poet as saviour of humanity which these suggest is extravagant, what is not absurd is the idea that poetry should imaginatively dramatize the intellectual and historic forces of the time. Shelley's ideas rest on the belief that the world we live in, with its politics, economics, institutions, laws, science, rich and poor, is an immensely tangled knot of habits, wills, dreams, prejudices, attitudes, and interests of human beings, a vast projected concretization of inner qualities of many human beings.

Since this is so, it is ideally reducible back to the qualities of existence, past and present, from which it derived. But although the forces of politics, interests, beliefs, habits, and so on, can be analysed, these are secondary effects of the human nature behind them, which remains irrational. If this were not so, then it would be the case that when the defective reasoning incorporated in social patterns was made clear, societies would resolve their problems on reasonable lines, as philosophers like Godwin thought they would. Some interested individuals, and some groups, doubtless might be afraid to do so, but it would be possible to persuade them that they had more to fear from being unreasonable than from being reasonable. Especially today, if human beings were rational, the main problems of the modern world could be solved in a matter of weeks. Knowing human nature as we do, even to say this is to say that within a few more weeks human beings would have created new problems.

There are extremely valuable systems of thinking for interpreting the public and private complexes of the modern world. Critics who complain about the decline of traditions, institutions, systems of belief and so on, forget that for the poet writing about the time he lives in, these are codes for interpreting the life around him, explaining human behaviour. The systems of Marx and Freud are, to the modern poet, valuable methods of interpretation, which dramatize the conflicts in society, and also in the psyche of the individual. If many beliefs and traditions have broken down it is not just because modern societies are materialistic, but also because they have ceased to provide satisfactory interpretations of human behaviour in modern life.

But useful as these instruments of analysis are, beyond the society which they revolutionize, the psychology which they adjust, there remains human nature.

Marxism is a philosophy of political and economic social analysis bound inseparably to a programme for putting the analysis into action. Most people would agree today that as analysis of the evils of nineteenth-century capitalism it is largely correct, whether or not they agree with it as a programme of action. But assuming the rationality of its doctrine of history, and that we accept the revolution as realization of reason through history, after the revolution we are still, as we have seen, left with political leaders, social engineers, who, putting into practice their system based on scientific politics and economics, have the same human nature as the leaders they have superseded. But they are given infinitely more scope for realizing it, owing to the increased efficiency of the police and thanks to technology.

Systems of political, sociological, and psychological analysis are therefore only instruments for enabling us to understand structures of society, economics, and psychology. To a certain extent they replace the old traditions and theologies. They are increasingly useful to the artist in the importance which they attach to symbolism, both in social institutions, and in a whole world of dream symbolism they have unveiled.

Apart from all this, they lack the wisdom of traditional and religious systems, to the extent that doctrines of perfectionism creep into their thinking. Communism is influenced by the idea that one day there will be perfect communist man; psycho-analysis by the idea of perfectly uninhibited and rational, psycho-analysed man: the one, abstract social man, the other the completely scientized individual.

We are brought back to the necessity of art because the acts of imagination which are poetry, music, painting, result from the immediate experiencing by means of the artist's senses, the whole of his being, of the circumstances of a time and a place. Art expresses the truth that despite all our systems of knowledge and analysis, to grasp, to get the feeling of our world, we are driven back on to ourselves, our own feelings. We cannot read what we feel off a chart, because we are not charts. Charts may be extremely helpful, but they are instruments. They are, indeed, part of the outside world which we have to comprehend. There is no doubt but Shelley was wrong in thinking that poetry could legislate for the social world. It was a crude error, for which he has received many reproaches. But he would not have been wrong if he had said that it can order inside worlds. And if it can order inside ones, it may, in the long run, at least influence outside ones. His error perhaps was a matter of mistaking the time-table. The answer to those who ask 'What can poets do to save civilization?' is not so much a plain 'Nothing', as 'Nothing in the given time.' Art is long and life is short.

But the ordering of inside worlds is important. They can be ordered because we can be sure that in understanding society we do ultimately have nothing to imagine except human nature. In the largest sense, the problem of poetry is to visualize the operation of human nature within magnifying and distorting circumstances—themselves the result of the concentration and accumulation of a great many human wishes and dreams—which produce the impression that we are dominated by nightmares and abstract forces.

For such acts of visualization we need help from outside systems which provide more or less mechanical, but nevertheless broadly correct, visual patterns. In the past there were traditional views. Today there are Marx, and Freud, and certain sociologists. Although there are abstracting tendencies in all of these, which encourage concepts such as that of 'social man', nevertheless the individual cannot understand his place in the modern world, unless he can make use of such maps. D. H. Lawrence, who could not bear the idea of charts, had to flee to primitive civilizations.

The modern movement began by being the struggle of imaginative man to hold within his own mind a picture of the whole world which was modern. Looking at it like this, I would say that the use of anthropology and mythology in *The Waste Land*, of psycho-analysis and Marxism in the early poetry of Auden, marked the turning point of the movement in literature. After this, literature ceases to attempt to use modern instruments of analysis to imagine the world. It turns back, uses analysis for the purpose of understanding only past literature. The creative movement becomes a movement in criticism, and starts to live off its own capital, the tradition. Writers cease to be moderns and become poet-critics, critic-poets and contemporaries.

PART THREE

NON-RECOGNIZERS, RECOGNIZERS, AND OVER-RECOGNIZERS

I

NON-RECOGNIZERS

B Y non-recognizers I mean those who do not recognize the modern situation, by recognizers, those who do recognize it, by over-recognizers those who recognize the modern to the exclusion of the past.

The Georgian poets, are, I suppose, the classic examples in English in this century, of non-recognizers.

The non-recognizer does not recognize the world of today, or the need to deal with it. He has the attitude to aesthetic enjoyment that the weekender has to the countryside. His true life, he maintains, is a world apart from the town, the office, the factory. What is 'real' for him is not all this world of material involvement but the moment when the train slides past the last houses of the city of a Friday evening, and the green fields begin. The cottage, the hawthorn bush glimmering in the darkness—ghostly reflection of the Milky Way—such nature, he decides, is going to be, for him, reality. The means whereby he earns a livelihood, the benefits he consumes as a result of other people earning theirs, the lives of the industrial population—all these are 'unreal', a nightmare imposed upon eternal values by frantic modern means.

The non-recognizers think there is a contradiction between modern life and poetic dream: that modern life can be got away from in the dream: that the dream is in some way beautiful, unworldly, 'ancient'.

The non-recognizers regard dreaming as an alternative to the nightmare of contemporary wakefulness. In the poetry of de la Mare there is a recurring image of England as the innocent dream of a child-like poet whose unconscious mind still inhabits a country which is a Garden of Eden, previous to the England of Blake's 'dark satanic mills':

> No lovelier hills than thine have laid
> My tired thoughts to rest:
> No peace of lovelier valleys made
> Like peace within my breast.
>
> Thine are the woods whereto my soul,
> Out of the noontide beam,
> Flees for a refuge green and cool
> And tranquil as a dream.

This is a ravishing poem true to the idea of an England still revealed in the countryside burdened with chestnut trees like castle walls, her green summer days and misted moonlit nights, her traditions still embodied in some moment which starts up out of the past like a sentinel—an English scenery and atmosphere which we identify with history. But of course it is not the England of industry and modern invasions. The 'truth' of the poem lies indeed in an imagery and a music (whose line appeals to the visual sense as well as to the ear) which make us aware of it as a vision, landscape we have seen, gossamer thought, all three of these together. Its strength is exactly the strength of that which is imagined and created in the poetry.

In one of his most tragic poems—written at the beginning of the First World War—*Motley*, reality invades de la Mare's dream, and it becomes nightmare:

> They are all at war!—
> Yes, yes, their bodies go
> 'Neath burning sun and icy star
> To chaunted songs of war,

> Dragging cold cannon through a mire
> Of rain and blood and spouting fire,
> The new moon glinting hard on eyes
> Wide with insanities!

The poem takes the form of a conversation between the Fool, Death, Love and Pity. The contrast it draws is between 'foul Satan' madness and 'simple happy' madness. A choice is implied between the dream or nightmare which derives from confrontation with real waking experience—the dream which is terrible awareness—and that which is dreaming about dreams—dreaming, that is to say, the dream of past poetry. De la Mare's poetry has many literary allusions: but they are not of the kind which uses the past as a cutting tool against the present: they are past literature become in the poet's mind the dream better than the surrounding world. This is the rôle played by the recollection of Ophelia's madness—the madness turned into the beauty of poetry—in the following:

> Nay, but a dream I had
> Of a world all mad,
> Not simple happy mad like me,
> Who am mad like an empty scene
> Of water and willow tree,
> Where the wind hath been;
> But that foul Satan-mad,
> Who rot in his own head.
> And counts the dead.

The 'simple happy madness' is a stage setting from *Hamlet*. The 'foul Satan-madness' is the waking madness of the Western Front. Such poetry is ingrown, mistletoe fashion, into the main trunk of English poetry. There, it is, within its limits, unchallenged. It might be the case that, a hundred years hence, de la Mare's poetry is read and the works of the 'moderns' forgotten. All the same, if this were so, it would be because history had shown the main task of a contemporary poetry—to imagine that which we know—was impossible in modern conditions, and that

M

poetry to be good today has to be 'minor'. What is crucial in de la Mare is his concept of dream activity as an escape of the mind of the poet into past poetry. Though one may disagree with his idea of what dreaming is, nevertheless he does make us realize that the essential nature of poetry is dream-work. He follows romantic, and—in some of Shakespeare's moods—Shakespearean precedent of exploiting the historic past as contemporary dream, fortress and granary of stored impressions, which are accessible to a modern, just as he uses childhood for the same purpose.

Walter de la Mare's poetry confronts us with a baffling question which would not have arisen before the twentieth century—how to describe his kind of dreaming. His dreams seem singularly pre-Freudian, out-of-date, to come from some region which is not that of his own subconscious sleeping. They have a purity and innocence which is unexpected in a twentieth-century dream. Yet Walter de la Mare's innocence was not of an unknowing kind. He was perfectly cognoscent of Freud, and his poems have many corridors and passages which open on to darknesses and night-mare. Childhood purity and innocence are to him one side of a medal on the reverse of which there is certainly evil.

His dreaming has a personal tone, a music individual to him; but it is not subjective or autobiographical. The reader does not feel that to analyse the dreams in this poetry would reveal much that is concealed about de la Mare's psychology. For one thing, they are not unconscious in that kind of way. De la Mare, one feels, knows himself very well, and does not write a poetry of involuntary unconscious self-revelation.

An epithet which would perhaps describe this kind of dreaming is mediumistic. It is really a reverie, a trance in which voices which are not those of the poet's ego speak. The voices are past voices, the voices of past literature. De la Mare's poetry is a medium whereby the spirits of past poets—or the spirit of past poetry—broods over itself. It is a murmuring like that of the spirit of the mother invoked by Yeats in *Easter 1916*:

That is Heaven's part, our part
To murmur name upon name,
As a mother names her child
When sleep at last has come
On limbs that had run wild.

In a country with a great history, a beautiful countryside, a great literature, one can imagine seeing ghosts, hearing in libraries in great houses the voices of dead poets. The past is stored experience and meditation, and although complete, because the actors in it are dead, for those who watch and listen intently, there seems a continuation of impulses stopped by death but still continuing within the stored words of works, a kind of overflow as from a reservoir.

The dream in Walter de la Mare is not sentimentalized, because it is impersonal, mediumistic. It is an objective dreaming of the moods, the seasons, the past, of England meditating over herself. It achieves one of the things that poetry can do, give voice to the past. His past is, it is true, recessive. His concern is not that which I have atrributed to Gerard Manley Hopkins, to reincarnate a faith and re-state it in the forceful terms of the industrial age. His ghosts do not speak a modern language, though they are not archaic either. His idiom, his metres, are such as to suggest that they speak to us in a language attuned to our ears, which nevertheless emphasizes the pastness of their lives, which have become our dream.

De la Mare's dreaming is not then made to seem sentimental by Freud because it is not personal, subconscious dreaming. It is the impersonal, mediumistic dreaming of the past in the mind of this purely devoted and attentive poet.

There is, however, a false kind of dreaming, in which the poet dramatizes himself as a superior being because he is a dreamer. This it seems to me is the defect of poetry of the kind of which *The Lake Isle of Innisfree* is an anthologized example.

In this famous poem of his early Celtic Twilight period, Yeats contrasts the Irish island with the 'pavement's grey' and the 'traffic's roar' of London. He will build 'a small cabin of clay and wattles made' on the lake shore, where he will 'live alone in the bee loud glade'.

In the dialectical language of the 1930's *The Lake Isle of Innisfree* is 'escapist'. But this seems dubious ground from which to attack a work of art. Why should the poet not escape from the traffic's roar, if, by doing so, he can fortify his own talent and strengthen our imagination?

The objection to this poem is on other grounds. *The Lake Isle of Innisfree* by substitution and implication sets up an ideal image of the poet, and through him, vicariously of an ideal reader, where strength ought to lie in the poetry itself. It substitutes for the limited but definite and concrete area of a created experience— 'a real toad in a real garden'—the vague, large, vulnerable idea of life lived for the sake of the poetic. It insidiously suggests that writing and reading the poem are a superior way of living. The poetic is elevated into a grail, the pursuit of which conjures up many ladies and gentlemen modelling their lives, or a corner of their lives, on an image which the poem suggests, of dedicated poetic life. The intentions and aura of the creator are substituted for the defined reality of the creation.

Walter de la Mare's poetry is, within its limits, impregnable because it remains on the far side of today.

But to create a world out of past values requires, of course, extraordinary consistency, courage, intelligence, powers of renunciation of the modern world.

All discussion about modern poetry is ultimately a debate about the relation of inner and outer worlds, the extent to which a certain ratio in past times of inner and outer life ordered traditionally can be maintained against the new and invading imagery of science, modern inventions, war, and societies which reduce the status of individuals to social units.

The modern world is forever busy transforming external

inventions and social systems into newer inventions and newer systems. But the modern view is that art, before it can become a 'criticism of life' must adapt to its own purposes, translate into its symbolic language, events and appearances explicitly modern. The 'non-recognizers' fail to make this adaptation, seeking indeed to avoid the issue by writing in conventionally accepted forms, used in conventional ways, choosing conventionally poetic subjects, and selecting from among their personal experiences, material in which the question of contemporary idiom does not arise. For them the modern is the banned world of the unpoetic.

In 1926, I. A. Richards summed up what seemed then a final judgement by a modern critic on the admired but regretfully dismissed poetry of de la Mare. His remarks are worth recalling because a good many young writers and critics would probably disagree with them today for reasons which are revealing of the extent to which doubt has been thrown on the aims of 'contemporary sensibility'. This is what Richards wrote:

> When in . . . *The Tryst*, for example, Mr. de la Mare does seem to be directly facing the indifference of the universe towards poor mortal longingness a curious thing happens. His utterance, in spite of his words, becomes not at all a recognition of this indifference, but voices instead an impulse to turn away, to forget it, to seek shelter in the warmth of his own familiar thickets of dreams, not to stay out in the wind. His rhythm, that indescribable personal note which clings to all his best poetry, is a lulling rhythm, an anodyne, an opiate, it gives sleep and visions, phantasmagoria; but it does not give *vision*, it does not awaken. Even when he most appears to be contemplating the fate of the modern, 'whom the words of the wise have made sad', the drift of his verse is still 'seeking after that sweet golden clime' where the mental traveller's journey *begins*.

Several assumptions of the modern point of view stand in judgement of de la Mare in this passage, and I think it is just these aims which have today been largely abandoned. One is, that modern poetry ought to awaken the reader to the situation of modern man in the scientifically revealed universe. Another is that after this awakening to the outside, to the not-self, poetry should then assist the reader to order the inner psychological structure of the inner self.

Today I think that writers have less inclusive, more limited and particular aims. Moreover, given the human condition in the world of atomic fission, some thoughtful readers may feel that de la Mare's use of poetry to contemplate a past where he withdraws—as it were with eyes wide open—into dreams, may offer the only consolation which will be possible to civilized beings in the future. De la Mare is exploring one of the potentialities of the imagination which began with the Romantics—and is especially conscious in Keats—of making out of poetry an alternative inner life.

Also it may not seem as clear today as it was thirty-five years ago that de la Mare's forms and idioms are dated. Young English poets are more likely to experiment with the kind of forms that Walter de la Mare used in considerable variety than to invent new forms.

For the time being, it is the modern manner that seems to have receded, and to date; the orchidaceous style of de la Mare, like a reverie of past literature murmured through half-sleep, seems no more and no less old world, than it already seemed a generation ago.

The idiom of young poets like Philip Larkin and Ted Hughes seems close not so much to that of de la Mare, as of his friend Edward Thomas. Edward Thomas might be described as having an easy conversational contemporary idiom realized in loose iambic patterns, either in blank verse, or seeming almost casually rhymed. He has few poeticisms and archaisms. He was as a young man a friend of Robert Frost, and the subsequent development of Frost suggests that had he lived he would have developed towards still more idiomatic speech used with greater self-consciousness, and stricter forms:

The rock-like mud unfroze a little and rills
Ran and sparkled down each side of the road
Under the catkins wagging in the hedge.
But earth would have her sleep out, spite of the sun;
Nor did I value that thin gilding beam
More than a pretty February thing
Till I came down to the old Manor Farm,
And church and yew-tree opposite, in age
Its equals and in size.

The observation is full of particularity, there is a personal tone felt throughout, the words chosen are precise and distinguished but without pedantry. If we can't quite think of this as equal with Yeats of the same period, or Graves, it is because the form—the pattern which separates material and rhythm and idiom from surrounding speech—seems adapted to what is described rather than its being transformed within the form. The manner remains a bit that of the note-book of an exceptional person and a close observer. But a young poet today might say: 'This idiom is as modern as I want without my having to be a modern.'

II

THE RECOGNIZERS

THE Georgians were, of course, finished as an influence by the time of the Great War, though several of the Georgian poets—notably de la Mare and Edmund Blunden—continued to write their best poetry, and Robert Bridges was still to publish *The Testament of Beauty*. In August 1914 Rupert Brooke hailed the war (as Rilke was doing in German) as a purification of the world of uncleanly materialism by the forces of poetry. It seemed the realization of the poetic. In an ideal action of right against might, the English soldier killed was to discover in the soil of a foreign land the mirror of his own beauty.

This attitude was shattered by the shells and mud of the Western Front. The immediate reaction of the poets who fought in the war was cynicism. The war dramatized for them the contrast between the still-idealistic young, living and dying on the unalteringly horrible stage-set of the Western Front, with the complacency of the old at home, the staff officers behind the lines. In England there was violent anti-German feeling, but for the poet-soldiers the men in the trenches on both sides seemed united in pacific feelings and hatred of those at home who had sent them out to kill each other.

There is a good deal of this hatred in the war poetry of Sassoon. The poet has become the poet-soldier identified with sacrificial youth, German as well as French and English, at the Western

Front. Poetry is youth, the middle aged and comfortable, not the Germans, are the enemies.

> If I were fierce, and bald, and short of breath,
> I'd live with scarlet Majors at the Base,
> And speed glum heroes up the line to death.

There was a modern style which seems hammered out of events themselves, the result of an immersion in the 'destructive element', the exposure to the action of the conflicts and forces and machinery, of this time, and not to an intellectual analysis of the poetic situation, nor through taking thought how poetry should adapt itself to the modern stature.

Recognition in Wilfred Owen's poetry is not head-work to evolve a new idiom, new forms. There is a general loosening of forms, and use of assonance to produce a minor key effect, but no intellectualization, no theoretic stylistic revolution. He had too little time to do other than adapt the means at hand. What is interesting is to note how well the Keatsian idiom can be twisted ironically to produce pity, terror and truth in lines such as:

> Whatever hope is yours
> Was my life also; I went hunting wild
> After the wildest beauty in the world,
> Which lies not calm in eyes nor braided hair,
> But mocks the steady running of the hour,
> And if it grieves, grieves richlier than here.

Keats could himself when writing about his illness and about his love for Fanny Brawne be almost as stark.

The irony in Owen is not the sophisticated irony of the poet mocking at events. It is, rather, his acceptance of the irony of events which mock at poetry. The poet makes his poetry partly out of admitting the force of the mockery, and partly by demonstrating that it can contain as much terrible reality as do events themselves.

He admits the mockery of poetry by events in the thoughts which return in many of his poems:

> But they are troops who fade, not flowers
> For poets' tearful fooling
>   and
> Heart, you were never hot,
> Nor large, nor full like hearts made great with shot . . .
>   and
> 'I shall be one with nature, herb, and stone,'
> Shelley would tell me, Shelley would be stunned:
> The dullest Tommy hugs that fancy now.
> 'Pushing up daisies' is their creed, you know.

Yet the lie of the poetic fancy is confronted by the poetic truth, the *terribilitá* of 'hearts made great with shot'.

> 'I mean the truth untold,
> The pity of war, the pity war distilled.'

In Owen's work the modern lies in the capacity of the poet, with rather little adjustment of the medium, to make poetry out of war.

Rimbaud thought that he should be exposed to the terrible reality of his time, allowing the cold and hunger and homelessness to strike poetry out of him. The poets and artists of the Western Front achieved this. There resulted works of terror and anguish which certainly represented the reality, even if they did not produce a style, and even though they remain somewhat isolated within modern English poetry.

I do not mean to draw a moralizing contrast between the works of Front Line poets and of non-combatants. All the same there runs through the poetry after 1914 and until the 1930's an implicit opposition between the attitudes of those who had suffered reality and those who intellectually apprehended it. The contrast is apparent if you compare, say, Ezra Pound's *Hugh Selwyn Mauberley* in which the human horror of the war is translated into the intellectual horror of youth slaughtered

> For an old bitch gone in the teeth,
> For a botched civilization

with the experienced horror of Owen's:

Foreheads of men have bled where no wounds were.
I am the enemy you killed my friend,
I knew you in this dark, for so you frowned
Yesterday through me as you jabbed and killed.

One discerns in this an underground theme of literature in
this century, the First World War contempt of the combatant
for the non-combatant.

* * * *

The non-combatants, feeling, as they did, the tragedy of the
war without experiencing it directly—were forced perhaps into
a position of exaggerated intellectualization. I have suggested
that imagism offered them the pattern for an intensely concentrated, objective, hard and impersonal kind of poetry, horrific
and yet unemotional. In imagist poetry, the distant object is seen
so clearly and in such isolation that it acquires an intensity which
makes up for the lack of immediate and personally felt experience.
Compare the poetry of Wilfred Owen with these lines by Pound
from *Hugh Selwyn Mauberley* about the same Western Front:

> Died some, pro patria,
>   non 'dulce' non 'et decor' . . .
> walked eye-deep in hell
> believing in old men's lies, then unbelieving
> came home, home to a lie,
> home to many deceits,
> home to old lies and new infamy;
> usury age-old and age-thick
> and liars in public places.
>
> Daring as never before, wastage as never before.
> Young blood and high blood,
> fair cheeks, and fine bodies;
> fortitude as never before
> frankness as never before,
> disillusions as never told in the old days.

Or, again, if you compare the immensely fabricated prose of Joyce which out of collected and selected carefully placed fragments of observation invents characters with the authority of immediacy in a passage such as the following from David Jones' *In Parenthesis* from which I have already quoted:

> Night-begotten fear yet left them frail, nor was the waking day much cheer for them. They felt each moment's more ample light, but a measuring, a nearing only, of the noonday hour—when the nescient trouble comes walking. Their vitality seemed not to extend to the finger-tips nor to enable any precise act; so that to do an exact thing, competently to clean a rifle, to examine and search out intricate parts, seemed to them an enormity and beyond endurance; as one, who, clumsied with fear or unnerved by some grief, seeks to thread needle or turn an exact phrase; for they were unseasoned, nor innured, not knowing this to be much less than the beginning of sorrows. They stood as a lost child stands in his fatigue, and gape-eyed, where tall Guardsmen, their initiators and instructors, moved leisurely about, well pleased with the quiet of the sector.

There is an influence of Joyce here and yet it is not 'literary' like Joyce.

The difference is between the work which comes out of life an object of experience, and that which comes out of intellectual comprehension of the experience. The non-combatant apprehends terrible reality as a mental concept.

Both positions are equally tenable. Competition between them, based on popular admiration for action and contempt for non-combatants, is irrelevant, though sometimes Mr. Robert Graves seems to appeal to such prejudices.

The work that is plunged in the destructive forces is affected as though by an electric charge. But when the charge is withdrawn, the writer or artist may no longer be capable of work of such power and authenticity. Thus it may happen that the poet who has been close to the most terrible experience and who has perhaps realized this in a work of power is, for the rest of his life, only able to create poetry that seems an echo of that which had immediacy. It is as though our century of the 'Western Front', concentration camps and atomic explosions conceals in the core of his history—like the fissionable atom—a truth which, if apprehended, destroys. Who hears too loud an explosion may be able to reproduce its effect on him, but later he is deafened and cannot hear the sounds of ordinary experience.

Robert Graves champions the soldier poet, the active combatant, against the poet who stays at home and sweats away at poetry about the fate of civilization in his study. He despises non-combatant poets from Virgil's day to that of the Second World War. In this, he doubtless represents one side of a real division which goes back to 1914–1918, when there were soldiers like Owen, Sassoon, Edward Thomas, Isaac Rosenberg, Read, David Jones, Blunden and Graves on the one side, and on the other non-combatants who gained esteem as voices of a disintegrated civilization, like Joyce, Eliot, Pound, Yeats and Lawrence.

Yet although virtues which are partly the result of participation in action show in the works of the first group of writers, and the lack of these qualities may be felt in the second group, the combatants cannot fully enter into the experience of our time. A characteristic of the twentieth century is that the destruction which hangs over the whole civilization is invisible, and if it comes, will destroy non-combatants as well as combatants; and since 1914, the appalling horrors which have taken place in concentration camps have left very few witnesses even of the facts, and almost no art by the victims. The most terrible, the most significant, and the most threatening experiences of modern history are overwhelming to those engulfed in them, whether they belong to a recent barbaric past which incredibly happened or a dreaded future which though incredible well may happen, which remains a mental terror, like a death sentence not yet carried out.

If one were to construct an image of the 'real' situation of being alive in our time it would not be of a First or Second World

War soldier, enduring horrors, wonderfully surviving and writing out of a deeper knowledge of events than his stay-at-home contemporaries. It would rather be of a man well fed, cared for by the state, comfortable, and admired, who sat at a typewriter on one side of a wall, on the other side of which there were victims of concentration camps doomed first to dehumanization and then to extinction. The expression of transcendence through art of this real situation would depend not on the suffering of the victim but on the capacity of the comfortably situated non-combatant to enter into, understand and invent a modern world of such events which included not only the victim but also himself.

War in our day is not just the experience of fighting. It is not even our famous wars—it is struggles going on across whole continents, sufferings that seem incommunicable, and which yet are felt as actuality affecting some, and as reality threatening even those who are far removed from action. This was true even of participation in two world wars. Although the combatants were immersed in the real fighting, beyond the fronts there lay the destruction of past values, and, above all, the emergence of invisible immensely destructive powers which pass through all lives, however we are situated, like invisible rays, waiting for the moment when they will actively destroy them. Therefore whether the poets and artists were combatants or non-combatants, the most consuming reality was invisible; but none the less operative, and growing every moment more powerfully destructive. The sensibility which was closest to the reality of our time had to be aware of the invisibility and by this I mean aware of the power struggles going on between governments, and the inventions being made in laboratories. But these forces, in their furthest potentiality, cannot be experienced, they can only be intellectually apprehended or intuitively felt. Thus, however we admire the work of combatants, it seems limited. It is the writers whose intellect has gone furthest into effects of the modern situation on civilization, or have felt most deeply conditions which they have not physically experienced, who seem to convey most the reality of our time.

The difference between Goya's *Los Desastres de la Guerra* (1810) and Picasso's *Guernica* (1937) is that with Goya the apprehension is the result of immediately experienced or immediately imagined terrible reality; with Picasso it is filtered through the mythology of the bull fight and heroic literature, both caricatured and distorted by consciousness of machinery. One has the feeling that Goya painted the greatest imaginable terrors of war. They remain imaginable because one can just envisage being a spectator even at the worst of Goya's scenes and coming away alive to be haunted for ever by them. But to witness the claustrophobic final horror which is *Guernica* would be to experience the screaming, floating moment of vision before extinction. It is a reality which passes beyond the barrier of the imaginable to the unimaginable and its images suggest therefore the transformation of the real into the unreal. Nor is this aim altogether unrepresentational because we are aware of experiences which seem just beyond the borderline of what we ordinarily think to be real—and if someone says: 'I went through a moment of unimaginable horror', we think that this might be described, but that if it were it would have to be in images that themselves were on the borderline of the unimaginable.

If a poet or novelist says 'My ambition is to write about the reality of our time' one does not think he means that he intends to portray just characters, behaviour, emotions, and scenery, but something which lies beyond these. One thinks of *reality* today perhaps as *power*, and one may also think that if an artist does not grasp this ultimate clue to our time, then his characters and the feelings, and even the nature he describes, are likely to be unreal. Thus in a world of revolutions, the novelist like Galsworthy who sees life through the eyes of his middle-class characters, who seem to take it for granted that their values are fixed, is open to the charge that his Forsytes are *unreal*, even though there may be people like them. On the other hand, a writer like D. H. Lawrence who, in his dialogue and in the way in which he imposes his own theories on his characters, sometimes seems to plunge into abysses of bathetic unreality, seems closer to reality than Galsworthy. This is because he describes situations in which his characters are themselves in search of a reality beyond their experience. This even has the curious result that Lawrence's unreal dialogue and situations produce an effect like that of distortion in modern painting in which the object appears to be distorted because its truth lies beyond verisimilitude.

The feeling then that the ultimate reality of our time is inapprehensible and can best be expressed by distortion of apparent reality, and the invention of systems, like cubism or vorticism—improvised ways of looking at things which 'for the time being' stand in for the true reality—is the result of our having 'contemporary sensibility'. It admits that the principle of reality in our time is peculiarly difficult to grasp, and that 'realism' is not an adequate approach to it.

DIALOGUE WITH A RECOGNIZER

A CRITIC who has not reacted against the modern move-ment towards academic traditionalism is Herbert Read. Primarily a critic of painting, he today is an exception among contemporary poets and critics in trying to keep open channels of communication between the arts.

A previous draft of this chapter began by being a consideration of Read as a critic who judged art (and, by implication, literature) entirely in the light of the relation of the work to the modern situation. In the course of writing it, I found that my remarks were taking the form of a debate with a position that I attributed to him. So I decided to turn this into a real debate by inviting him to answer what I had written. What follows is therefore partly a dialogue between him and myself. (In the course of re-writing, I have slightly modified the original position I took up, wherever I thought that what I had written would simply be misleading.)

My account of Read considered as Recognizer (I first called him the Over-Recognizer) began as follows:

'The Non-Recognizers are those who refuse to attribute poetic significance to what is specifically characteristic of the modern scene and who cling to hallowed poetic shrines, hallowed poetic living. The Recognizers (Over-Recognizers) are those who think that there is at any given moment an ideal completely correct contemporary attitude—like an image projected by historic circumstances upon the sensibility of the artist—and that the only work worthy of their serious attention expresses this image. Herbert Read is the outstanding example of a Recognizer.

'Almost any example of his occasional critical articles contains some passage revealing his consciousness of his position as a kind of time-diviner. Let him loose in an exhibition of contemporaries and he will point to the work which exactly projects the attitude suited to that particular day of the month and year. Writing of an exhibition of paintings by young artists held in Rome in the summer of 1955, he queries the list of exhibitors chosen by the English judging committee:

> Suppose we each made our ideal list—would it then differ in *general character* from the actual list? I do not think so. It might have included an abstract painter—but this would merely have brought it more into line with the lists from other countries.
>
> Not that abstraction, in the usual meaning of the term, is characteristic of this younger generation of painters. Of the purism, or absolutism, that we associate with names like Mondrian, Ben Nicholson, or the recent work of Victor Pasmore, there is hardly a trace. Instead we have various forms of the formless—paintings that look like a scraped palette, arbitrary scribbles in colours that have the dramatic flourish of a signature, and do indeed signify a personality, and nothing but a personality. This type of painting, which has been given the name of tâchisme (French, *tâche*—stain, spot, blot) is the only face that the atomic age presents to the world—a face of blank despair, of shame and confusion.

'In the 1930's Herbert Read was writing that the only way to paint was in the manner of Ben Nicholson's squares and circles. At the opening of the London surrealist exhibition in 1936, he jumped on to a chair and declared the "revolution of the word". In 1940, he was the ardent supporter, in poetry, of the New Romantics and Apocalyptics. A month to month diary of his critical opinions since 1918 would be an illuminating commentary on the art history of our times.

'Such a time-table would show many apparent inconsistencies, volte faces, absurdities. But Herbert Read might reasonably claim that the inconsistency lay in the development of modern history which is not continuous but violent, abrupt and contradictory, and demands constant adjustments of their strategy from artists. Throughout everything, he has remained loyal to the idea that every day he must rediscover and re-state the ever shifting relationship of contemporary sensibility to the time in which we live. The critic who in 1930 thought that the correct reaction of creative sensibility was shown in the purist squares and circles of Ben Nicholson, whereas in 1955 it was to produce "arbitrary scribbles" must surely think of the artist as a kind of seismographic needle (a self-respecting kind of needle with a conscience which, when there are earthquakes, records thin and exact lines in waves, but which, if asked to record an atomic explosion, very properly declares that it has no alternative but to produce ink blots and scribbles).

'One might describe Herbert Read's criticism as an attempt to interpret a really modern work of art as, ideally, a line on a graph recording the reactions to the development of history of some artist, and corresponding to another line on a graph which is the critical mind of Herbert Read. Occasionally, he writes résumés in which he puts his views in perspective and sums up the direction of art movements. But in these, as in his articles, he is always dominated by the idea that certain works are correct because they are "modern" and that certain other works, however good they may be by some standard he does not recognize, are incorrect because they are not "modern". And it is he who defines what is "modern".'

I break off at this point noticing that Herbert Read writes in the margin of my text: '*No. I merely accept the existential situation.*' This seems a good place to let him answer my argument. Other things that I wrote are apparent from references to them in his letter:

'I believe, as I think you do, that the critic's main task lies in the interpretation of his time; his subsidiary task is to re-interpret the past for the understanding of the present.

'That granted I, as an art critic (a term I never acknowledge, but there is only the French alternative, *écrivain d'art*) must try to interpret for the public each artist or phase of art that comes up for my consideration. Interpret implies explanation, appreciation, and so far as aesthetic quality is concerned, judgement.

'In this activity I must take care not to involve my personal tastes and predilections. I might even have to explain sympathetically an art I do not personally like—for example, expressionist art in general. But explain I must, if I am to be a critic and not just a writer who exhibits his personal tastes and predilections ("adventures among masterpieces" etc.). I claim that I am an objective, even a scientific critic, and in no way to be confused with uncritical enthusiasts.

'As for my personal tastes, it is absolutely unjust to imply that they have changed. As they began to form from the age of twenty-one onwards, so they have grown and been established consistently in my sensibility. They are not exclusively "modern". I admire Piero della Francesca with the same sensibility that I admire Ben Nicholson; El Greco with the same sensibility that I admire Soutine or Kokoschka; early Gothic or Mexican sculpture with the same sensibility that I admire Henry Moore.

You may say that these admirations are inconsistent. I deny it. I affirm that my sensibility is "open" whereas the sensibility of many of my opponents is "closed" by prejudice, convention and self-interest.

'In a more general sense, I think your misrepresentation of my critical attitude arises from an over-simplification of the complexity of the modern period—the modern epoch in art is superficially incoherent, but from the beginning of the Romantic Movement onwards to the present day there is a unity in its multiplicity. The unity is that of the liberated psyche trying to achieve integration in the creation of objective works of art (reification of the emotions); the multiplicity is that of many experimental but not inconsistent attempts to achieve such intergration. The only "split" is between the various levels of the personality; unconscious, ego, super-ego. What remains consistent (and I have repeatedly insisted on this) is the aesthetic criterion: there is no art, realistic, expressionistic or abstract, unless there is unity, harmony, integration of the elements of expression. I have insisted so often on these values, that I deserve to be called a classicist! It is therefore absolutely false to say that I acknowledge "no debt except to contemporary vision, constantly improvising its own self-sustaining standards above an acknowledged abyss".'*

'The Abyss is there, gaping wide, but the work of art, to adopt Erich Kahler's simile, is the Tower we construct to avoid a giddy descent into it. But it is a tower of many mansions—some little better than mud pies, others of brutal concrete, others aery and graceful, some piercing the clouds. The critic has to distinguish all these styles of architecture.

'You do not find a similar figure to guy in the world of literature, and it would be interesting to ask why. Eliot, Richards, Lewis—they are all too ambivalent for your purposes. That, from my point of view, is their weakness, and in one or two references to Eliot you seem to agree that it is a weakness. Paradoxical as it may sound, I would claim that my art criticism is far more consistent than the facing-two-ways attitudes of these literary critics. The New Criticism I regard as a retreat into the funk-hole of "objective analysis"; an incapacity to estimate contemporary values. It has killed modern poetry, whereas modern painting and sculpture remain vital. I don't claim the credit for this, but the whole arena of modern art has a dynamic freedom that is lacking in literature (drama excepted perhaps). A "new criticism" of modern art, is perhaps not unthinkable, but happily it does not exist.

Herbert Read's reply fills in my idea of the Recognizer.

'The critic's main task', he writes, 'lies in the interpretation of

---

* The remarks which I sent to Herbert Read concluded with this sentence.

his time'. By this, I suppose he means that the critic forms his own view of what is modern, that is of how the time should be interpreted, and judges contemporary works by this. In his Preface to *A Concise History of Modern Painting*, he explains his exclusion of 'such painters as Edward Hopper, Balthus, Christian Bérard . . . (who) certainly belong to the history of art in our time', on the grounds that their work is not 'specifically modern', and he goes on to define what he means by 'modern':

> 'I have already described this style as 'complex', but for all its complexity (which also implies variety) it has a unity of intention that completely distinguishes it from the painting of earlier periods: the intention, as Klee said, not to reflect the visible, but to make visible. That is, at any rate, the criterion of modernity I have adopted, and my exclusions are determined by it.'

The real difficulty here seems to be to discover a criterion which justifies Herbert Read's criterion. For it would seem to most readers, I think, that even Klee was not laying down a clear principle by which you can distinguish works which 'make visible' from those which 'reflect the visible'. Herbert Read's principle is puzzling when used to include the painting of Edward Munch, James Ensor, and Fernand Léger, while excluding that of Henri Rousseau. One sees here the predicament of those who consider that modern art interprets or presents the modern situation, and who think that past tradition provides no objective standard by which present work can be judged.

If Herbert Read does offer a 'criterion for justifying his criterion', it is perhaps a psychological one. The unity of the modern epoch of art which began with the works of the Romantic Movement is 'that of the liberated psyche trying to achieve integration in the creation of objective works (reification of the emotions); the multiplicity is that of many experimental but not inconsistent attempts to achieve such integration.'

Instead, then, of appealing to the standards laid down by a body of past works from which may be deduced objective standards,

Herbert Read appeals to the psychology of the unconscious ego. This process is perhaps that of trying to base objective standards on the Jungian hypothesis of there being a shared subjectivity of the collective mind. But the standard by which the works are judged, the unconscious patterns which they express, are derived from study of the works themselves, and the aesthetic argument is circular. The works are being approved by standards which a certain type of artist himself supplies in his work.

It is true though that ultimately all standards are derived from a body of work. But on the assumption that the modern experience and practice are totally cut off from the past, then one can only judge modern art by modern examples.

Herbert Read goes on: 'There is no art, realistic, expressionistic or abstract, unless there is unity, harmony, integration of the elements of expression. I have insisted so often on these values that I deserve to be a classicist!'

One sees what Read means, but his claim to be a classicist seems curious. The fact that one admires qualities of harmony, unity, etc. which one finds present, say, in the Parthenon frieze, and also in the painting of Paul Klee, does not make one a classicist. A Romantic is not a classicist because he admires the romantic qualities in classical art. What makes for classicism is not just observing rules of classical proportion, but interpreting into modern terms a tradition which lies in a past classical age and 'unity, harmony, integration of the elements of expression' are not a tradition, they are, rather, mysterious qualities of judgement present in the human consciousness wherever there is art. A tradition is an attitude to life outside art, which, nevertheless, is observed in classical art. That someone expressing his own subjective taste, which may be representative of the interior lives of his contemporaries, discovers relations in his work which have an affinity with those of classical works does not make him a classicist.

The idea implicit in the minds of Recognizers is that there is a gulf which divides the past from the modern. It is the sense of this

abyss which persuades Herbert Read that in judging the contemporary he has to have standards that derive from the situation
made visible through sensibilities that are entirely contemporary:
so that when he writes that he admires Piero della Francesca with
the same sensibility as he admires Ben Nicholson, he does not
mean that there is a continuous line of tradition which connects
two such widely separated artists, but that it is the same Herbert
Read who admires them both and that there are mysterious
qualities of harmony, purity and scale common to both. Herbert
Read is an explicit, trained and cultivated sensibility acquainted
with art of all times and places, an expert of the *Musée Imaginaire*
of Malraux which connoisseurs today carry round in their heads.
They admire classical Greek art and negro art because they discover in them the same qualities of harmony, proportion, etc.:
but this does not make them belong to the same tradition. The
problem of the external gulf in history which has caused a break
in the tradition is reconciled within the wholeness of and unity of
the sensibility.

At any rate this point of view is (as Herbert Read would agree)
the opposite of that which we find in the New Critics, whose
attitude is that at all costs we must find our way back into the
authentic, objective and external achievement of past tradition,
back to the values of living of these traditions. But the New
Critics have confined themselves to literature: as Herbert Read
points out, there is no New Criticism of painting.

The Modern Movement at its climax, which was just before
the First World War, was a movement of all the arts. This meant
in fact that it was a movement of painters followed by poets:
Picasso by Apollinaire in France, Gaudier Brzeska by Ezra Pound
in England. Its aims and values were those of painting, the idea
being that, in order to make a revolution of taste, the artists must
through their sensibility, and in the invention of their images,
reflect the experience of that modern world, speak its language
in order to correct and change it.

The principles of modern art criticism do in fact resolve themselves into taste, accompanied by a good deal of scientific-seeming analysis. 'Plastic values', 'significant form' etc., are only high-sounding names for the taste which approves the form and finds it significant: taste argued with a powerful apparatus of analysis, and appealing in the end to an instinctual judgement justified presumably by modern psychology. The extreme eclecticism of the modern view of art—resulting from the great increase in the number of things seen in excellent reproductions—justifies the idea of a common denominator of taste by which all art can be judged, and makes impossible the search of standards within any one tradition to judge its past, which could also be applied to its present and future.

Literary standards are traditional ones. And whereas the mystique of taste continues to be the basic criterion for judging the visual arts, comparison with the analysed and elaborate tradition has become more and more the standard for criticizing literature, entrance into the tradition, the aim of the creative. The modern movement arose from a confusion of the aims of painting with poetry (and perhaps also with music). It disintegrated as a result of the separation of the arts, perhaps due to the reassertion of the difference intrinsic to each.

PART FOUR

THE REVERSAL OF THE MODERN

I

TRADITION-BOUND LITERATURE AND
TRADITIONLESS PAINTING

CRITICS of visual arts and of music describe in words—that is to say, a system of signs other than those made by brushes on canvas or chisels into stone or notes of music—those characteristics of painting or sculpture or music which can be described and analysed. Visual artists and composers can disregard critics on the ground that the medium of verbal criticism bears so indirect a relation to the medium in which they make something.

Poets are in a different situation. With the development of so-called scientific methods of criticism they are made ever conscious that criticism of poetry is in the same medium of work as the art which they practise. 'Close analysis' is useful to critics and readers. But for the poet there is the danger of the disintegration of poetry into paraphrase, examination of technique, influences, all analysed in the vocabulary of criticism. The poem risks becoming fragmented into the words explaining what it means and how it is written, and although critics would be the first to admit that the poem is different from and never can be even the most complete analysis, the modern student often reads the analysis into the poem, rather than the poem first and then the analysis. If he himself becomes a poet, he may proceed from a critical analysis of his projected poem to the writing of the poetry.

Did not the imagist poets (perhaps without their fully realizing that they were doing so) attempt to write an unanalysable kind of poetry, close to painting, when they adopted their techniques for concentrating on the creation of an image rather than a statement? Although themselves critically minded, they advocated a kind of poetry which could not be completely paraphrased, and the kernel of which was an unanalysable word-picture. Yet their influence developed critical consciousness far more than it did poetical creativeness. Every poet-critic produced ten critic-poets.

The imagists tried to turn poetry into word-painting or sculpture. They wanted to release poetry from the burden of past conventions and traditional ways of thinking by concentrating upon reproducing the image which springs naked into the mind from the impact of modern life. Yet the most intelligent of them soon realized that poetry could not be completely modern and new in the way that the other arts could be, because it uses as its material words which are old and social, and which only to a limited extent can be used in new ways. The limitation is imposed by the fact that the meaning words have outside the poem has to be maintained—even if it is stretched—within the poem.

If the literary medium were to become 'new' to the extent that the material a painter works with, or even the instruments for which a composer writes, can be revolutionized for the purposes of his art, then literature would become not merely divorced from 'life', but from language, its own terms, within which writers work. A medium which was entirely special to literature would cease to mean in the way that words do, and if an art could be made from it, would be calligraphic or onomatopoeic, approaching the condition of painting or music. There have, of course, been attempts to produce a poetry of typography or of sounds, totally devoid of prose meanings, notably by the dadaists, and by Kurt Schwitters. And the tendency to invent a special literary language of images, symbols, or sounds, separated within the poetry as far as possible from associations outside and from prose

meanings, runs through symbolism, imagism, extremes of autotelic expressionism, and the experimental poems of Gertrude
Stein.

It seems plausible to make entirely new paintings and sculpture
out of new materials: but in literature such an attempt could only
succeed if it produced a completely new art. For literature is an
art whose basic condition is that the medium used—words—is not
special to the art. Within poetry the meanings of words are both
more exact and more extended than they are in social discourse.
They correct meanings which are abused outside. But words as
they are used outside literature also might be said to exercise a
critical watch over the world inside poetic language. Idiomatic
speech outside can show that the language inside poetry is artificial,
has become too conformist to past literary conventions. But the
criticism of the literary conventions by the unprecedented idiomatic life is usually unwelcome to literary critics.

A sculptor might be stimulated by some entirely new invention
—a sputnik, say—and interpret it in a work of new materials and
new techniques, isolating it as an unprecedented visual event. A
writer could certainly write a poem about a new invention but
only in material—words—that could not be unprecedented.
Language of its own nature repudiates a complete break between
past and present. A 'revolution of the word', in the sense of the
words changing completely their sense and becoming something
else, is one kind of revolution that is impossible, a revolution in
human nature being perhaps another. Dictionaries contain the
material with which writers work, and they are overwhelmingly
traditional. It may be theoretically possible to discover an entirely
new form in which a poem might be written, but form is only one
aspect of a poem, and its unprecedentedness would only make a
superficial break with the unavoidable continuities of grammar
and usage.

There is an opposite, and, as it were, complementary error to
that of those who think that a literary work could be new in the

way that painting, sculpture and music can, and that is of those who think that modern creativity must be tied to the values of certain established masterpieces. The exponents of the Great Tradition argue that modern conditions are unprecedented and incapable of producing literature of any value. The only hope for the future of literature lies in writers studying the works of the Great Tradition produced at a time when the organic life of the community was reflected in certain exemplary poetry and fiction. Surely this attitude must imply that writers must work within the context of the literary language hallowed by tradition and avoid the language which has been corrupted by unprecedented modern circumstances. But for a writer at any given moment in history the potential material of his art is the whole of language surrounding him in his circumstances. In effect both views—the view that writing can be entirely new and the view that it must be attached to the values of critically interpreted selected reading matter—limit creativeness, the first by separating the modern from the past, the second by separating the past from the modern. Language, the material of literature, is neither completely new nor completely traditional. It is always evolving and accumulative.

*　　*　　*　　*

In painting and music, the cards with which the game is played can be replaced by a new pack. In literature, the pack can only be reshuffled, though sometimes new cards are added.

I have suggested that the imagists had, when they were still a literary movement, a tendency to make poetry into a branch of painting. The poetic image may have a meaning which cannot be paraphrased or explained any more than can a painter's image. Dadaists and surrealists deliberately set out to write poems which had no paraphrasable meanings.

James Joyce is often confused with these 'experimentalists'. But although in the long run the tendency of his work was to produce a purely literary language, his aims were as different as possible from theirs, and the difficulties his work offers are of an entirely different kind. The difference between Joyce and Gertrude Stein—with whom he particularly hated to have his work associated—can be summed up by saying that her tendency was to produce a non-language; his tendency was to produce a literary language, extremely difficult to comprehend because it was packed with meanings, the clues to which are almost inaccessible.

Joyce attempted, in *Finnegans Wake*, to invent a language in which several themes can be combined in the chords of portmanteau words formed from other words in several English tongues and fusing meanings on several levels. The ideal reader of *Finnegans Wake* (a figure whom Joyce had constantly in mind) should be equipped with knowledge including all the referents—languages, places, history, autobiography—to which the work refers. Given all this, he would find *Finnegans Wake* by no means impenetrable. It would appear to him a complex, difficult, translucent and paraphrasable work, as capable of ultimate extensive elucidation as *The Divine Comedy*.

Joyce will continue to challenge critics not because he invented an opaque new language but because he combined the available resources of several languages, and of immense learning, and idiosyncrasies of special information, into a whole which, though ultimately transparent, is very difficult to elucidate. The difficulties he presents are of immense complexities of meaning whereas the difficulties of Gertrude Stein's work are of brutish simplicities of meaninglessness.

I think then that the tendency of Joyce is to invent not a language tending to turn writing into music so much as a literary language comprehensible only to specialists. Sometimes the international language of *Finnegans Wake* is defended as foreshadowing a world language, as it were the tongue of the world literature which Goethe prophesied. It seems unlikely though that the populations of Common Market Europe will speak the language of *Finnegans Wake*. Language cannot advance beyond the development of average idiom, except in the direction of a specialized literary language.

There is today a rather common assumption (deriving from generalizations made by critics which go unchallenged) that Joyce, Eliot, Pound, and even Hopkins are 'idiomatic', without its being clear what this means. It is true that they are not 'literary' in the manner of Swinburne, Patmore and Wilde, who cultivated exquisite styles which were sensitive to their public school and university education, but unrelated to the way in which contemporaries talk in pubs, or discuss ideas in philosophical debates, or put forward theories in laboratories. What the moderns undoubtedly did, was to draw upon the rhythms, the colour of language used by those less catastrophically well educated than themselves, and by those who would find the Edwardian literary idiom quite inadequate to discuss the hard realities with which they had to deal.

Yet I question whether the absorption into modern poetry of a good deal of the idiom of the street and of scientific and philosophic discussion makes modern poetry in the completest sense idiomatic. It seems to me that the idiomatic is a language in which it should, ideally, be possible to conduct a dialogue with the people from whom the idiom is borrowed. It should be recognizable by those from whom it is derived as being about them, and not seem to be their involuntary contribution to an élite speech which they cannot understand. I doubt whether the ploughman or blacksmith coming from that part of Wales would recognize himself in Hopkins' poems. Nor do I think that Lil whose husband got demobbed would recognize her locutions in *The Waste Land*.

The distinction I am trying to make will be clear if I add that I think that ideally a character in a poem by William Barnes, or Thomas Hardy, or Edward Thomas, or Wilfred Owen, or in a novel of D. H. Lawrence, would recognize his idiom of thought, and conversation in the writing of any of these writers.

All the moderns did was to invent new literary idioms brought up to date by the intelligent awareness of writers like Joyce, Eliot and Pound, of the nuances of contemporary idiomatic speech. They absorbed and selected idioms, parodying them, turning them to ironic effect. They were writing not so much for those who belonged to the modern world as for those who, hating it, knew about it, could think in its terms. In the work of these writers there was an increased sophistication of language reflecting a consciousness of the way in which contemporaries think and feel. This was an immense gain.

Nevertheless the language of modern poetry still remains to a great extent that of a literary élite. The mandarins have absorbed into their converse highly intelligent, ironic—and sometimes even appreciative—echoes of and references to the world that goes on outside. Yet fundamentally they are agreed in being opposed to the aims of this world, even when they feel a bit humiliated by the unparalleled penetration and flight of its scientific thought, its philosophic reasoning. They are secretly intrigued by the idea that they might in their own medium produce works as difficult, inventive, intellectual as scientific theories. They have caught the tone of modern idiomatic speech to express in it their hatred of modern life.

What the idiomatic writing of Eliot and Pound did was to break through the crust of poeticisms which enclosed the Edwardians and Georgians. It enabled poets to write about modern ideas in a language open to the sights, sound, phrases, habits of thought which were contemporary.

Probably the aim of this idiom was that which Eliot described as the achievement of Dryden who, he writes, 'for the first time established a *normal* English speech valid for both verse and prose, and imposing its laws which greater poetry than Dryden's might violate, but which no poetry since has overthrown.'

But the moderns—as distinct from the Wellses and Bennetts and Shaws who were contemporary without being modern—were writing for trained readers, poets writing for critic-poets.

They transformed the literary medium into one which could discuss the kind of ideas which Tennyson also grappled with in *Locksley Hall* and *In Memoriam*—but too poetically—in an idiom which, inside the club of writers and readers, was ironically responsive to the non-literary language spoken outside.

The Joycean obscurity is the result of the writer treating his work as a form of specialization. The formula is only communicable to the ideal reader who has devoted his whole life to understanding it, and yet it is about the world which concerns all men, and it may, in its results, shake the world. This means that the language, however much it may exploit current idiom, does so in an esoteric way intelligible only to the most devoted readers. If 'school of Joyce' writers were the only poets and novelists, within a hundred years there would be a special literary language for the élite, removed from idiomatic speech, however much the mandarin language might ironically borrow from the currently idiomatic.

*   *   *   *

In one respect the machinery of dream and metaphor of *Finnegans Wake* is close to modern painting. For the central mythology of some of the best modern painting derives from the concept of metamorphoses. And in *Finnegans Wake* there is constant metamorphosis: the waker changes into the sleeper who in his dreams becomes the landscape and his own and all history.

In modern painting the idea of metamorphosis dominated the surrealists, in the work of Max Ernst, Salvador Dali, and André Masson (in the phase of his surrealist drawings *Mythologies*). The most effective of Picasso's series of etchings is the illustrations for Ovid's *Metamorphoses*. And the theme of metamorphosis runs through Picasso's work from 1930 onwards. What is most enduring about surrealism—a movement so riddled with charlatans and amateurs—is the idea of a collective modern subconscious dreaming mind whose forever changing fantasies grotesquely transform the appearances of actual living. 'Surrealist' became an accepted epithet because it seemed to explain the phenomenon of the most irrational and extravagant inner dreaming becoming realized in outer history. The blitz provided innumerable examples of the dreams projected on canvases and in the poems of the surrealists in the twenties and thirties becoming the external reality in the forties.

We still look at surrealist painting. But I doubt whether anyone today reads surrealist poetry, and the attempt in *Finnegans Wake*, to use language as a medium whose nature in itself is perpetually transforming, is that which, even more than the difficulty of the language itself, makes sustained reading of Joyce's book so difficult—perhaps impossible. Painting is the art best adapted to the mythologies of metamorphoses, largely because it is an art whose own nature can undergo the most fundamental transformations in harmony with, on the one hand, the dreams and the historic condition of modern man, on the other, the most advanced techniques of representation. Language can describe, define, explain, represent change, but only in words which themselves cannot be metamorphosized. The endeavour to invent a metamorphosizing language runs into two dangers: the first is that the writing will cease to become an art of verbal meanings and become merely typographical arrangements of painterly signs, the second that it will become the private literary language of an esoteric clique.

Modern poetry presses at a barrier beyond which words might shed their meanings and become *things*. As I have said, early in the present century imagist poets tried to write a kind of poetry which made a complete break with the past. They had the aim which Herbert Read attributes to modern visual artists: 'a unity of intention that completely distinguishes it . . . from earlier periods.' But it became evident that a completely new poem would consist only of a pattern on the page, or an image unrelated to meaning outside itself. This would lead to the abdication of literature. Thus the development of modern poetry has been for poets to turn away from the invention of poems as visual objects to an interest in the extension of poetic meaning in traditional forms and language. The shift of aim can be shown by comparing, say, Eliot's *Preludes* with *Four Quartets*. In *Preludes* the tendency is to write a poem in which a situation, though related to modern life, is isolated within the poem and has there a meaning as impression or image concentrated in the poetry itself. In the *Four Quartets*, meanings borrowed from theology, philosophy and literature, flow into the poetry, threatening at times to dissolve it in ratiocination. A way of putting the difference might be to say that the tendency of *Preludes* is to produce a concentrated essence of poetry in which the unpoetic elements of prose experience and ideas have been eliminated: the tendency of *Four Quartets* is to attack surrounding ideas and experiences by using the poetic concentration as a solvent which can purify and test them. But perhaps the second attempt would not be possible unless the elements of pure poetry had first been isolated.

*   *   *   *

The question most often asked today about a considerable poem or novel is 'Is it in the line of the tradition?' The question that should be asked about a painting is: 'Is it, although entirely different, analogous with some past work which we admire?'

It would be to praise a visual artist to say that he had a power of observation, a sense of harmony, a transforming imagination, similar to that of a great master. But if we say 'he is in the tradition of' we are in danger of applying to painting our way of thinking about literature. The idea, supported by Ruskin, that the pre-Raphaelites went back to a tradition of which the master was Giotto, today seems only comprehensible in the context of the nineteenth century.

Epstein, standing before one of the great African sculptures he had collected, is reported to have said: 'We shouldn't in any way wish to imitate this. What we want is to make something which, in relation to our own time, is as strong.' It is difficult to think of a poet claiming that he could establish a relationship traditional by analogy with negro tribal poetry. The thought could at once suggest to him the lack of connecting line between African languages and English. (A reader may object that there is the influence of tribal Africa in *Sweeney Agonistes*, *Gold Coast Customs* and *A Handful of Dust*. But in all of these the African influence is not by way of literature but of African sculpture and jazz.)

Literary influences are communicated like sap that reaches from the soil up through the trunk and branches of a tree into the leaves. Visual influences flash their messages directly across spaces and centuries dividing different cultures. A contemporary interpretation like that suggested by Epstein's remark can make all visual art of the past available to the living artist. And the values of the visual arts—where these consist of proportions, harmonies, combinations which the critic discovers in works of all periods and cultures—are universal in a way in which those of literature can scarcely be generalized.

Epstein's remark is justified, though a little dangerous, because 'to be as strong as this, in relation to our own time', sets up an ideal of strength which can only indirectly be realized in a society by no means primitive. What is needed is audacious tact of interpretation. It is exactly this which is the greatest achievement of modern art. It distinguishes Picasso's *Les Demoiselles d'Avignon* and some of the sculpture of Henry Moore from the archaism of the pre-Raphaelite returns to models of earlier and healthier times. Picasso exploits the primitive to produce effects which are entirely modern. He evokes the 'strength' of the negroid against a civilization which has the 'strength' of machinery, and in doing so indicates that in some way industrial civilization has returned to the crudely primitive.

Language barriers have not collapsed between the literatures of different modern countries. We are today no nearer the world literature foreseen by Goethe than he was in his day. In some ways we are further from it. But we live today in the midst of world painting, with the advantages and the disadvantages for visual art that the almost uncontrollable intercommunication of artistic influences between contemporary cultures entails.

When modern literature was closest to painting, Joyce, Pound, Eliot and Wyndham Lewis had an attitude towards tradition, which was that of the visual artists. The reaction against the extremes of futurism was concomitant with the splitting up of the international all-the-arts movement into its components. The writers turned back to tradition because they turned back to language which cannot—as can the media and symbols of painting—reinvent its own terms.

Painting, as I have pointed out, can, and does do so, as, to a lesser extent, does music. Hence we get the situation whereby, in their old age, Picasso and Stravinsky remain moderns with what Harry Levin (in his essay *What is Modernism?*) calls 'that metamorphic impetus, that systematic deformation, that reshaping spirit which must continually transpose its material and outdistance itself in a dazzling sequence of newer and newest manners.' Whereas of T. S. Eliot's development he writes: 'Witness T. S. Eliot, whose career has been a literary parallel to Stravinsky's or Picasso's. Since his conversion to the Anglican Church and his naturalization as a British subject, we have come to view him as a living embodiment of tradition. Yet he emerged as an experimentalist, whose problematic endeavours startled and puzzled his early readers.'

The difference is not just that between artistic temperaments but between the development of arts, which can metamorphosize their own media and meanings, and the art of language. If Joyce continued to be metamorphic until the end of his life this was partly due to the fact that he had a scientific approach to literature as pure invention, and partly that his writing tends towards music. Pound, whose *Cantos* have been described as metamorphic, is the modern poet who has remained closest all his life to painting. Eliot, who of his generation has always been most concerned with words and least involved in the other arts, has become the most traditionalist.

Painting is then the modern art *par excellence*, with all the advantages and the appalling risks of its extremist rôle. Painters are freer even than composers (who are limited)—unless they write *musique concrète*—by being dependent on interpreters who have received academic training. The composer has to consider the orchestra and the box office. The painter is free to use whatever materials he can afford. He is backed by dealers selling to connoisseurs who often require above all else that new painting should be experimental. They have learned that in the visual arts the experiments of the early part of this century have proved the most lasting modern works.

Painting is, as Wyndham Lewis pointed out in *The Demon of Progress in the Arts*, peculiarly exposed to the dangers of extremism. An obvious example lies in the undermining not just of academic standards but of traditions of training in art. Painters of the early part of the present century used techniques they had acquired from an academic training in order to destroy the standards and abandon techniques of the academies. Picasso, Braque, Matisse, and artists of that generation, show in their distortions of anatomy a release from the standards of their academic training. But their inexactitude has the exactitude they had learned in the academies. Since these masters had the appearance of throwing away or rebelling against an academic training, art teaching has itself been discredited. Few young artists bother about learning techniques which they will then throw away. The freedom of those who rebelled against an imposed discipline has been succeeded often by the freedom of those without discipline. The area of modern painting had now become one of total freedom; and it is in consequence an area which receives into it amateurs and the self-taught on the same terms as professional artists.

I wrote above that literature is kept traditional by the conservative nature of the medium, language; and that writers are made aware by the very fact of using words that if they press language to the point where it no longer means what it does outside their writing, then the words they use break away and become simply letters and noises.

I also wrote that painting is not like this, because the medium used by painters is used simply for the art within which they are free to change the medium, if they can produce what they consider better results by doing so.

If we ask what makes a painting a work of visual art, the answer is not that it is painted in tempera, oils, or that it is a collage, or made of plastics, or sand, or rusty nails. It might achieve its effect by any of these means. The only proviso would be that it had to relate, however remotely, to some aim of artists in the past. If it did not do this, then the connecting line which placed it in the continuity of things called works of art would be broken, and there would be a new object which was not a painting or sculpture able to be judged by any existing standard. If it had no such connection with the past, there seems no point in calling it a painting or sculpture and the artist a painter or sculptor.

The claims made by certain critics—notably by Harold Rosenberg—for American action painting seem to be that action painters are painting (or non-painting) pictures (or non-pictures) which have no connection of aesthetic aim with any pictures painted before.

What action painters (according to Mr. Rosenberg) appear really to be doing is simply adding to the number of objects in the world some rather special things they make which are not 'about' anything, but which simply happen as the result of the contact of the action painter with the canvas. As he puts it in his famous essay *The American Action Painters*:

> At a certain moment the canvas began to appear to one American painter after another as an arena in which to act—rather than as a space in which to reproduce, re-design, analyse or 'express' an object, actual or imagined. What was to go on the canvas was not a picture but an event.

The painter no longer approached his easel with an image in his mind; he went up to it with material in his hand to do something to that other piece of material in front of him. The image would be the result of this encounter.

'A picture that is not a picture' is not meant to be looked at, at least not as people have looked at pictures in the past, to perceive the painter's statement about the object, or to see how he gives 'a new twist' to the 'game of the tradition'. The painting simply exists, it is not an expression of anything except the event of the painter doing something with material in his hand on it. (If the metaphor sounds onanistic, perhaps it is meant to do so. One is put in mind of a sexual act which produces a stain but does not result in a birth.)

Statements (quoted by Mr. Rosenberg) of painters themselves about their action paintings add to the impression that these works are events which add to the world objects, as little related as possible to anything itself to previous art objects; 'My painting is not Art; it's an Is.' 'It's not a picture of a thing; it's the thing itself'; etc.

The important question arises of by what standards can you judge a completely self-sufficient object, which refers to nothing except the moment in which it happened. Mr. Rosenberg is not very helpful about this. He appeals not to any previous criteria of art (that would be to give up the whole case of 'action painting') but to our feelings and to patterns in our psychology which may correspond to the 'tensions' set up in the painting:

> The test of any of the new paintings is its seriousness—and the test of its seriousness is the degree to which the act on the canvas is an extension of the artist's total effort to make over his experience.

This may well be true; and it is why one respects American painting. But as argument it seems self-defeating, because it is difficult to conceive of seriousness which is not 'about' something outside it. Seriousness is seriousness about things and conditions. Seriousness is not a pure condition of emotion. It is not just an 'is'. Also 'to make over his experience' seems like saying— or rather avoiding saying—'a way of communicating an experience which the artist has to express'.

Possibly the process which Mr. Rosenberg is trying to describe is the negation of existing standards of painting and of judging painting, so that art and the standards by which it is judged are re-invented as their opposites. He writes of action painting:

> It follows that anything is relevant to it. Anything that has to do with action—psychology, philosophy, history, mythology, hero worship. Anything but art criticism. The painter gets away from art through his act of painting; the critic can't get away from it. The critic who goes on judging in terms of schools, styles, forms—as if the painter were still concerned with trying to produce a certain kind of object (the work of art), instead of living on the canvas—is bound to seem a stranger.

In all this I seem to detect ghosts of Hegel and Marx—the negation of the negation—who have been banished from communist societies. This is sympathetic. It is nice to meet them. But having abolished all the standards by which visual art can be judged, Mr. Rosenberg then tells us that 'the new painting calls for a new kind of criticism, one that would distinguish the specific qualities of each artist's act'. So the critic is necessary after all, which is a relief, because Mr. Rosenberg is himself a critic. And having told us that the one thing the action painters don't want to do is to sell their paintings, one reads on knowing that, partly as a result of Mr. Rosenberg's writings, they are at the top of the art market—which is a relief, because after all they have to live.

What is serious about Mr. Rosenberg's argument is that it puts forward the ideal of completely traditionless art. Having discerned this in the work of the action painters, he is up against the difficulty that all our standards for judging painting derive, however indirectly, from past painting. A completely new art would be one completely without criteria by which to judge it. He therefore has to invent traditionless criteria for traditionless artists applied by traditionless critics. Here we run into the problem of language—the terms we use—being traditional, for to call action painters artists, and their critics critics, and their works paintings, is to apply to them terms which are bound up in traditional art-meanings. What Mr. Rosenberg really means is that the anti-artists should be judged by the anti-critics for their anti-paintings.

A further difficulty now arises that none of the categories of critical judgement that could be applied to these works could, given Mr. Rosenberg's hypothesis, have any meanings that were not denigratory: for they would inevitably connect them again with the tradition, and with 'modern art', which Mr. Rosenberg despises. He therefore is reduced to having to discuss these paintings as though they were pictures used in Rorschach tests, taking from them readings of the psychological tensions of the painters.

Nothing of what I have written above is meant as an attack on the school of American painters, whoever these may be. I say 'whoever these may be', because Mr. Rosenberg may mean ones different from Jackson Pollock, Kline, Rothko, and others I would expect him to mean. His painters may even be imaginary, ideal ones, invented for the purpose of his argument. More probably, they are real, slightly unsatisfactory ones, none of whom quite come up to the ideal goal he has set for them. For an extraordinary thing about this essay on *The American Action Painters* is that he does not mention in it the name of a single American action painter.

The great interest of his argument is that it holds up the vision of an art completely shedding its past, and becoming a new art. In doing this he really states a challenge for artists: is this what they intend to do? Is it really the tendency of painting today, to cease to be visual art, and become something which in effect would be quite different, an entirely new art: for if it completely shed the tradition then none of the existing art terminology—all of which is derived from the past—would apply to painting any longer. The word 'painting' itself would be merely confusing.

I think that in reality the painting of the American school has succeeded because it is not as traditionless as Mr. Rosenberg imagines. Nevertheless, I think that it does describe a tendency. Action painting, and the theories attached to it, indicate that some painters may abandon painting and start a new art. This will perhaps turn out to be closer to decoration, as it exists now, than to painting.

When the moon split off from the earth (if it ever did this) the earth was still left, so if anti-painting splits off from painting, painting is left. The problem of painters is really how they should relate their work to the tradition. Mr. Rosenberg makes this clearer than it seemed before he wrote by implying that there are alternatives: get back into painting, or get out altogether. He thinks painters should get out, but others will draw the conclusion they should get back in. As, in an unexpected and rather light-hearted way, the 'pop' painters seem to be doing. They are getting back into the tradition by way of illustration and attaching words to their works—returning to the painting with a story.

It seems to me possible that just as, in the early phase of the modern movement, poetry turned to paintings in order, through the concentration on the creation of a pure image, to release itself from conventions, so painting may have to turn to literature to rediscover standards. Something of the kind seems already to be happening in the work of Francis Bacon whose paintings, in addition to their having technical qualities which are entirely modern, are literary in the sense of providing criticism of their contemporary subjects and in using distortion, in the treatment of human figures, to suggest a cruelly compressed terrifying narrative.

II

HATRED AND NOSTALGIA IN DEATH'S
DREAM KINGDOM

IN the twenty years between 1910 and 1930, much of the writing of those whom today we think of as conservatives was influenced by the *avant garde* which Roger Shattuck characterized
in *The Banquet Years*:

> In its early demonstrations, the avant garde remained a true com-
> munity, loyal to itself and its time. To a greater extent than any time
> since the Renaissance, painters, writers, and musicians lived and
> worked together and tried their hands at each other's arts in an
> atmosphere of perpetual collaboration. It was their task to contain
> and transform the teaming excitement, the corruption, and ideal-
> ism of this stage-struck era.

You cannot read the letters of Ezra Pound, or even of D. H.
Lawrence; Eliot's review of *Ulysses* in *The Dial* ('*Ulysses*, Order
and Myth'); the aggressively advanced manifestos of Wyndham
Lewis in magazines called by names such as *Tyro* and *Blast*; Robert
Graves' and Laura Riding's *New Bearings in English Poetry*;
Richard Ellmann's account of Joyce's ambition to write about
the whole of modern life in his recent biography of Joyce; without realizing that in this early phase a chief aim of most of these
writers was to make a new modern literature which would transform the techniques, the ideas, the appearances, the material of
the modern world into great art. For Ezra Pound, Herbert Read

and Wyndham Lewis, these aims were connected with the perhaps quixotic one of transforming modern man—through the influence of painters and poets co-operating with architects and designers—to revolutionize the appearance of urban industrial civilization through art. People should be stimulated to live in a world made beautiful by technology directed by artists (this is what was meant by 'advanced').

What are today regarded as the traditional aims of literature interpreted in modern idiom, were then regarded as the use of traditionalist themes to underline the modern. Today *Ulysses* is discussed as Homeric myth; but when it was first published the classical model which is now looked on as its goal was regarded as its point of departure.

Eliot, in the *Dial* article referred to, hailed Joyce as the inventor of perhaps the only feasible method of ordering contemporary experience—namely by using the Homeric myth to manipulate 'a continuous parallel between contemporaneity and antiquity'. He saw the Odyssey myth as underlying Joyce's laying bare of 'the immense panorama of futility and anarchy which is contemporary history'.

And yet inseparable from this will to be absolutely modern, there was an intense hatred and contempt for modern life. In the works of the most characteristically modern writers contemporary civilization was represented as chaotic, decadent, on the point of collapse, anarchic, absurd, the desert of non-values. Yeats, Eliot, Wyndham Lewis, Pound, all abhorred the idea of progress, hated the industrial age. They had invented their modern idiom and forms in order to express disgust with the modern world.

Hatred is rarely quite convincing, and at its most intense, in Carlyle, Baudelaire or Stefan George, it seems a bit meretricious. What seems poignantly felt is the passionate nostalgia which colours so much modern writing.

Someone should write a history of nostalgia, comparing the nostalgic feelings of the post-industrial revolution literature, with

that gilding of previous eras, golden ages, which in the past produced rebirths and revivals, but which since the beginning of the
nineteenth century produced only hatred and despair. The
Renaissance used to be regarded as a rebirth of the classical
European spirit as the result of the then recent discovery of masterpieces of classical antiquity. The modern nostalgia is not so much a
rebirth as a burial of the contemporary world under the heaped-up
memories of the past.

The modern nostalgic feels that an irreparable break has taken
place between the past and the present, in society and in man's
soul. The dubious material gains of progress have been made at
the price of stupendous spiritual loss. The nostalgic modern sensibility, looking back on the past, is like Othello viewing Desde-
mona strangled on the bed. He has thrown away all that is
precious and valuable in his life in his pursuit of a self-condemned
aim. In the circumstances of his abasement, his memoried love
expresses itself in a self-accusing cry. In himself he sees

> One whose hand
> Like the base Indian, threw a pearl away
> Richer than all his tribe.

The murdered past is reborn as vision more precious than anything the present has to offer. The contemporary scene becomes
simply a torn fabric through whose rents the past burns with
illumined clarity—more real than any inventions, discoveries,
riches, false shows of happiness, the materialist future can bring.
The nostalgic sees with double vision at one and the same time the
passionately desired yesterday and the hated today. Nostalgia and
hatred are two sides of the same medal.

This unparalleled modern nostalgia doubtless has its roots in
the industrial revolution—when Goldsmith saw the village and
green of Auburn made into a desert, Blake the blackening of
England's green and pleasant land, covered by the 'dark Satanic
mills'.

It was the time of heart-rending comparisons between the

country as it was and the town squatting upon its hills and fields, between Merrie England and the Black Country. What gives force to the pre-Raphaelite movement, William Morris handi-crafts and those evocations of Monastic or Elizabethan England which begin with Carlyle, Ruskin and Morris, and collapse into self-parody with Chesterton and Belloc, is the scene laid in the past set against one in the present. Here is Carlyle, turning from nineteenth-century England to evoke the scene of a twelfth-century monastery, in *Past and Present:*

> Within doors, down at the hill-foot, in our Convent here, we are a peculiar people—hardly conceivable in the Arkwright Corn-law ages, of mere spinning wheels and Joe Mantons! There is yet no Methodism among us, and we speak much of Secularities: no Methodism: our Religion is not yet a horrible restless doubt, still less a far horribler composed Cant; but a great heaven-high Unquestionability, encompassing, interpenetrating, the whole of Life.

*   *   *   *

Nostalgia and hatred are aspects of the modern literary move-ment which have a long history. They provide the connecting link between Eliot and Pound with the 1890s aesthetes and, beyond them, with Carlyle, Ruskin and Morris. The passage in the 'Fire Sermon' in which Eliot superimposes a vision of the Thames near London as it is today upon the Thames evoked by Spenser's 'Prothalamion' employs a method of contrast between past and present which Ruskin witnessed with his own eyes, a juxtaposition of the rural and the industrial which he dramatizes in his lecture on *Modern Manufacture and Design:*

> Just outside the town I came upon an English cottage, or mansion, I hardly know which to call it, set close under the hill, and beside the river, perhaps built somewhere in the Charles's times, with mullioned windows and a low arched porch; round which, in the little triangular garden, one can imagine the family as they used to sit in old summer times, the ripple of the river heard

faintly through the sweetbriar hedge, and the sheep on the far-off wolds shining in the evening sunlight. There, uninhabited for many and many a year, it had been left in unregarded havoc of ruin; the garden gate still hung loose to its latch; the garden, blighted utterly into a field of ashes, not even a weed taking root there; the roof torn into shapeless rents; the shutters hanging about the windows in rags of rotten wood; before its gate, the stream which had gladdened it now soaking slowly by, black as ebony and thick with curdling scum; the bank above it trodden into unctuous sooty slime: far in front of it, between, between it and the old hills, the furnaces of the city foaming forth perpetual plague of sulphurous darkness; the volumes of their storm clouds coiling low over a waste of grassless fields, fenced from each other, not by hedges, but by slabs of square stone, like gravestones, riveted together with iron.

Here, what in Eliot, Joyce, and Pound is a contrived method of contrasting nostalgic past and hideous present, is the writer's direct observation.

Victorian nostalgia of this kind was tempered with reformist passion, or with social optimism; it did not take the twentieth-century form of utter hatred for the present, and contempt for progress. With the Victorians nostalgia gave rise to a desire to reconcile the beauty of the past with improvement of the present: hence Ruskin's teaching art to men at working-class colleges, Morris' manufacture of furniture and fabrics, and Matthew Arnold's polemics against the industrialists—whom nevertheless, as a liberal and progressive, he supported in politics. The Victorians were sentimentally and aesthetically, in their various ways, often medievalists. They wanted to plan for a future which got back to a period of monkish living, handicrafts, Gothic architecture, castle keeps.

The literary modernists of the twentieth century, often American expatriates coming to Europe in the search for values, and finding 'an old bitch gone in the teeth' and 'two thousand battered books', did not direct their nostalgia towards a sentimentalized picture of Catholic medieval Europe. In Eliot the past is of

certain points ('Little Gidding,' 'Burnt Norton', etc.) inhabited
by those who were rooted; the present is inhabited by people who
are ghosts, men of straw, rootless. We contemporaries are, as it
were, condemned to be ghosts, because we live in the world of
industrialism and fragmented values: and if we know in our
hearts that we stand outside the present, feed with passion upon
images of past history, then we are still ghosts, haunting the past
and unreal in the present, differing from our contemporaries only
in being more self-aware.

I think that in some ways, though not in all, nostalgia has been
one of the most productive and even progressive forces in modern
literature. Nostalgia of the kind which was excited in the minds
of a good many Europeans during the nineteenth century, and
then transmitted to some Americans in this one, is a demonic
force, driving its victims on from one position to another. To be
sufficiently aware of the past is to be aware of the present; for
nostalgic images are vivid by contrast. Passion for the past is a kind
of spiritual homesickness contrasting these grey walls with that
bright South. The Mediterranean represents the nostalgia of the
West.

The driving force within nostalgia is that it is a passion which
must be constantly correcting itself, and I think that this correcting process has contributed to the demonic force of certain modern
writers. Carlyle, Ruskin, and Morris hated industrialism and tried
to reconcile social reform and progress with a medievalist revival.
This was not an ignoble aim but it was unreal towards both past
and present. The aesthetic movement of the 1890's was a much
more sophisticated and spiritual nostalgia, because it yearned for
Renaissance genius, art, and ideals, not for the stage settings and
handicrafts of a past period. The weakness of the aesthetes was
that the disdain of their pose in the face of their public was not
matched by any sense of proportion about themselves. There was
something ludicrous about superior, languid, effete Paters and
Wildes identifying themselves with the ancient Greeks and with

Michelangelo. Pound and Eliot provided their own nostalgia with the most powerful defence of all: elaborate irony directed at a persona in the poetry which could be identified with the poet himself (e.g., 'Prufrock', 'Hugh Selwyn Mauberley'). What this irony accomplished was more than to put the poet in the position of one who mocks himself before the reader can laugh at him. It put nostalgia itself into perspective, by making it appear not just as hatred of the present and yearning for the past, but as a modern state of mind, a symptom of the decline that was also modern: 'In the room the women come and go / Talking of Michelangelo.' The cunning complexity of the self-mocking attitude, which is nevertheless presented as the only civilized one possible in a barbarian age and therefore justified above all other possible ones, has never been better conveyed than in the opening lines of Pound's *Pour l'Election de son Sepulchre*:

> For three years, out of key with his time,
> He strove to resuscitate the dead art
> Of poetry; to maintain 'the sublime'
> In the old sense. Wrong from the start—
>
> No, hardly, but seeing he had been born
> In a half-savage country, out of date. . . .

The modern nostalgic was adept at defending his own poetry and poetic personality, but it is possible that by being too cleverly defensive he undermined the position of the modern in literature. A passionately felt and strategically postulated nostalgia provided him with reason for coming to no sort of terms at all with contemporary values of progress and science in his work. He built for himself a heavily armoured up-to-date defence system of idiomatic language, within which he could withdraw into the endless underground workings of *Finnegans Wake*, or withdraw from the modern altogether into critical examination of the great achievements of the past tradition, or into some form of religious orthodoxy.

I suppose that at all periods certain outstanding men have acted out, in the present, rôles which seemed to them reincarnations of heroes living in a more heroic past. The French Revolutionaries had a passion for thinking of themselves as Romans; but I think this was because they felt that they lived in a period which they paralleled with the triumph of the Roman republic. They were living again the past history which they had given the energy of their revolutionary fervour. The peculiar modern disease is for certain individuals to feel that their genius, which belongs to another historic period, receives no nourishment from the present. They imagine themselves in fifth-century B.C. Athens or Renaissance Florence, and this becomes a fantasy which is to them the most intense reality of their being.

We owe masterpieces to this mental living of a light that casts a double shadow. Golden-age nostalgia has always inspired poetry. But it also leads to a lack of reality which is fatal to lesser talents unable to grasp their real limitations. They feel frustrated by contemporary life, and yet at the same time they are only able to lead an intangible phantom existence in the past.

The reader of Oscar Wilde's recently collected letters, and of the now complete *De Profundis*, will note that although as the result of appalling suffering Wilde grasped many truths about his own personality—so that his imprisonment and later unhappy life acquire significance if one sees them as paths he had to follow if he was to confront the truth about his own nature, and get away from Society—what he never grasped completely was the limitations of his talent. He thought of himself as a poet—which he was only feebly and intermittently—and a philosopher— which he was not at all. He also thought that the work which reveals the deepest mystery of his art—*The Importance of Being Earnest*—was a mere *jeu d'esprit*. The reason he could be so confused was that he clung to a concept of his own genius which had nothing to do with his time: of genius that made him another Oscar Wilde, the friend of the friend in Shakespeare's sonnets, the companion of Socrates, a Renaissance artist walking the streets and squares of Botticelli's Florence. He clung to this picture so passionately that even when he doubted his behaviour he could not altogether get away from the idea that all his deeds were justified by his belonging to a cult of beauty not of this age, but of Greeks, Renaissance Italians, and Elizabethans.

No decade seems too remote to us—so impossible to take seriously—as the nineties. This is so true that it is difficult to realize that the *fin de siècle* nostalgia, the identification with the past implying total hatred of the present, remains scarcely altered in Pound, the Eliot of *The Waste Land*, Yeats, and, surprisingly, in the last poems of Lawrence:

> What do I care if the smoking ships
> of the P. & O., and the Orient Line and all the other stinkers
> cross like clock-work the Minoan distance!
> They only cross, the distance never changes.
>
> And now that the moon who gives men glistening bodies
> is in her exaltation, and can look down on the sun
> I see descending from the ships at dawn
> slim naked men from Cnossos, smiling the archaic smile
> of those that will without fail come back again,
> and kindling little fires upon the shores
> and crouching, and speaking the music of lost languages.
>
> And the Minoan Gods, and the Gods of Tiryns
> are heard softly laughing and chatting, as ever;
> and Dionysos, young and a stranger
> leans listening on the gate, in all respect.

This feeling that the dead had a life more living than any which is possible in the conditions in which the writer lives today, corresponds in the twentieth century to the song of the sirens. We are beguiled by this singing. It fills us with a longing for the unattainable past. Yet at the same time it directs such resentment against the present that our whole world seems fit for nothing better than to be dashed, with us in it, against the rocks.

The view seems today to be gaining favour among younger English poets and critics that Pound and Eliot were an alien incursion of American influence into English poetry, interrupting its true line of development, that of the Georgians. Myself I doubt whether even Owen and Graves would have awoken English poets from the Georgian doldrums back to which some of them today seem to be harking: but whatever worth is attaching to the argument, it is wrong to see in Pound and Eliot only an American invasion into English poetry.

I question their view not just because Pound and Eliot represented much more the introduction of French symbolist influences than of Whitmanesque ones into modern English poetry, but because what comes nearest in their early work to a message was its sophisticated reinforcement of European nostalgia. They spoke not so much in the language of the mid-West as that of Greeks and Romans. Pound lends to the dandified exhausted European spirit of Hugh Selwyn Mauberley, intellect, irony, power of exact quotation, awareness of modern art. Those who were out of touch with the time, while barricading themselves behind sly self-denigration, suddenly rose immensely above it, and saw it as not just decadent but tragically catastrophic.

They wrote modern poetry to reject modern life. They were spiritual inhabitants of an Elizabethan or Italian Renaissance world. They were able to express nostalgia in a new way, and with the force of an outsider's coming all fresh and new to an old world. It fell to the American poets to write the swan songs of Europe after the first world war:

> But where is the penny world I bought
> To eat with Pipit behind the screen?
> The red-eyed scavengers are creeping
> From Kentish Town and Golder's Green;

> Where are the eagles and the trumpets?

Buried beneath some snow-deep Alps.
Over buttered scones and crumpets
Weeping, weeping multitudes
Droop in a hundred A.B.C.'s.

The contrast in *The Hollow Men* is not just the metaphysical religious one between the living who are exiled in life from the true life which is in death, but between historic life and historic death. The real life lies with the dead because they belonged to a history more living than any who live in our history can be. 'For We are the hollow men / We are the stuffed men / Leaning together / Headpiece filled with straw.'

★ ★ ★ ★

Wyndham Lewis was, it seems to me, a striking example of the clash in the mind of an artist between the wish to be modern and *avant garde*, and hatred of modern life—a hatred which ultimately included contempt for that very modern art which he practised and expounded. But perhaps it is misleading to write here of a 'clash': for the conflict or contradiction is as it were incorporated in the modern literary sensibility. Wyndham Lewis began as a modernist with the tendencies I have called futurist. He advocated his own 'movement' called Vorticism, which owed something to futurists, something to the theories of T. E. Hulme, something to cubism. He stood for a highly formalized, depersonalized art, in which the painter incorporated into his vision the forms of machinery and did not indulge in the sentimental humanism which Lewis criticized in the work of Picasso. He wanted an art of mechanized will. He also believed strongly in the propaganda and politics of art, which had to be conducted if possible by methods of modern publicity: agitation, intrigue, an air of mystery, press releases, the creation of a public image of the artist, etc.

At the same time, with all this, Lewis did not regard himself as belonging to contemporary civilization at all. With one side of him—that which did his vorticist paintings, carried on his campaigns, called himself the Enemy, and produced a polemical magazine of that name—he was as 'advanced' as a Man from Outer Space. But with the other, he regarded himself as the unfortunate victim of a Time Machine accident which had catapulted him, a man of the Renaissance, writing from what he called 'the standpoint of genius' (by which he meant that of Leonardo), into the twentieth century.

An anecdote is revealing of his real self-image. In the late thirties he painted my portrait. When the work was finished, I saw him examine it carefully for some minutes. Then he said, half to himself: 'It is as beautiful as a fresco of Raphael.' This remark did not come, I am sure, so much out of vanity, as out of a sense that the Renaissance was the world to which he really belonged. At heart, he was really the Renaissance-haunted man of the nineties.

The deepest motivation of Wyndham Lewis came from the nostalgia of a man who secretly feels he belongs to another age, and who therefore despises his contemporaries and his surroundings.

One result of this view of himself is that his books are haunted by a shadowy presence—of whom Pierpoint, in *The Apes of God*, is an example—of the man of genius outside this time—clearly yours truly. This demi-god never quite consents to materialize and be altogether himself in a world of shadows, above which he is the reality, the final court of appeal, the point of view of genius. As a result of Pierpoint's immanence, Lewis himself never consents to take the kind of trouble which would set his work fully in the context of current human intercourse. The time in which he is living is simply not worth the trouble of a man of Renaissance genius, he seems always to be saying. He prefers rather to keep up the air of mystification—if his readers were worth bothering about he would show them a thing or two. Even his great productivity of books, put together apparently with an air of haste, seems the result above all of impressing himself and others with his Renaissance energy. In one of his magazines— *The Enemy*, I think—he printed a reproduction of the corrected proof of the revised edition of his novel *Tarr*. It is significant— and impossible to think that Lewis had overlooked the resemblance—that the proof was exactly like one of the famous corrected proof sheets of Balzac.

Does one not discern the operation of the poet's acting out before a public whom he disdains the myth of his earlier age of genius, in Ezra Pound's *Cantos*? With Lewis, the sense of belonging to another era, the reluctance to do more than mystify the present one, takes the form of a kind of programmatic hurriedness. With Ezra Pound it is excessive familiarity with and allusion to the men and works of the past as though they were his contemporaries.

When nostalgia of this intensity is applied through action to contemporary history, it is—or it was—Fascism. The attraction of Fascism for these writers was that it seemed a programme for using entirely modern techniques to impose upon twentieth-century society the patterns of pre-industrial society. The sirens of nostalgia sang the speeches of Mussolini.

III

THE NEO-TRADITIONALISTS

I HAVE been arguing that the reversal of the modern movement in poetry was implicit in the very nature of language itself, which is traditional. The writer who wishes to be entirely new has to limit himself to a very small part of language—that which corresponds to new experiences and phenomena—or to invent a new language—with the result that he finds himself turning language into sounds or calligraphic signs, or at best, into a special literary language for an élite.

Secondly, I have argued that ever since the early nineteenth century there has been a passionate nostalgia in writing which has greatly influenced poetry, and for which I find it difficult to find a parallel in the past.

In all this, I am concerned principally with describing the reversal of the modern movement, and not with making critical judgements. It is indeed difficult to judge nostalgia. In the past it has always provided themes for art, and in the present century it has produced masterpieces. However, for a contemporary, excessive hatred of the time in which he lives and passionate self-identification with the School of Athens, or the artists of the Renaissance, endangers his gifts. It leads to that lack of self-criticism which one finds in writers as gifted even as Pound, and as the remarkable, though less gifted, Wyndham Lewis. In them the lack is all the more striking because both were distinguished critics. But the projection of one's aesthetic self into a time not one's own leads to a dismissive attitude towards one's own time, and therefore to a total disregard of any current standards by which one's own work might be criticized.

It is clear that with Lawrence his nostalgia was symptomatic of the hysterical side of his nature; this hatred of modern ugliness which was so profound that he was all his life in flight from it, first to countries other than England, then to continents other than Europe, and finally into times remote from modern history. Joyce was probably not so nostalgic as Eliot's account of his using the Homeric myth to parallel the modern chaos suggests. We are not to assume that he condemned the modern chaos. He simply created it within a vision in which the development of history was circular and the modern world of night-town was only a part of life. After *The Hollow Men* Eliot strikingly breaks with the theme of nostalgia. Up to then he is certainly concerned with the situation of life in historic time, and he shares the modern hatred of the present, and longing for the past. But in *Ash Wednesday*, and his later poetry, he is concerned with a quite opposite subject matter: the place of man in eternity. Although he still exploits the past-present contrast, and appears to condemn the civilization of 'a thousand lost golf balls', social despair does not have the same relevance within the context of his religious affirmation.

In Pound and Lewis one feels that a fallacy is embodied in their somehow violent preference for the past over the present, their hatred of modern civilization, their contemptuous view of most of their contemporaries, their willingness to support causes which use modern technology in order to re-establish forms of living to which they attribute the achievements of the enviable past.

This nostalgic fallacy is also present, I think, in certain modern critics, notably those whom I shall here call the *neo-traditionalists*. I shall try to demonstrate this in the next chapter.

I call them this in order to distinguish them from *traditionalists* —

as the term has been used in the past—and what I call *revolutionary traditionalists*. In the past a traditionalist in literature was taken to be someone who held views which, he believed, had been handed down to him from the past, and who observed standards and forms which he derived from these, in his writing. Although there was a sharp distinction between the traditional past and the untraditional present, it was assumed that you could unreflectingly be a traditionalist by loyally interpreting the past and waging mental war against the present.

One result of the ambivalent modern literary movement was that such unreflecting traditionalists became regarded as lax guardians of the high standards of the past, supporters of hollow conventions, slovenly betrayers of the values which they supposed themselves to represent. Pound and Eliot were what I call revolutionary traditionalists; and *Ulysses* represented for them, perhaps a bit perversely, the true tradition, though standing on its head. The revolutionary traditionalists, in their criticism, studied, examined, re-evaluated the masterpieces of the tradition. And it was assumed that, from their writings, the pure seed of these works, which they had planted in their souls, brought forth flowers which, however unrecognizable to the miserable armies of hack critics and English professors (vitiated by over-indulgence in Shelley, Keats and Byron), were in fact the true blossoming of the tradition.

*   *   *   *

Although there was a clear distinction between the revolutionary traditionalists and the neo-traditionalists, there was also a tendency for some revolutionary traditionalists to become neo-traditionalists. The balance of creative consciousness was always precarious in the work of poets who wrote criticism. The poet-critic tended towards the critic-poet.

Recently there has been a good deal of hindsighted comment on the ambiguity of statements of T. S. Eliot which, when they were made, seemed revolutionary, but in retrospect, and in the light of Eliot's later development seem, rather, positions taken up in preparation for his Christian orthodoxy. The famous metaphor in his essay *Tradition and the Individual Talent* conceals behind its solid statuary the balancing of scales which may fall to one side or the other:

> The existing monuments form an ideal order among themselves, which is modified by the introduction of the new (the really new) world of art among them. The existing order is complete before the new work arrives; for order to subsist after the supervention of novelty, the *whole* existing order must be, if ever so slightly, altered; and so the relations, proportions, values of each work of art toward the whole are readjusted; and this is conformity between the old and the new.

If one exercises one's imagination on translating this into real monuments, one sees how shifting the metaphor really is. Supposing the monuments are real statues: Greek sculpture, Medieval sculpture, Michelangelo, Bernini, Canova, Rodin, Henry Moore, Brancusi. One's reading of this arrangement would depend on whether one decided in one's mind that Moore and Brancusi were in, or outside, the tradition, which is the organic inter-relationship of the first six figures. If one decided they were inside then one's interpretation of the tradition would be 'revolu-tionary'. If one excluded them (on the grounds that they were creating visual images out of 'unprecedented' conditions), then one would be, perhaps, a neo-traditionalist.

What Eliot does in the metaphor—as in many of his statements —is make Eliot the critic give Eliot the poet an extremely large loophole through which to escape into his own interpretation of 'the new, the really new', a phrase meant to mystify the reader.

This is an example of the intelligent and subtle procedure by which Eliot has left the uncreative critics and exegesizers of his work stand clasping the stuffed bird that is the image he has helped them make of himself, while the real, the poetic, ever-self-renewing bird flies away.

So in the composition of the poet-critic there is a tug-of-war between poetry and criticism. With Arnold, the critic tended to get into the poetry. Eliot, with the example of Arnold before him, was determined that this should not happen, and has marvellously prevented it from happening, in his poetry: the philosopher, the theologian, the pedant is sometimes there, but never the 'critical consciousness'.

A far more powerful pull against the modern was just that hatred of the modern world which I have described. In the early work of Joyce, Lawrence, Eliot and Pound, there is a straight-forward willingness to regard the modern scene as being made up of hard, brutal, ugly appearances, which the poet was neverthe-less determined to melt down and transform into strange and beautiful images, music harshly mechanical, yet disturbing, in his poem-novel or his poem. In their later work, all these writers turned away from that external scene of the modern—the poetry of the city, of the machine—which had at first fascinated them with its challenge. They become interested in ideas, or in levels of consciousness where the outside world is but a menacing evil on the fringe of a universal dream, a transforming ecstasy of love, or a compelling and timeless orthodoxy.

There seems something almost inevitable about this develop-ment, as though to lose interest in the world of actuality were a stage of maturity. The same acceptance of the modern city as a challenge and the later turning away from it that characterized an earlier generation, was in a later one paralleled in the develop-ment of Auden, who in his early work seemed the poet of mechanized civilization, but who in his later poetry only intro-duces the imagery of the world of machinery to treat it with contempt and boredom.

However, it is in the early stages of attacking the outer scene that these writers seem most nearly part of a general movement.

There is a feeling of sharing a heroic enterprise, conquering the bastions of the factories and engines, in this phase. Giving it up is, among other things, the abandonment of a common cause. One feels, and feels rightly, that the support given to *Ulysses* by Pound, Eliot and Virginia Woolf was of an entirely different nature from the loyal protestations backing the 'greatest prose writer of our time' given to *Finnegans Wake*, when it, as *Ulysses* had been, was 'work in progress'. The reason surely is that *Ulysses* was a noble attempt to resolve the intractable material of a hostile industrial age into the language of the imagination, and to relate it to the epic past. *Finnegans Wake* was felt to be the deep research of a specialist so far ahead of his contemporaries, that his experiments might not be understood for generations.

For these reasons, when the moderns ceased to attack the external world, they split apart. The sympathy that existed between them was the mutual esteem of specialists, not the enthusiasm of an advancing army. One result of this splitting up was the emergence of the school of critics, in England and America, who founded whole systems on the statements and revaluations of the generation of revolutionary traditionalists. They codified and tabulated what they themselves sometimes referred to as 'the critical asides' of Eliot and Pound, taking up these crumbs that fell from the poets' table, mixing them with much reading and research, and then baking them into their indigestible cakes, which had little of the pungency and taste of the original remarks. It is these whom I call the neo-traditionalists, as distinct from the revolutionary traditionalists.

The revolutionary traditionalists were eclectic, drawing on the whole European Hellenic and biblical culture, and sometimes going still further afield to the art and literature of China and other parts of Asia, to Buddhism as well as Christianity. The neo-traditionalists narrowed down their interest in the past to the channels of tradition they regarded as available for conversion into critical dogma, determining the taste of students of English literature. The revolutionary traditionalists were primarily concerned with making discoveries in past literature which could be useful to them in their own work, with removing obstacles to their own understanding of the past, to their own development, and even to their success as part of a general modern movement. They were polemical, and generous, in the manner of literary men, ready to forgive those they had attacked when the attack had served its purpose. This failure to take their own polemical positions altogether seriously shocks the neo-traditionalists who are disturbed when Eliot, having 'dismantled' Milton, later explains that to do so was merely a necessary stage in the development of his own poetry; or, having cast scorn at Shelley's chorus from *Hellas*, and the *Ode to a Skylark*, proceeded to put a speech from Shelley into the mouth of a character in one of his plays, and to pronounce Shelley the most Dantesque English poet.

Neo-traditionalists attempt to systematize their values into criticism that is not only literary but educative. They not only criticize but teach a vigilant and aggressive distrust of all values which derive from contemporary conditions. They start off from the assumption that nothing good can be written if it proceeds from the circumstances of disintegrated modern culture. They teach a double act of critical awareness. The reader must be critically discriminating in what he reads from the past, and also be critical of all the values of modern society.

He must choose to experience the past by training himself to be a discriminating critic of its literature. He must train himself to analyse destructively its advertising, its mass media, the whole machinery of appeal that surrounds its consumption of consumer goods civilization. He must learn to understand that we are living in an age of no values except commercial ones. He must distrust progress, science and the age of technology.

Next, he must learn that the true values are those of the tradition; that they are attached to a social pattern whose day is past; that the only way of getting into touch with the tradition is through reading its masterpieces, studying them, analysing them, developing in himself a capacity to extract from them that awareness of moral and aesthetic distinctions which is repudiated by the conditions surrounding him.

The idea of the necessity of choosing the tradition and rejecting the world of advertising, journalism, propaganda and consumer goods, is stated with succinctness in *Culture and Environment*, by F. R. Leavis and Denys Thompson, a book which might be described as a primer of neo-traditionalism. This book has had considerable influence among educators throughout the world.

In the passage which follows, the authors are discussing George Sturt's *The Wheelwright's Shop*. George Cook and Turner are wheelwrights:

> At the centre of our culture is language, and while we have our language tradition is, in some essential sense, still alive. And language is not merely a matter of words—or words are more than they seem to be:
> 'From the beginning civilization has been dependent upon speech, for words are our chief link with the past and with one another and the channel of our spiritual inheritance. As the other vehicles of tradition, the family and the community, for example, are dissolved, we are forced more and more to rely upon language.'
> (I. A. Richards, *Practical Criticism*, pp. 320-1.)

> . . . If words are our chief link with the past they depend for their life, vigour and potency on being used in association with such traditions as the wheelwright's and that represented by old Turner —such traditions as died when George Sturt's shop became a garage and his Surrey village a suburb. And such traditions are for the most part dead. The decisive use of words today is, as we have seen, in association with advertising, journalism, best-sellers, motor-cars and the cinema. How this kind of association differs in its effects from the traditional kinds we have also seen. It now becomes plain why it is of so great importance to keep the literary tradition alive. For if language tends to be debased instead of invigorated by contemporary use, then it is to literature alone, where its subtlest and finest use is preserved, that we can look with any

hope of keeping in touch with our spiritual tradition—with the 'picked experience of ages' . . . as constitutes a surer taste than any individual can pretend to. True, it is only in individuals that tradition lives; it is you and I who make judgements and exhibit taste, just as it is George Cook who handles the tools. But 'in watching Cook putting a wheel together I was watching practically the skill of England, the experience of ages': just as a good critic or a cultivated person of sure judgement, is exhibiting more than merely individual taste.

Few would disagree with the remarks of the authors, and their citation of Richards, about the role of language. Nevertheless, the general line of their argument seems to me negative. Nor is it the same as that of Richards. The difference between his arguments and theirs is revealing.

What Richards means, surely, is that, with the breakdown of the 'values of tradition', language becomes not only our chief link with the past but also with one another, and the present. Today, more than before, it is essential that language should be kept pure: that it should be so, it must be strengthened through keeping open the channels with past literature. But it is clear, from Richards' other writings, that he thinks that there should be a contemporary poetry open to unprecedented, apparently traditionless modern experience. He thinks that the future of poetry depends largely on the willingness of poets to accept a world of unbelief and scientific fact as the conditions within which it can be written. He puts forward in his famous essay on *Science and Poetry* the theory that the old myths of past poetry can still be used if it is recognized that they refer not to metaphysical statements believed to be literally true, but to the complexities of human psychology (much as Freud uses the Oedipus myth not because he believes in the story of Oedipus but because it dramatizes the relationship of son to parents in the familial situation).

Richards' theories perhaps raise as many problems as they attempt to resolve. But I am not here concerned with them. My point is that he thinks of modern literature as having to be based on the acceptance of the whole modern situation. What Leavis and Thompson do, and what Leavis and his followers today continue to do, is to separate an area which consists of great books and contemporary criticism—a pipe line supposedly leading back to the world of 'the organic community' in which there was a traditional pattern of living (represented, in the passage quoted, by the wheelwrights)—from contemporary conditions, which are traditionless, and represented by 'advertising, journalism, best-sellers, motor-cars and the cinema'. 'The decisive use of words today is . . . associated with these things,' they say. Therefore within the developed area of debased modern language, literature (by which they mean past literature) is the only means by which we can keep in touch with the tradition.

My objection to such thinking is that past literature does not deal with the present situation, nor does it contain the words and language which express it. If literature is forced back on to that period one or two centuries ago when there was a supposed convergence of the stream of living with the stream of poetry, it simply has to abandon all the places and ways of acting, all the words and phrases, which are the expression of living today. The world as it is—by which one means also the world of language as it is lived and spoken—would in that case remain an unredeemed, abandoned area. The 'elect' would be those who had no dealings with this area, who for their spiritual living did not use its language or think its thoughts, and who as far as their occupations and positions are concerned would have to be teachers and students of English literature in schools and universities. They would only be modern in directing a campaign based on their study of past literature against everything that had happened since the time when the approved books were written; everything, that is, except the writing of criticism.

Leavis and Thompson have an almost entirely negative attitude towards the present. They argue that a literature rooted both in the tradition and in contemporary living can only occur in a kind of community which no longer exists and that today cannot exist. Literature must derive from past literature. True, the tradition lives in the individual; but nevertheless the individual in the 'organic community' is more than himself. No one can be such a tradition-fortified individual today, unless through his training in criticism.

Today—Leavis and Thompson argue—no one can be the transmitter of traditional values except by acquiring them through education in past literature:

> The very conditions that make literary education look so desperate are those which make it more important than ever before; for in a world of this kind—and a world that changes so rapidly—it is on literary tradition that the office of maintaining continuity must rest.
> But literary education, we must not forget, is to a great extent a substitute. What we have lost is the organic community with the living culture it embodied. . . . Relics of the old order are still to be found in remote parts of the country, such as the Yorkshire Dales, where motor-coach, wireless, cinema and education are rapidly destroying them—they will hardly last another decade.

(This was published in 1930 so we can assume that the tradition today is derelict.)

Much of the later criticism of Leavis is based on developing these views. In a recent pronouncement, he states:

> It is only in a coherent, educated and influential reading public, one capable of responding intelligently and making its response felt, that standards are "there" for the critic to appeal to: only where there is such a public can he invoke them with any effect. A great fact of the literary history of our time is that such a public no longer exists. (*London Magazine*, March 1955.)

And a few lines further on, in the same communiqué, we are told of W. H. Auden:

> . . . he can only bore and exasperate. He could be taken for a poet of satisfying creative achievement only by those who are so much of

the cultural conditions he represents that they cannot criticize them—they cannot believe them to be new and unprecedented.

The geographical and historical pattern of this way of thinking is now apparent. Geographically, there was an England of the tradition which produced the works of the Great Tradition. In 1933, when *Culture and Environment* was written, we were told that this only survived in a few patches (the Yorkshire dales) and would vanish within the decade. The prophecy has been fulfilled, the geography of the tradition has been swallowed up by the new history of the disintegration.

What we are left with then is teachers and critics who keep open the channels to the history of the tradition that once had a geography of its own. Only dealings with the history preserved or conserved in literature are allowed. Any geographical jaunts by a poet which take him to areas beyond the redeeming influence of the critics of the school of Leavis—to America, for example—are simply excursions into an area of modern damnation called the 'new and the unprecedented'. Hence condemnation of America in Leavis' recent Richmond lecture, as an area from whose conditions nothing of cultural interest can emerge.

*   *   *   *

My objection is principally to the view that literature is the *only* means of connecting the values of the past with present conditions; with, added to this, the further proviso that by literature is meant the works of the great tradition, as interpreted by critics of 'sure judgement' and 'more than merely individual taste'.

To make my own position clear, I must try to explain how I think of tradition.

Most people, I suppose, visualize tradition as monuments or ruins, with associations attached to them, ingrained habits of thinking, institutions hallowed by time and still surviving, patterns of living and behaving associated with the past, and so on. I mention these assumptions in order to show that people have an idea, perhaps accepted unthinkingly, perhaps thought out, of tradition.

When one associates tradition with past values, and sees that it is challenged by changing conditions, and that it also challenges them, then one begins to form a picture of the action of tradition within life. Ideas about this are a generalized poetic thinking. People imagine, for example, forces like rays coming from the past, and entering into the present and future.

Matthew Arnold's insistence that there have to be accessible ideas current in society for it to be possible that 'important poetry' should be written, is a vision of those ideas streaming through the environment. Eliot's metaphor of the hierarchy of past and present monuments is another. Yeats thought of tradition partly as the Great Memory—something like Jung's idea of the Collective Unconscious—and partly as aristocratic life.

Different kinds of poetic visualizing of tradition can exist side by side, and contribute to our own thinking about it. Essentially tradition to each of us, when it has been separated from crude conventional acceptance of established views, and from social distinctions, is our vision of the living relationship of the past to the present.

I do not mean that all our pictures are of anything like equal value. But I do mean that it is possible to think in different ways about tradition as a living force. It is vulgar and wrong, though perhaps high-minded, to think that the tradition can be encarcased in the Hundred Best Books, a six-foot book-shelf, or the approved works of the Great Tradition.

Traditions of course fall into certain classifications of time and place. But they only 'live' in the minds of contemporaries, to the extent that they are understood and imagined by them. Yet to select a period and say 'this was our true tradition, the rest was false' is to exercise an entirely contemporary selective judgement, and to tell little about the past except its relevance to our present situation. It may be necessary for certain writers to do this. The Romantics rejected the Augustan, because it was necessary for them to do so in order to write their own poetry—to breathe, one might say. Eliot when he was young rejected Milton because he found the Miltonic influence in current English poetry and criticism stifling. But Eliot was equally right later on to change his attitude to Milton, when his own writing was no longer threatened by Miltonic influences. But we can be sure that when we make some such judgement as 'the puritan revolution is the true line of the tradition', we are making a judgement not about the past but about ourselves in the present.

*   *   *   *

To 'visualize' the place of tradition in life, we must remember the deception imposed on us by our idea of intervals imposed on history by human generations. It is of the nature of life that we should be victims of the illusion that what happened yesterday has infinitely less bearing on our thoughts and actions than what happens now. The past seems to us dead, because those living then are dead, and therefore we think of it as having to be redeemed or resurrected. The past seems to belong to memory and not to flesh and blood.

A moment's reflection shows us however that there is another scale of change besides the flesh and blood measurement of generations. There are architecture, books, works of art, and the vast majority of man-invented things which make up what is called civilization. Any living generation is made up only of flesh and blood tenants inhabiting the houses of the dead; living on their ideas, reading their books, looking at their pictures. And after us, other tenants will occupy the libraries and galleries.

This gives us another scale of change: not flesh and blood, but bricks and stones, and canvases and paper and institutions. A city can be imagined as a brick and stone body. It would be difficult to say how long are the generations of cities—in fact, they vary immensely—before the parents have died and child cities grow up from the ruins. But even in modern times we could measure such change in hundreds of years. All we need note here is that there is a time when traditions get cut off, when a history becomes a prehistory, because connections between the living and the dead have become too far extended. Life blood is no longer flowing along the withered veins.

But if you compare the generation of the city's life-span with that of the lives of the inhabitants, you get an idea of the ratio between tradition and the lives of those now living.

Tradition, in the widest sense, is simply that which is both handed down and capable of exercising an influence on contemporary life.

Now what is handed down is a great many things, some good, some bad. Some of them are realizations of the wisdom and creative energy and perception of those who have lived in the civilization: of the values they lived by. Usually when we speak admiringly of 'the traditional' we mean those crystallizations into palpable objects of experiences felt, values lived by, faiths held, by people living in the past. Yet there are other traditions, not altogether so obviously to be admired: for instance there is a low-life tradition running from the poetry of Villon onwards, and to be found in the comedies of Shakespeare as well as in Defoe. Since this gave rise to some of the most truthful reflections on the nature of existence, and some of the most vital works ever written, it lends a kind of authority to writers today who choose to be against all the institutions and all the respectabilities. Doctors of literature should remember this.

Everything handed down is, as I say, strictly, traditional. We do not like to think so because some of it is useless and bad, some of it dead wood, some 'the dead hand of the past'. What we mean when we talk of there being traditions is forces emanating from those patterns of the past which have, or which we think should have, a beneficial influence on our lives. In thinking thus we are recognizing that the dead are simply people the same as, or perhaps better than, ourselves, who lived in different circumstances of the same history. To some extent we may judge that those circumstances enabled them to lead lives better than our modern ones, and for this reason we need all the more their wisdom. We may feel that they would be critical of our circumstances. Here, of course, the fact that there were people living in circumstances not our own, is a very great advantage for us. It gives us in terms of history a bifocal view of ourselves in our time. We can view life as our own and also theirs. We can play with the idea that if we lived in their time we would have some of their qualities, and ask ourselves whether, if they were living in ours, they would be able to resist what is bad in our conditioning. We cannot really *think* ourselves into the past, but we can speculate.

We draw broad lines of ideas, judgements, values, which we derive from the achievements made by those living in previous times. We feel these to be forces capable of being adapted, in our creativity, and directed, in our criticism, against the values of our own time.

But the more we select from traditions, the more we are, in a sense, exercising our own contemporary interpretation of them. We choose one past rather than another out of the immediate needs dictated by our own time and place. If we select with sufficient passion of intensity, and with obsessive concentration on our own problems, we achieve the very reverse of what we may have set out to do. Instead of learning from the past, we imprison ourselves within the contemporary interpretation. A striking example of this happening is the Marxist interpretation of all historical conflicts as the class struggle which has been going on for hundreds of years and reached its culmination in our own era. In the Marxist interpretation, the past leads to the present, but there is nothing discoverable in the attitudes of past philosophy or religion or literature which could provide a corrective, or alternative way of thinking to the latest development of Marxism, or even throw much light on present history. The aim of Marxism is, indeed, that the past should provide no such escape route from the present. The Marxist philosophy makes it impossible to say 'They were wiser than we are.' It is only possible to say: 'If they had had our scientific understanding of history they would have interpreted their struggles exactly as we, in the light of our superior science, do for them now.' The past simply affirms the necessity of the present. Thus even Christianity, which would be a crime of thinking in our time, can be forgiven retrospectively as a stage in the development of the class struggle. But it would not be possible for Marxists to say that Dante or Shakespeare, just because they were free of the ideological interpretations of history of our time, were able to see into the human nature that produces a Stalin, for whom the scientific theory of history can provide no satisfactory explanation. The selective interpretation of the tradition tends to imprison us in the present.

I do not suggest that modern 'scientific' analytic criticism has the effect of imprisoning us in the contemporary systems of explication of the past. But it does shut a good many doors by narrowing down the concept of the tradition to the view of the modern critic, approving that which can be analysed with his instruments of criticism, and submitting contemporary literature to the same standards which the critic has discovered in the past. But what he has found in the past is to a great extent the reflection of his own contemporary analysis. What seems to be advocated by F. R. Leavis in the passage which follows (from *The Common Pursuit*, the essay on 'Literature and Society') is a kind of vicious circle, in which the literary critic is set as watchdog over the past to derive from it values which he then imposes on the present:

> . . . It needs stressing that where there isn't, in the literary critic's sense, a significant contemporary literature, the literary tradition—the 'mind' (and mind includes memory)—is not fully alive. To have a vital literary culture we must have a literature that is a going concern; and that will be what, under present conditions

of civilization, it has to be. Where it is can be determined only by
the literary critic's kind of judgement.'

The literary critic, then, is interpreter of the past, and judge of
the present. It would seem that there was grave need of a critic to
set over the critic: but this is not a policy specifically recommended
by Dr. Leavis. The whole of the past is narrowed down to the
critic's view of what is literature. He admits that the works of the
great tradition did not, when they were written, emerge simply
from the womb of previous literature, under the surveyance of
the critic (who was remarkably lacking, in the most vitally creative epochs). They came out of the lived conditions of values
projected into the communal patterns which were of those times.
And the justification of the critic's great authority today is that
there are no such patterns. It does not follow, however, that we
should be well advised to go back to those times, believe in the
things they believed in, try to work out in our modern society
beliefs and philosophy which are adaptations of theirs. The suggestion that the critic—since he makes such free use of literature
as a stick to beat 'present conditions of civilization' with—should
have a philosophy, a view of life, beliefs from which literature—
and perhaps also criticism—derive annoys the critic extremely:

> . . . It is no doubt possible to point to valuable writing of various
> kinds representing various kinds of alliance between the literary
> critic and the philosopher. But I am not the less sure that it is
> necessary to have a strict literary criticism somewhere and to
> vindicate literary criticism as a distinct and separate discipline.

Well, if this is so, and if the area of impressions received from
literature by the critic does not stray an inch outside the discipline
that is criticism, why use literary criticism as an instrument for
making moral judgements, and why recommend that the main
effort of a university education should be the study of literature—
which means, in fact, teaching students to be literary critics?
Literature is, of course, a line connecting with the past; and it

connects not with a selected past, but with all the past that it makes accessible to us. Criticism must certainly be concerned with what is carried along the ducts of literature out of past into present living, but why insist that literature is the only connection with the past? If present conditions are unfavourable, it seems important that there should be the fullest communication not with a selected part of the past, but with the widest possible life of other times into the widest possible one of our own. I confess that the idea of limiting the tradition to a few dozen books analysed by critics who are also teachers of English literature, and who know almost nothing of foreign literature, nothing of the other arts, gives me a sense of choking claustrophobia.

It is inevitable that poets and critics should have some selective view of the past which they claim to be the one and only true tradition. Indeed modern circumstances more and more dispose contemporaries to seek for ancestors. The search began already with Keats, and the pre-Raphaelites. But while one recognizes the inevitability of such a choice it should not be forgotten that the necessity itself, and the selecting, arise from a contemporary situation and to a great extent are decided by it. The more dogmatically held the view that such-and-such is the line of the true tradition, the more likely is it to spring from a contemporary need which exploits the past for the purposes of the present. The tradition is not as tidy as the traditionalists would have it. It has the variety, dividedness, confusion even, of life around us, and one sees it at its most lively and controversial, in the battle of styles, themselves based on different past traditions, which forms the old quarter of any great city.

IV

THE NOSTALGIC FALLACY

THE neo-traditionalist position which I have been considering can be summarized as follows:

1. *Positive aspect.* Language was in a healthy state when it
sprang from the conditions represented by the wheelwright's
shop—the organic community.

2. *Negative aspect.* No language that springs from the cultural
pattern represented by advertising, radio, cinema, etc., can
provide the conditions to produce literature of value and interest.

3. *Deduction.* Therefore the main task of literary criticism and
education today is to construct channels (purified and tested by
literary critics) back to the time and place in which the use of
language sprang from the traditional pattern of living.

4. *Conclusion.* The reservoir into which the living stream must
flow out of the past is universities watched over by English
teachers who are trained critics, and in which English is the main
subject of study.

It seems to me that the positive side of this argument—that it
treats literature seriously and draws attention to the position of
language as the 'centre of consciousness (and conscience) for our
civilization' is largely cancelled by the negative side—that, in
rejecting contemporary conditions where they have not already
been redeemed by contact with the tradition, it condemns
the creation of new work to a law of diminishing returns.

But the most serious objection is that it sets up in the concept of the tradition itself a nostalgic fallacy of vicarious living. For the basic assumption of the argument is that qualities of living individuals are decided by the pattern of the environment. If this assumption were not implicit, there would indeed be little sense in the whole argument. The organic community must have been better because the people in it were better. If they were not better, or worse, than present-day contemporaries, their conditioning would be of no import. But their conditioning made them better just as the conditions that prevail today make us worse.

Putting the argument in another way, it means that if the organic community were somehow restored, we would become different, and writers would perhaps be able to write master-pieces without the supervision of professors of English literature.

Here what is fallacious in the evangelistic aspect of neo-traditionalism links up with the extreme nostalgia of Hugh Selwyn Mauberley in a twentieth-century version of the nineteenth-century nostalgia.

Reduced to its simplest terms the nostalgic fallacy is a variant of the proposition: 'If person A could become person B, then he might still retain the consciousness, still live in the conditions and still enjoy the advantages of being person A.'

Or, another variant: 'If Wyndham Lewis were living in the Renaissance he would be a Leonardo: since he lives in the twentieth century he considers himself a Leonardo forced to be Wyndham Lewis with his modern consciousness and blaming the conditions which frustrate his genius.'

Or, another variant: 'If, living in conditions which are totally destructive of traditional living, I study the chosen works of the tradition, then I become part of the organic life which was that tradition and which is crystallized in those works, in spite of my being modern and living in conditions which make the traditional living and creativity impossible.'

The fallacy contained in the idea of the organic community is that it attempts to turn literature into a vicarious form of living in the past. It also separates the spiritual life of those contemporaries who are critics and students of the great tradition, not only—as is inevitable—from the conditions in which those who were in the tradition actually lived, but also from the beliefs and attitudes to life which enabled them to write as they did.

When we arouse ourselves from the superiority complex of Great Traditional thinking, we see that we do not and cannot transport ourselves through the study of literature into the past organic community spiritual life, because to do so would mean our living in that time, which is unthinkable. If the conditions of our present way of living are totally destructive of traditional creativity, then we cannot live traditionally by using literature as a channel back to the life of the tradition. If the contrast between traditional living—the wheelwright's shop—and untraditional living—the garage—is so final, then the garage simply cancels out the wheelwright's shop and it is false to use literature as a means of pretending to ourselves that we who read books and write criticism can belong to the life that is irremediably cut off from us. The traditional has living meaning only if one believes that one can live it not just as a literary critic or a student but as a person accepting—for better or worse—the contemporary conditioning facts of life, and accepting oneself as a modern person.

In terms of crude reality—shaking off again the spell of the concept of the Great Tradition—would any writer or reader or literary critic living today choose to live in the towns and villages of the England in which Blake, Cowper, Clare and Smart went mad through poverty, neglect and frustration?

Perhaps the village church, the Latin, Greek and Bible, the squirearchy, the pattern of the community, the handicrafts and carpentering, might indeed simplify, direct, organize, nourish individual vision, enable us to communicate freely. But to resist discouragement, distress, pain, brutality, cynicism, worse than many things in our century, and equally disruptive of the totality of vision, we would have to acquire qualities of courage and toughness which those men had, and that to us are unthinkable, because it is unthinkable to *be* their existence. We should not beguile ourselves with envying past conditions; we should confront ourselves with the impossibility of *being* the past, and then turn back into this life, our being, our conditions.

C. H. Waddington, contributing to the discussion of Snow's *The Two Cultures*, recently pointed out:

> Literary intellectuals who criticise the scientific revolution should remember that were it not for the improvement in medical care and nutrition that science has brought, only half of them over thirty would still be living. The major results of science in those parts of the world in which it has been applied, are firstly, that there are many more people alive, and secondly, that they live much longer. Try to imagine yourself back in a situation, say two or three hundred years ago in England, in which you and your wife could only hope to rear to maturity about half the children she bears. Would such a situation be borne by anyone who is not provided with a crust of insensitivity to human values which we find difficult to imagine, but which must, one supposes, have been general among our ancestors who found their most amusing Saturday afternoon entertainment watching public hangings at Tyburn?

Extreme nostalgia of the nineteenth- and twentieth-century variety can only make us think that our conditions are totally destructive of the values we care for, so that we feel nothing but hatred for our own time and envy for other times, and we use literature as a means of exacerbating these feelings in ourselves.

As I have pointed out, the idea of the Great Tradition submits creativity—and perhaps also, in the long run, even criticism —to a law of diminishing returns. For if it is true that we become every day ever further removed from the social conditioning in which the creative values of literature once derived from the pattern of organic living, then our connection with our roots will become ever more tenuous. The flower that is contemporary writing is separated by an ever longer and more tenuous stalk from its roots in the community that flourished— one hundred, two hundred, five hundred—years ago. At the end of this long pipe line even the critics themselves will produce works more and more desiccated (are they not doing so already?) in which the ever more remote works of the approved longer and longer lost tradition, of the time when a happy geography was married to a happier history, are ground to ever finer and finer dust.

The reader of Keats' letters may feel that the poet's circumstances were more discouraging than those of any more recent poet of comparable genius. Keats' work is characterized by his immense faith that the imagination which creates poetry can also create values of life which are an answer to the circumstances of a world where 'men sit and hear each other groan'. As confirmation of this faith he certainly required to belong to, or be accepted by, some kind of a community. He found this conviviality in Leigh Hunt's circle, and he doubtless owed the first flowering of his talent to the friendship of other men who believed in his genius and who shared the same ideal vision of the imagination: J. H. Reynolds, James Rice, Haydon, Charles Dilke, and the rest. But his letters show his gradual disillusionment with Leigh Hunt's friends; and the undermining of his faith in the transforming power of the imagination, by the actual circumstances which sap the life capable of sustaining vision— the illness and early death of his brother Tom, the certainty of his own early death, his disappointed love.

Keats is sufficiently near for us to think of his mind as more or less contemporary; and thinking this we can also think that had he lived in our century he would have been better understood, better cared for by his contemporaries, spared the appalling calamities that killed him in an age of less confused values.

In the end, perhaps the problem looks different to the critic and the poet, a fact which has been blurred over by the near-identification of the critical with the creative consciousness since

Matthew Arnold wrote about the function of Criticism. To the critic it appears only that behind the disorder that is life there is an order of values handed down by tradition at a particular time. Most life experience appears to be experience of disorder. The critic sees the poet as interpreting traditional values into the apparent disorder that is life. In doing so, the moral structure of his poetry is provided by the pattern of tradition woven into the life of the community. The existence of this pattern also enables the poet's readers to recognize in his work the realized significance of which, without it, they are only dimly aware. In the absence of the pattern of values accepted by the community the poet lacks a structure to work on.

To critics this easily appears to be the whole of the matter. The critic's mind operates upon existing structures. When they are not in evidence, it seems to him that the task of constructing the background of values becomes more important than the endeavour to carry on creating in a cultural void. Or if he feels that it is impossible to undertake such construction, then he thinks that criticism should take the place of both the structure and the poetry.

I do not think the problem will take exactly the same form in the minds of poets, however much they may be aware of it, with that part of their minds which shares the preoccupations of critics of the problem. But to poets the problem is that of focusing their experiences within a unifying vision. The vision is not something given beyond question by society. Even in the 'organic community' it would have to become, for the poet, as it was for Blake, something he discovered and imagined for himself. Before experience can go into a poem it has to be re-invented and personalized within the imagination of the poet.

This means that for poets institutions of moral order cannot be ready-made solutions for their poetic problems, as they can be for the critic who looks to society for a reflection of the order which he finds in an approved masterpiece. For poets the structure of ordered beliefs and values provided by society has to become personal to their experience before it can operate in their poetry. Moreover the presence of such a structure is only one difficulty solved. There may be other problems entirely personal to them, which are equally difficult to solve. I have tried to suggest that the critic feels the need of what might be called secondary and fixed ideas or beliefs, realized in creeds, institutions, and patterns of behaviour, which prepare for and support poetry. But poets, before all else, are in need of primary values which are their own personal qualities, which no one can give them, and which societies cannot altogether provide.

I think that poets when they write their poetry, although they are aware of the problems raised by critics, are really concentrating on something other than the cultural situation (unless, indeed, this is the subject of their poem). They are occupied with focusing their experiences within a unifying vision. And this kind of concentration is not accomplished for them by their cultural conditioning even when it is favourable. It requires a kind of attention in which the creator is alone with the object of his creation, whatever his circumstances. Conditions may be more or less favourable, but the artist is always to a greater or less extent creating the very conditions out of which he creates. If there are no, or few, or minor poets, the critics, coming afterwards, find their reasons for showing the conditions to have been unconducive to creativity. If there are great poets, then reasons can be found easily enough in the surrounding history to justify their existence. The only thing that really makes art possible is there being artists. In this sense at any time or place a work of art is a miracle.

V

POET-CRITICS AND CRITIC-POETS

MATTHEW ARNOLD is the unacknowledged legislator of twentieth-century criticism. His lecture *The Function of Criticism at the Present Time* started the process which has ended in criticism today having perhaps a more important position than poetry. In his lecture Arnold begins by dealing with what he feels will be the objections of his Victorian audience to his thesis: their conviction that creativity is 'superior' to criticism. His argument might, in fact, have been clearer if he had dismissed the question of which activity is higher, and put forward the consideration that poetry is no more in competition with criticism than with politics or philosophy. So he concedes that 'the critical power is of lower rank than the creative'. Then he proceeds to render this generalization irrelevant, and to pull the carpet from under the feet of the poets, by declaring that just the same 'the exercise of the creative power in the production of great works of literature or art . . . is not at all epochs and under all conditions possible; and that therefore labour may be spent in attempting it, which might with more fruit be used in preparing for it, in rendering it possible.' Clearly he feels that he is living in such a time.

The word 'important' like the discussion of 'which is superior', covers up a vital question: whether, superior or inferior, more important or less important, poetry does not at all times do something which criticism cannot do. This question remains present within more recent developments of criticism.

Poets tend to think in metaphors, even when they are critics. And just as Eliot, when he thinks of the tradition, tends to think of a museum with statues in it, and a new statue introduced, which alters the relations of all the statues to one another—so Arnold tends to think of the stage and scene shifting.

His picture suggests actors on a stage with scenery and lighting, and the language and action decided by a powerful current of ideas proceeding from the producer, who provides the intellectual atmosphere which the actors (the poets) require in order that they may improvise their lines.

As regards ideas, poets are parasitic—or, as Arnold puts it:

> the elements with which the creative power works are ideas; the best ideas on every matter which literature touches, current at the time. At any rate we may lay it down as certain that in modern literature no manifestation of the creative power not working with these can be very important or fruitful. And I say *current* at the time, not merely accessible at the time; for creative literary genius does not principally show itself in discovering new ideas, that is rather the business of the philosopher. The grand work of literary genius is a work of synthesis and exposition, not of analysis and discovery; its gift lies in the faculty of being happily inspired by a certain intellectual and spiritual atmosphere, by a certain order of ideas, when it finds itself in them; of dealing divinely with these ideas, presenting them in the most effective and attractive combinations, —making beautiful works with them, in short. But it must have the atmosphere, it must find itself amidst the order of ideas, in order to work freely; and these it is not so easy to command. This is why great creative epochs in literature are so rare. . . .

The operative word here is surely 'atmosphere', since one can hardly maintain that the centuries in which appeared the theories of Evolution, Relativity and psychoanalysis have been lacking in ideas. But the ideas are rather inaccessible and not current, we would expect Arnold to say, wondering whether he does not mean something else—productive, or noble, or meeting with general consent—since surely the debate between the evolutionists and the religious provided a current atmosphere of ideas.

And in the present century, one wonders still more whether it is not a defect of the literary mind today if it feels the lack of ideas. Darwin, Marx and Freud surely provide a powerful intellectual atmosphere. As with so much literary discussion, one finds oneself convinced by the truth of the symptoms and therefore disposed to agree with the diagnosis, and yet wondering whether the problems are adequately stated.

Arnold was a poet, not happy about his poetry. It is not hard to see what he was thinking: it is the nineteenth century which prevents my poetry being as good as it should be; perhaps my more important task is preparing the way for the poets to come.

Eliot's essay *The Function of Criticism* is largely an answer to Arnold, coming from a poet who takes for granted much of Arnold's view about what is wrong with the age we live in, but who nevertheless wants to write poetry. He has no intention of spending his life in the 'more important' task of shifting intellectual scenery. In answer to Arnold, Eliot substitutes for the figure of the poet who resigns his once-superior vocation in order to pursue the now more important one of critic, a new figure, a kind of centaur—the poet-critic. 'Matthew Arnold distinguishes far too bluntly, it seems to me, between the two activities: he overlooks the capital importance of criticism in the work of creation itself.' At some point there is a junction of the critical and creative. 'The critical activity finds its highest, its truest fulfilment in a kind of union with creation in the labour of the artist.' But he makes a distinction, which has not always been observed by his followers, between the poet-critic and the critic who would like to equate criticism with poetry. 'I have assumed as axiomatic that a creation, a work of art is autotelic; and that criticism, by definition, is *about* something other than itself. Hence you cannot fuse creation with criticism as you can fuse criticism with creation.'

However, despite the characteristic escape clause with which

Eliot the critic supplies Eliot the poet, he has provided a fusion, a junction, common to critic and poet. And a great deal of traffic has passed over this, most of it moving from poetry into criticism. Matthew Arnold suggested that poetry might replace religion, but often criticism seems to have replaced poetry *and* religion.

Eliot says that Arnold distinguishes too bluntly between criticism and poetry. Yet if we followed up the implications of his own characteristic aside that poetry is 'autotelic', whereas criticism is about something other than itself, we might consider that in his view the difference between criticism and poetry is greater than in that of Arnold. For if Arnold makes too much distinction between criticism and poetry, he seems also to blur that between poetry and prose. Arnold does not say that poetry is 'autotelic', that is having ends of its own, being about poetry itself: he says it has the faculty of 'dealing divinely' with the ideas with which criticism is primarily concerned: the ideas that ought to be provided for it by the mental climate of the time. Altogether one might think that Arnold was asking for a classical age. His view seems to be that poetry should be partly illustrative and partly discursive of current ideas with which it 'divinely deals'.

Another difference is between Arnold's and Eliot's conception of criticism. For Arnold, criticism is concerned not only with literature but also with the values and ideas in society outside poetry but without which poetry, in his view, cannot function so as to be 'important'. Criticism is largely concerned with the current ideas of which poetry is 'synthesis and exposition' but in which it is deficient as 'analysis and discovery'. Criticism for Arnold is not just literary criticism. It is also moral and social criticism.

Eliot argues that the critical faculty operates within the poetry. He thinks that Arnold overlooks the fusion of criticism and creation in the poem. It is a truism that if, after a poem has been written, a critic analyses it, the critic only discovers those qualities which the poet has put into the poem. In creation the creative and critical faculties are, as it were, reverse and front of the same object. Creation and criticism are in a relationship like that of positive and negative poles of an electric current. Creation is, as it were, the critical principles of the poet in action. And criticism is the passive application of the same principles to the work achieved.

This is self-evident. Criticism would have nothing to criticize unless creation already embodied, to a greater or lesser degree, critical standards.

Nevertheless Arnold's and Eliot's views have both of them altered the attitudes of poets and critics coming after them, towards criticism and poetry.

For Arnold's remarks pose the question of whether there are not, and should not be, 'ages of poetry' and 'ages of criticism'. If the conditions of the time are not propitious to creation, then criticism must fill the vacuum left by society by keeping open connections with past values by way of the study of literature. Criticism becomes more 'important' than literature.

And Eliot's remarks make way for the idea that poetry is translation into imagistic and magical language of values which are also those of criticism. One might conclude that the ideas released into poetry are paraphrasable back again into prose. I do not think this is what Eliot means, but his parenthetic qualification of what is essential to poetry, its being autotelic—the saving clause which prevents the critical and the poetic being the same—gives rise to misunderstanding.

It is significant that both Arnold and Eliot were writing not just as critics, but also as poets.

This goes some way to explaining what Eliot finds unsatisfactory about Arnold's observations. Victorian poets were very worried because the scientific ideas which agitated their contemporaries were difficult to assimilate in poetry. The endeavours of Tennyson and Browning to expound and analyse these ideas could only lead to the conclusion that the ideas of the time were unsuitable to poetry. Arnold himself was more successful than most of his contemporaries in stating in poetry his intellectual and moral distress. Yet behind even his poetry there is the strain of prose realized with difficulty as poetry. It was inevitable then that Arnold should think that perhaps prose thinking had better be in prose.

The reasons for Arnold's 'blunt distinction' between criticism and poetry is that in his time, and for him, there was such a distinction—at any rate according to the way in which he thought of criticism, and of poetry.

Eliot, in admonishing Arnold, may have been thinking also of his own poetry. The great stylistic achievement of Eliot and Pound was that their poetic idiom succeeded in dealing with the very problem—the lack of current ideas available to poetry, and the condition of civilization which this implies—that persuaded Arnold that poetry could not be 'important'. It made poetry out of the situation unconducive to poetry. For Arnold criticism was about poetry and about the condition of society which produced or failed to produce current ideas accessible to poetry. In the kind of poetry which Eliot to some extent represented, poetry is often about criticism.

I should underline here that Eliot remains in his criticism—a bit slyly perhaps—mysterious about the nature of poetry, or—to put it better—he makes qualifying asides to the effect that 'autotelic' poetry remains a mystery, 'language rich and strange'. Temperamentally, I should say, Eliot does not think for a moment that criticism can be more 'important' than poetry.

Thus criticism of the present state of civilization, and the idea of the necessity of critical values which would 'prepare' for poetry, 'render it possible', become themselves the theme of poetry. In *Hugh Selwyn Mauberley* as in Eliot of the same time, there is criticism of the society whose 'current ideas' are not assimilable in poetry.

*　　*　　*　　*

Poets did not accept the rôle which Arnold assigned to them of having to give up while the critics prepare their future way. They were ready to do the scene shifting themselves—perhaps even while they were writing their poetry.

The twentieth-century reply to Arnold Matthew is the poet-critic, who does not throw in his poetic left hand and devote himself entirely to being a critic with his right. He plays out, as it were, his act in a very 'advanced' theatre, in a modern play in which there is only one actor—himself—on the stage. All the props and scenery are improvised by this soloist. While saying his lines he is also ready to run off the stage and fetch a chair, a bowl, a vase, a pistol, a piece of string, or some other essential prop.

For the poet-critic improvises his own intellectual climate, his critical values, even his supporting beliefs. He pauses in the writing of his poetry to systematize his ideas—in order that he may write more poetry—Pound in manifestos, Yeats in the mystical philosophy expounded in *A Vision*, Eliot in his critical essays—or he writes, like Auden, different ideologies into different phases of his work. Or having studied the principles of ambiguities in the poetry of others he studiously injects them—like Empson—into his own poems.

Of course, he does not always get away with his double rôle. We pay for the consequences.

One is that the supporting ideas tend either to separate from the poetry, or to harden within it, so that the poetry becomes more and more an abstraction, or illustration, of the ideas. There are signs of the separation of theory from practice in the more sententious passages of *The Four Quartets*, still more in the very painstaking traditional parallels (drawn from Greek tragedy) forced into *The Family Reunion* (*The Eumenides*), and *The Elder Statesman* (*Oedipus at Colonus*). There is a stiffening of the intellectualized dogma in some of Auden's later work.

The fusion into poetry of the ideas postulated by the poet,

seemingly not hindered by the intellectual and spiritual atmosphere unfavourable to 'the grand work of literary genius', has
introduced a tension of opposites—concrete image and metaphysical abstraction—into modern poetry. Yeats transformed
himself from being the minor poet of the early to the major one
of the later poetry, having constructed a philosophical system
whose ideas, images and affirmations he could raid for his poetry.
It would be interesting to speculate what Arnold would have to
say about poems deriving from a system of ideas that Yeats
himself admitted to be a store-house of metaphors and symbols
for his poetry.

The poet-critic was destined to be gradually superseded by the
critic-poet. Perhaps, though, the development of the latter was
already implicit in the work of the poet-critic. For the great
recurrent theme of the poet-critics in those works, written at the
beginning of this century, which are like mighty epitaphs on the
struggles that had rocked the nineteenth century, and written in
the idiom of the twentieth, is the swan song, the end of our
culture, enclosed in a doomed civilization. It was the theme and
the impossibility of carrying on beyond the celebrated disaster.

In Eliot's earlier and middle poems the obsessive idea, crystallized in some image of immense concentration, occurs—'the
awful daring of a moment's surrender'—suggesting, even more
than the open references to decline and disintegration, the supreme
effort of the creative and critical intelligence to grasp, in a single
act of fused imagination and intellect, the whole past and present
of civilization. It is the illumination within a burning instant of
stillness and silence before the final explosion.

★   ★   ★   ★

The poet-critics did not provide solutions to the problem of
the lack of current ideas available to be presented 'in the most
effective and attractive combinations', raised by Matthew Arnold.
Instead, they made the crisis of poetry, the necessity of criticism,

the themes of their poetry. They converted a cultural vacuum into a tragedy, and made the lost values the theme of their poetry, much as Henry James in *The Ambassadors* makes Strether's defective experience of life and love become his vision of the young Chad's immersion in these things, a vision more poignant than the real love his young friend has but is incapable of imagining. They showed that in art the vision of what a civilization has lost, and of its having had its past, can compensate for the absence of these things through being tragic.

Yet of its very nature end-game bars out the future. A masterpiece may erupt from the waste land but it does not lay the foundations for further masterpieces. On the contrary it draws credit on the suppositious bankruptcy of the future—otherwise it would not be the waste land.

Thus the modern period which produced such masterpieces as the novels of James' last period, *The Waste Land*, *Ulysses*, etc., dramatized the problem of the lack of current ideas, without providing ideas to prove that the future lay in creation and not criticism. Indeed the criticism which justified *Ulysses* and the imagists produced creative work which in its turn led to more criticism.

To a great extent modern critics accomplished the task of filling the gap between the breakdown of cultural values and poetry unable to achieve important results without a coherent background of ideas, which Arnold assigned to them.

The *Scrutiny* critics and the American New Critics performed a service to literature in that part of their work which consisted of close attention to the ways in which writing reflects past influences and creates its effects. They designed categories for analysing the very complex organization of a poem or novel. They tore away the speculative vagueness, the romantic afflatus, which surrounded criticism at the beginning of this century, when a work was discussed for the emotions it aroused in the critics, the pleasant or unpleasant sensations suggested by its subject matter, for its aura of intentions rather than its achievement.

Modern criticism brought the past close to us, in bridging, by a structure of interpretation, the gap between the reader and the work, and in giving writers a more serious, intellectual and precise approach to the tasks of writing.

Yet Arnold thought that the main task of criticism should be to prepare the way for a new poetry. This hope was justified to a certain extent in the work of the poet-critics who wrote their own criticism to justify their own poetry. But in the long run it has not been fulfilled. Perhaps Arnold was mistaken in thinking that criticism alone could create the conditions for a new great period of poetry.

VI

THE MODERN AND THE NOW

THE modern movement, in literature at any rate, looks today like past history. If this is so, the reader may well ask—why discuss it?

The reason for doing so is that it made a challenge which even now, when some of the works in which writers tried to meet it seem dated, is still there. The challenge was to meet the experience of living in a world of conditions which in many ways seemed unprecedented with an art based on acceptance of the separateness of that world from the past tradition.

In order to do this, a great many techniques, devices, attitudes were called into being. There were also the attitudes to the past adopted by writers who wished to write fiction or poetry as modern as the experience of the contemporary world. There was a way of being traditional which was modern. I have tried to show, though, that this consisted not of going back into the tradition, but of reinterpreting it, in order that it might provide ways and techniques for seeing and transforming the modern material. The moderns did not go back into the tradition, they brought it forward as an instrument with which to attack the present.

One reason why the modern movement remains a challenge is that the greatest moderns treated the experience of the modern world as a unity. They sought to create works which expressed the experience of a present which was distinct from all the past, as a whole. They did so because they felt that the quality of something unprecedented about the conditioning of industrial societies, somehow altered all relations of the individual to his environment. Everything experienced in the twentieth century was, as it were, coloured or tainted by belonging to this century, and there was no way of escape, whether into natural scenery, or the past.

Thus Lawrence was being modern when he went to nature not as a Wordsworthian alternative but as life force, dark gods, sex, destructiveness, weapons of the unconscious or primitive instincts which could be used against machinery and industrial civilization. In the same way, the past in Ezra Pound's *Cantos* is not roots returned to, but nostalgic vision reinforcing hatred for the modern world founded on usury.

The moderns used nature, used the past to give power to works which were both made out of and directed against the whole of modern life. What held them together was not a philosophy or a belief but some all-including emotional attitude towards the present—hope, hatred, despair. These emotions are not so contradictory as may appear because, as I have suggested, the modern movement had connections with the nostalgic aestheticism of the end of the nineteenth century. Hope, hatred and despair can converge in faith in the transforming power of art, which, if it cannot save external society, can perhaps redeem inner life.

The characteristic gesture of modern genius was to produce vast, all-inclusive works, mansions themselves containing many mansions, but without foundations. Foundations were not planned, partly because a modern house should be made of materials that need no foundations, but more significantly because the attempt to build foundations meant inevitably reverting to beliefs or philosophies which were fragmented, partisan, not capable of dealing with the modern experience as a whole, and for that reason reverting to the past.

An illustration of this is provided by comparing *The Waste*

Land with Eliot's later, religious poetry. In *The Waste Land* the poet accepts the chaos of modern civilization, and this is enclosed in the all-inclusive gesture perhaps of despair which overshadows most of the poem, perhaps of hope ('O Lord thou pluck'st me burning') with which it ends. (Whether the poem is despairing or hoping depends on whether you view the state of consciousness it reveals from the standpoint of time or eternity. For, in fact, in Eliot's work there is always this division between time viewed as chaos and eternity as order.)

The Waste Land has a kind of finality which is about modern civilization itself. It is a vision of the whole seen through the European mind at the end of its tether. After *Ash Wednesday*, Eliot is preoccupied with constructing spiritual foundations, and that which made his poetry part of the modern movement in its heroic visionary phase is less in evidence. One may prefer the *Four Quartets* to *The Waste Land* and yet feel that there has been a certain withdrawal from the material of modern life.

I think it was the aim of the moderns to accept the twentieth-century experience, in this world, as it is, in its ugliness, its anti-poetic qualities, and transform it into all-inclusive art, which was, and still is, a challenge, uttered in the spirit of Edmund at the end of *King Lear* throwing down his gauntlet. The confrontation, to be fully tragic and heroic, must be of the past apprehended as the vision of the civilized city with the chaotic non-civilization of industrialism.

Within the modern movement itself there were defections from the idea of the modern as such a confrontation of past with present, such an envisioning of the modern situation as a whole-ness. Futurists attempted to break all connecting links between past and future, Gertrude Stein produced her stuttering language which was meant to sustain a 'continuous present', there were experiments of little more than technical interest.

Carried out programmatically in a few works of heroic dimensions (*Sacre du Printemps*, *Ulysses*, *The Waste Land*,

Guernica, etc.), the great modern achievements were wagers which made gestures, invented methods, but laid no foundations for a future literature. They led in the direction of an immensity from which there was bound to be a turning back, because to go further would lead to a new and completer fragmentation, utter obscurity, form (or, rather formlessness) without end. One could not go further in the directions of fragmentation, obscurity, and inclusiveness than Joyce.

The wager was of a kind that made art dependent on external events, ends of revolutionary hope or total despair. Thus in its most productive period the modern movement was borne up on the idea of its being an international inter-arts alliance, the expression in music, painting, writing and the ballet (an art form in which all these met) perhaps capable of combining with more or less anarchist revolutionary politics and transforming the world. If, as some expressionists hoped, the world was renewed, then there would be a new art—of the kind that Rimbaud had already prophesied—based on the visions of a new life. Alternatively, there might be the end of civilization, in which case art was the vision of a drowning man whose consciousness realized the memory of the whole of past civilization within the present catastrophic moment.

So the modern movement was attached to two possible alternatives: the transformation of the whole of civilization within a revolutionary vision inspired by art, or the end of civilization. If neither of these happened, then artists were confronted with the problem of how to go on. Yeats prophesied the entry of our civilization into the period of final darkness in the year 1929. In that case, 1929 might be for Yeats and his contemporaries the climatic moment of exalted vision: but by the same token, after 1929, the prophecy which had produced the great work of Yeats' last period also demanded the collapse of art afterwards, or at least a withdrawal of artists into less apocalyptically great positions.

The withdrawal was then inevitable. Instead of sitting on the battlefield and 'waiting for the end,' which might be either a victory transforming the whole of history, or a defeat ending all history, the poets have had to take up positions, acquire dogmas and philosophies, consolidate technical innovations, simply in order to continue their own work.

But this has involved a strategic withdrawal from the 'far-out' position of the modern movement of the vision of the whole fatality of the modern experience. The most symptomatic expression of this withdrawal was the dominating rôle played in poetry since the early thirties by criticism. That the critics whom I call the 'neo-traditionalists' wrote 'new' criticism does not make their researches any less a withdrawal. To see this, it is sufficient to contrast their attitude to the past to that of the writers I have called here 'revolutionary traditionalists'. The 'revolutionary traditionalists' (among whom I would reckon Gerard Manley Hopkins) were in the position of equipping the forces of the past tradition with modern weapons in order to fight industrial civilization. Joyce *used* the parallel with the Homeric myth in order to *realize* Dublin night-town. The neo-traditionalists have done the reverse of this: they have used modern sophisticated critical scholasticism in order to withdraw into a past which has been strengthened by an up-to-date critical terminology.

Today there are the beginnings of a reaction against the reaction.

* * * *

It is encouraging that writers are beginning to challenge the myths which have formed the background of criticism. Here, for example, is John Wain, in *Declaration*, commenting on the picture of the collapse of values which has been such an article of unfaith in the criticism of the past thirty years:

Everyone always speaks of the twentieth century as an epoch of rapid change, so rapid as to be without parallel; old people, interviewed by the local press on their ninetieth birthdays, are always asked what changes they have seen, and always give the appropriate answer, the one that is expected of them; nothing, wherever they look, is what it was, or where it was, when they were young.

But when we look at this change in all its proliferation of detail, the most striking thing is not its extent, its completeness, but its lumpy and patchy quality.

He goes on to describe the attitude of people who thought of the 1914–18 War as the final catastrophe to the values of civilization:

In their youth, it had seemed that the rigid crust of conventional life was cracking from top to bottom; a few more holes punched in it, and it would be nothing but a heap of crumbs. And behold! everything had somehow drifted back into something like the old shape; things like marriage, and private property, and war, and the division of the world into nations, and the Church, and the public schools—there they all were, the same as ever! To such people, the twentieth century must seem like one long tragic swindle. It isn't a new situation; an exactly parallel sequence of events happened in the lifetime of Wordsworth; he had just that glimpse of a new world, with

France standing on the top of golden hours,
And human nature seeming born again.

That's the trouble with new starts. Human nature is always seeming born again, and always growing up into much the same kind of shape as it always had.

In much criticism of this kind, tinged with sociology, there is a breakdown of the monolithic fable of Great Traditional criticism.

Richard Hoggart, in *The Uses of Literacy*, fills in the background of a picture of the industrial North of England where the agricultural workers were put into barracks of slums during the nineteenth century, their local traditions and distinct culture destroyed. He argues that nevertheless the workers, through temperament and through the pattern of their family life, resisted their new environment and retained more traditional attitudes than might be expected.

The Uses of Literacy hardly contradicts *Culture and the Environment* in the picture it gives of workers deprived of the physical bases and environment of their local culture. But it extends and humanizes the picture, portrays the human beings concerned as well as the desolation of their past, the moral emptiness of the distractions offered to them in the industrial towns. It sees the North of England towns as places in which although, to the visitor, the community may seem swamped by the mass of slums and their inhabitants, in fact for most of the slum-dwellers their own street and its immediate neighbourhood became their village.

Mr. Hoggart's book is in itself a sign of promise for the future. It has a wide charity which indicates the perhaps rather shallow and broad, rather than narrow and deep, soil in which a new culture might take root. By his charity, I do not only mean that he has—as in fact is the case—always a considerate and courteous tone. I mean also that he does not divide his contemporaries into approved well-read sheep and disapproved ill-read goats. He sees present-day culture as a subject for study and inquiry rather than dogmatic acceptances and dismissals based on standards set up by literary critics. His wider context of criticism is patient examination of the new media, such as television, instead of contemptuous dismissal of them.

I do not mean to set up Richard Hoggart against writers like Leavis and Thompson, who—whether or not one agrees with the way in which they do it—are in this century fighting the battle against philistinism fought by Arnold, Morris and Ruskin in the last. I must, however, distinguish his attitude, which includes hope for the whole culture of modern industrial society, from that of the authors of *Culture and the Environment*, which offers its grain of comfort only to those educated to be literary critics. One significant distinction is that Auden, the poet whom Leavis dismisses as dealing only with the new and unprecedented, is the poet most quoted by Hoggart.

It seems to have required a whole new generation of young writers from the industrial towns to repudiate the legend that they have no tradition. They have done it, I have pointed out, in their part sociological part literary criticism. They have also done it in the theatre, with the plays of Osborne, Wesker, Pinter and others.

They have not done it in poetry, and I think the fundamental reason for the present low pressure of poetry in England is a simple one: that poetry has become the most self-conscious of the arts, the one in which the analytic consciousness has come most close to the creative one. The poets who survive are those, like Larkin, who, sensitive and gifted, can make an art of their very self-consciousness: or those, like Ted Hughes and Thom Gunn, who combine great awareness of technique with an obsessive and assertively tough subject-matter.

*   *   *   *

Assuming that the development of modern literature is not in a circle but a spiral, it might be said that we are today at that point in the spiral which is above the turning reached thirty years ago. The young English playwrights and novelists, conscious of being representatives of an emergent class, correspond to Bennett and Wells, whom, indeed, they look back to. The young English poets, with their personalist poetry of limited aims, look back across the confusing political poetry of the 1930's, the despairing affirmations of Eliot, Yeats and Pound, to the Georgians cultivating their gardens.

Of course there is a great more to it than that. There is modern criticism which has added self-consciousness and consciousness of technique to the young poets. Their Georgian poems seem to have been sent to a laundry run by the new critics. Just as the nostalgia of Hugh Selwyn Mauberley is far more sophisticated, ironic, and critically self-aware than that of Pater or Ruskin, so the Georgian themes of Philip Larkin or Ted Hughes are treated more intellectually than in the poetry of Edward Thomas or Walter de la Mare.

Another parallel—also with a great difference—with the situation early in the century is that today there is a dominant academic criticism in poetry from which the liveliest talents are breaking away. It is true that this criticism itself derived from a revolution in poetry. Yet this was also true of the academic criticism in the early part of the century whose standards derived from successive waves of the Romantic movement. The characteristic of the criticism against which there was the imagist revolt was that it defined what were the appropriate subjects, forms and idioms for poetry. The neo-traditionalists, with more intelligence and sophistication, in effect do the same thing. Just as in the early part of this century the subject-matter of the realist novels of Bennett and Wells was considered unpoetic, so, today, the kind of subjects chosen by Osborne, Wesker and Arden for their plays are ruled out from that intellectual poetry which bears the stamp of the new academicism of the universities.

Notably some American poets—Lowell and Roethke—having absorbed the new criticism—have broken away from it. Essentially they both write a poetry which consists of the passionate and dogged pursuit of obsessive images attached to their most personal feelings. Their poetry breaks the bounds of a new academicism just as that of the early imagists broke those of the old ones.

What strikes one as an element of 'greatness' in this poetry—particularly in the writing of Robert Lowell—is that these realized images of his personal life and attachments established a deep connection with a world in which there are sensual delights and private obsession, and also atomic bombs and concentration camps.

With the difference that he is writing in the 1960's, Robert Lowell seems unique in facing things in his own personal life which are also significant of the most public contemporary world, and realizing them in concrete imagery, in the manner which is the extension of Pound's and Eliot's aims forty years ago. The point is demonstrated, surely, in these lines from *Fall 1961*:

> Back and forth, back and forth,
> goes the tock, tock, tock
> of the orange, bland, ambassadorial
> face of the moon
> on the grandfather clock.
>
> All autumn, the chafe and jar
> of nuclear war;
> we have talked our extinction to death.
> I swim like a minnow
> behind my studio window.
>
> Our end drifts nearer,
> the moon lifts,
> radiant with terror.
> The state
> is a diver under a glass bell.

★ ★ ★ ★

The significance of the modern movement looked back at from today is not just that it produced some masterpieces, nor that it extended the boundaries of idioms, techniques, and forms, but that in certain works a fragmented civilization was redeemed within the envisioned memory of the greatness of its past. To achieve these poignant states of remembering great unifying beliefs and art while confronting chaos and destruction, safe positions of sheltered certainty were avoided, whether they were based on the kind of reasoning which goes with belief in progress and technology, or on religious dogmas. I. A. Richards, when he saluted the idea of a poetry severed from all belief, was wrong in thinking that this would provide the philosophic basis of a future poetry, but surely he would have been right if he had suggested only that the abandonment of metaphysical positions, the acceptance of a moral and cultural void, was the position which made possible the compressed epics of a fragmented culture. A vacuum of unbelief was filled with the incantations of an age of belief.

And in a sense the decline of the modern movement leaves another vacuum waiting to be filled with different works written out of the same mixture of hope and despair in face of our history. For that potentiality of destruction, which has become identical with the very concept of modern civilization, is still the great unifying reality of our culture, behind all else. What is so fragmentary in other respects is single in this one of final negation. Thus to ignore the universal threat which makes opponents one, and ideologies, and all the means they use, similar; and which gives the primitive cultures a certain moral superiority over the complex and advanced ones, is like concentrating on the part to shut out the realization of the whole. For this reason, against the achievements of the modern movement, the sociological novel, the political play, poems of personal relations and decisions, or of animals and nature, however solid their achievements, seem too evidently the results of limitations consciously imposed to shut out realizations which can scarcely be denied on the less conscious levels from which the greatest work springs. Perhaps a deliberate, conscious, limited, cautious poetry of experiences, carefully chosen and rationally explored, is inevitable today. But the works of the modern movement stand behind us not only by reason of their being so much more ambitious but because they wrestle with the universal predicament that is still our world.